Children as Victims

Dedicated to Julie Kennison and Sue Goodman

We owe our gratitude to the contributing authors who have provided their own distinctive perspective on children as victims. We also owe particular thanks to Terry Pizzala, Isabelle Brodie, Jayne Mooney, Peter Turner, and to past and present Criminology colleagues and students at Middlesex University who have helped shape our thoughts and ideas. From Learning Matters we would like to thank Di Page, Jonathan Parker and Greta Bradley for their support, encouragement and constructive feedback as the book took shape.

To order other titles from Learning Matters, please contact our distributor: BEBC Distribution, Albion Close, Parkstone, Poole, BH12 3LL. Telephone: 0845 230 9000, email: **learningmatters@bebc.co.uk.**

You can also find more information on each of these titles and our other learning resources at **www.learningmatters.co.uk.**

Children as Victims

PETER KENNISON

ANTHONY GOODMAN

Series Editors: Jonathan Parker and Greta Bradley

First published 2008 by Learning Matters Ltd

© Sally Angus, Chris Bourlet, Caroline Chatwin, Gwyn Daniel, Anthony Goodman, Sue Goodman, Nic Hinrichsen, Peter Kennison, Caroline Metcalf, David Porteous 2008

British Library Cataloguing in Publication Data
A CIP record for this book is available from the British Library

ISBN: 978 1 844 45136 4

Cover and text design by Code 5 Design Associates
Project Management by Swales and Willis Ltd
Typeset by Swales & Willis Ltd, Exeter, Devon
Printed and bound in Great Britain by TJ International Ltd, Padstow, Cornwall

Learning Matters Ltd
33 Southernay East
Exeter EX1 1NX
Tel: 01392 215560
info@learningmatters.co.uk
learningmatters.co.uk

FSC
Mixed Sources
Product group from well-managed
forests and other controlled sources
Cert no. SGS-COC-2482
www.fsc.org
© 1996 Forest Stewardship Council

Contents

About the authors

Sally Angus

Sally is a Lecturer at Middlesex University within Social Work and teaches research methods, youth justice and is on the practice teacher award scheme. She has worked for Enfield Victim Support since the early 1980s and supported victims of crime. Sally was also a victim liaison volunteer and panel member of the local Youth Offending Team (YOT). She is a member of the National Victim Support steering group currently looking at and designing training material to support young victims of crime. Her PhD research considers how YOT practitioners respond to children's needs as victims of crime perpetrated by other children.

Chief Superintendent Chris Bourlet

Chris was the Deputy OCU Commander in the Child Abuse Investigation Command between 2002 and 2006 and held the child protection and policy portfolio. He sat on the National ACPO Child Abuse Working Group and the London Child Protection Committee. He was also the Staff Officer to the Director of Serious Crime at the time of Victoria's death. He remains a member of the MPS Every Child Matters Programme Board representing Borough policing. As a result he has been in a unique position to witness the changes in policy, practice and reorganisation taking place within child protection in the MPS not only from a strategic perspective but also at Borough level as well. Chris has 19 years' police service in the MPS having worked in a range of uniform and detective roles. He is currently a Borough Commander in South West London.

Caroline Chatwin BA (Hons) Psychology, MA International Criminology, PhD

Caroline is a lecturer of Criminology in the School of Social Policy, Sociology and Social Research at the University of Kent. There she teaches courses on 'youth and crime' and 'criminal justice in modern Britain'. To date, her published work has reflected an interest in drug policy-making at the European level. More recently, she has become involved in the study of cultural and sub-cultural aspects of drug-taking and party behaviour within subsections of the UK dance scene.

Gwyn Daniel

Gwyn is a systemic psychotherapist and social worker who has worked for many years within the NHS in Child and Adolescent Mental Health, most recently at the Tavistock Clinic, London. She is founder and Co-Director of the Oxford Family Institute. Her publications include (with Charlotte Burck) *Gender and Family Therapy*, (with Gorell Barnes, Thompson and Burchardt) *Growing up in Stepfamilies* and many articles in professional books and journals. Her clinical and training specialities and interests include working with families in the context of violence or parental mental illness and working with children whose parents are involved in court disputes.

Anthony Goodman BSC (Hons), PG Dip. Social Administration, PG Dip. Social Work, CQSW, MA Deviancy and Social Policy, MSC Social Science Research Methods, PhD

Anthony Goodman worked as a probation officer for 15 years in a number of different settings, including a period in Holloway Prison where child protection issues could be a serious concern. More often with the women prisoners, as was evident in working with both male and female offenders in the community, there were disturbing histories of child abuse. These experiences in their many manifestations had not been diagnosed by professionals, who had chosen by default or design to ignore the symptoms. The damage this caused was long-term and enduring. He was involved in multi-disciplinary child protection training from a probation perspective. He has worked at Middlesex University for the past 17 years, based initially in Social Work and then moving into criminology where he leads an applied criminology Masters programme. Anthony is a Principal Lecturer and he has written a book on substance misuse for Learning Matters and currently is researching on the transmission of drinking cultures amongst the young, for the Joseph Rowntree Foundation.

Sue Goodman Cert. Ed, PG Dip. Special Educational Needs, MA in Education (Special)

Sue is a Research Fellow in the Centre for the Study of Crime and Conflict at Middlesex University. Sue has taken part in research projects focusing on Youth Justice, Hate Crime, Community Safety and issues around work/life balance. Sue has also researched children's services in a number of London Boroughs through the Children's Fund. Sue was a teacher for 40 years in a large inner-city multi-cultural primary school, and in recent years she was assistant head teacher and Special Needs Co-ordinator. Sue is also volunteer counsellor with Careline, a charitable telephone crisis counselling service. Sue is chair of 'Newham Crossroads', a voluntary sector agency which provides care support workers for a variety of family problems. Sue is also a school governor.

Nic Hinrichsen BA (Hons), CQSW

Nic trained and worked as a social worker and specialised in children and families. His background is as a Local Authority social care practitioner and manager experienced in residential and field social work; court social work; specialist services (intermediate treatment); Youth Justice; and as a reviewing officer and service manager. He has worked extensively in Social Services, Youth Justice, Education and Youth Services and was formerly Chief Executive of a service-provider charity, working with vulnerable and 'at risk' young people, young people in the criminal justice system and young people leaving care. He is a consultant specialising in strategy and policy development, business analysis and assessment, business processes, procedures, and quality assurance in governance, management and operational service delivery in not-for-profit sectors.

Peter Kennison BA, MA Criminology, Dip. NEBSS, PhD

Peter is a Senior Lecturer in the Department of Criminology and Sociology at Middlesex University. He is also Undergraduate Programme Leader for Criminal Justice and Criminology, and Policing. His research and teaching interests include policing and police accountability; community safety; crime and disorder; and child protection. Peter was a police officer in London for over 25 years and his insider perspective has given him a valuable insight towards practice experience in child protection.

Caroline Metcalf BA (Hons) PhD

Caroline's PhD awarded in 2006 was entitled *Making Sense of Sex Offenders and the Internet*. The thesis focused on the way Internet sex offenders are understood within the criminal justice system, that is, those professionals working and dealing directly with Internet offenders. Its contribution to theoretical Criminology relates to the social construction debates surrounding how child sexual abuse is understood and how this is contingent upon historical, cultural, legal, political, economical, media and value-laden doctrines. Caroline is currently **a** Programme Specific Facilitator for the Probation Service. Caroline is responsible for assessing people's suitability for the sexual offending treatment programme and delivering Sex Offender Groupwork Programmes. These programmes are based on cognitive behavioural principles and are delivered in a community-based treatment programme for offenders who have committed sexual offences.

David Porteous BA, MA

David is currently a Senior Lecturer in the Department of Criminology and Sociology at Middlesex University. He is Programme Leader for MA Criminology: Crime Conflict and Control; BA Youth Justice; BA Criminology and Psychology. David teaches a variety of subjects at undergraduate and postgraduate level including criminological theory and research, international comparative criminology, youth crime and youth justice. His recent research has focused on violence involving young people as perpetrators and victims and on the effectiveness of the youth justice system in meeting their needs.

Glossary of terms

ACMD   Advisory Council on the Misuse of Drugs
ACPC   Area Child Protection Committee
ADHD   Attention Deficit Hyperactivity Disorder
BCS   British Crime Survey
C&FCS   Child and Family Consultation Service
CAF   Common Assessment Framework
CAFCAS   Children and Family Court Advisory and Support Service
CAIT   Child Abuse Major Investigation Team
CAMHS   Child and Adolescent Mental Health Service
CDA   Crime and Disorder Act 1998
CMU   Crime Management Unit
COPCA   The Catholic Office for the Protection of Children and Vulnerable Adults
CP   Child protection
CPS   Crown Prosecution Service
CPT   Child Protection Team
CRB   Criminal Records Bureau
CRIS   Crime Recording Information System
CSSR   Council Social Services Responsibilities
DfES   Department for Education and Skills
DOH   Department of Health
DSM   Diagnostic and Statistical Manual of Mental Disorders
ECM   Every Child Matters
EPO   Emergency Protection Order
FGC   Family Group Conference
FGM   Female Genital Mutilation
GBH   Grievous Bodily Harm
HMIC   Her Majesty's Inspector of Constabulary
HMSO   Her Majesty's Stationery Office
HOC   Home Office Circular
Hydra   High-tech Multi-Agency Critical Incident Exercise
IAG   Safeguarding Children Independent Advisory Group
ICS   Integrated Children's System
IMPACT   Information Management, Prioritisation, Analysis, Co-ordination and Tasking
ISKCON   Hare Krishna church or International Society for Krishna Consciousness
LCPC   London Child Protection Committee
LSCB   Local Safeguarding Children Board
MAPPP   Multi-Agency Public Protection Panel
MIT   Child Abuse Major Investigation Team
MIT   Major Investigation Teams
MPS   Metropolitan Police Service
NAYJ   National Association for Youth Justice
NOS   National Occupational Standards

NPIA	National Police Improvement Agency
OC&JS	Crime and Justice Survey
OCU	Operational Command Units
PCLO	Police Conference Liaison Officers
PEP	Pastoral Education Plan
RI	Religious Institutions
SCIP	Safeguarding Children involved in Prostitution
SSD	Social Services Department
SIDS	Sudden Infant Death Syndrome
VS	Victim Support
YJB	Youth Justice Board
YOT	Youth Offending Teams

Introduction

This book sets out to understand the phenomenon of child abuse in an inter-disciplinary way. In doing so this publication uses a variety of professionals and academics who illustrate the importance of viewing child abuse within the contexts of social relations, processes and interactions. Therefore any studies or methods used here originate from the specific subject area located within a variety of disciplines e.g. sociology, criminology, psychology, social policy, health, education, social care, social work, community safety and the police. Furthermore, the contributors outline and explain the various changes that have occurred in their specialist areas, not only in terms of practice, policy and the law, but also in respect of their agency roles and responsibilities.

In Chapter 1 Caroline Metcalf and Peter Kennison introduce the book by discussing and unpacking the concepts of 'child, childhood and child abuse'. The chapter considers these key concepts in terms of social constructs that attract differing ideas, beliefs and assumptions from observers, researchers, practitioners and academics alike. Lack of consensus is a constant problem. The chapter explores the doctrines and debates that evidently influence and 'bring life' to the social constructivist perspective of child abuse.

Chapter 2, by David Porteous, focuses on the relatively under-researched phenomenon of children as victims of street crime. The chapter is divided into three sections. It begins by suggesting that children's experiences as victims of crimes such as robbery and assault have at least until quite recently represented something of a blind spot – the omission of children from most British Crime Surveys being an example. The chapter then summarises what is known about children as victims of street crime, describing patterns of victimisation identifiable from quantitative research and the experience of street crime as evidenced in qualitative studies. Finally, the chapter reflects on the implications of current knowledge for criminological theory and for youth justice policy and practice.

Caroline Chatwin critically reviews recent research of parental use of alcohol and illicit drugs in Chapter 3. The chapter considers recent statistical information on drug use and drug users which reveals a continuing upward trend in the use of licit and illicit drugs among the general population. In line with this increasing general trend, the number of parents and carers of children reporting problematic use of these substances is also increasing. This chapter seeks to explore the growing public and governmental awareness of this issue as a potential problem. There has been a recent 'explosion' of research in this area. Evidence suggesting that the children of parents/carers displaying addictive behaviour patterns can be disadvantaged is examined, and contrasted with quantitative research documenting the opposite. She concludes the chapter by making recommendations for policy-making in this sensitive area.

In Chapter 4 Caroline Metcalf explores the issue of child abuse and the Internet by focusing on social construction debates surrounding the child sex offender. The rising number of individuals downloading child abusive images on the Internet is of significant concern, one which has heightened speculation and debate. The chapter takes a look at these individuals and the activity in which they engage, the need for this to be understood by academics, politicians, professionals, the media and the public. It presents the current political debates about child sex offender risk and, in particular, its underpinning in Conservative neo-liberal rhetoric that New Labour have perpetuated in similar fashion. It draws on the impacts of recent events, namely the Soham murders and Operation Ore, which have directly influenced the political agenda regarding the way sex offenders are managed in the community. In particular, the chapter refers to one community project funded by the Home Office, Circles of Support and Accountability, which neatly illustrates the current attempt to reintegrate sex offenders into their local area by directly involving members of the same community. Furthermore, Caroline examines the political debates surrounding the demand to 'name and shame' registered sex offenders. Despite the growing trend to give victims of crime a 'voice' by focusing primarily on their welfare needs, the Government's reaction to sex offenders residing in the community is very much reflective of 'offender focuses'. The impact on understandings of 'paedophile' risk may be marked by public knowledge of such offenders who inhabit the community we live in.

In Chapter 5 Sally Angus discusses the issue of child victims and the role of youth offending teams in delivering restorative justice to young victims of crime. Children and young people not only make up a great proportion of suspects in criminal matters, but also of victims of crime. The role of the victim in the criminal justice system is also taken into account where it has travelled from the periphery of the criminal justice system to (virtual) centre stage. The Crime and Disorder Act 1998 and the Youth Justice and Criminal Evidence Act 1999 introduced for the first time into English law the concept of restorative justice. This process in principle allows victims of crime to be engaged more fully in 'their' crime. The newly formed youth offending teams are required to have a victim focus in all work they undertake with young people who offend. This illustrates the concept of restorative justice and how involving victims has proved somewhat problematic – a cultural challenge for those practitioners working in youth justice. The chapter shows that research undertaken in youth offending teams has revealed some reluctance on the part of practitioners to consider restorative justice and its application to work with young offenders. Other research indicates that many crimes committed by young people are against their peers, particularly crimes of violence.

Chapter 6 by Peter Kennison concentrates on the issue of child protection in the religious context. This chapter helps define the nature of faith, religion and the church within the context of child protection and plots its contemporary history. It shows how in many cases individuals within the church have abused their duty of care with respect to children and young people, not only in the UK but abroad also, by hiding and denying its existence. Yet denial by religious groups relating to child abuse as its defence mechanism has often worked in the past to deflect blame. The religious setting has included an element of secretiveness, and when accusations of abuse have been made it has acted as many other institutions have done, and tried to cover up the problem. This chapter explores how in some cases within the religious setting, steps have been taken to improve child protection measures.

Chapter 7 by Peter Kennison concentrates on the police and partnership failures in the tragic case of Victoria Climbié, a 9 year old child who was killed by her carers. The policy 'Every Child Matters', that has been regularly updated, was inspired by the lessons learnt from the failure of agencies to protect Victoria Climbié. Using examples it focuses on the failure of the police and other key agencies involved in child protection to work individually and collectively to safeguard the welfare of this child. Throughout the public inquiry chaired by Lord Laming, evidence was presented which surprised spectators as to the levels of incompetence in the police, health and social services. It critically examined the central importance of the relationships of agencies working together as partners involved in child protection. The chapter graphically illustrates that when partnerships fail, the true nature of any organisation and its interconnections can be viewed. The chapter reveals the fault lines and causes that show how lessons can be learnt for the future.

Chapter 8 by Gwyn Daniel deals with child abuse and the health service and projects a view from the health perspective. Since the theme of this book is of children as victims, it quite naturally places great emphasis on the powerlessness and vulnerability of children. In this chapter Gwyn discusses how we talk with individual children whose abusive or otherwise adverse experiences lead professionals to be concerned for their safety and wellbeing. She argues that focusing on them only as powerless victims may not be the most helpful approach. There is inevitably a tension between the way that children's victimisation needs to be witnessed and documented at the macro level of policy and social action and the more complex, subtle and personal processes that infuse the micro level of our professional interactions with individual children.

Chapter 9 deals with primary school education and child abuse taking a teacher's standpoint. It is written by Sue Goodman and Anthony Goodman. In this chapter the writers argue that children rarely and spontaneously report abuse and more often than not it is unusual to see physical signs of abuse in the school setting. Suspected sexual abuse is often manifested by inexplicable behaviour such as withdrawal, attention seeking, challenging or aggressive outbursts. When challenged, the child may become disturbed or withdrawn. The signs will be brought to the attention of the designated child protection member of the school, often the head teacher, who will need to make the decision whether to pursue this further. Children may express anxiety about going to particular places of worship, club, homes of other children etc. but not be able to express why. As parents/carers are seen every day at the school gate the school is aware of the dynamics between the parent/carer and their child. Parents/carers may not be aware of this or not wish to know of how their children behave or if something is worrying them. At the end of the day the child may display reluctance to go home and the school has the dilemma of what to do. The process of how this can be taken forward within the school will be discussed, as will how the school links in to working with other agencies.

Chapter 10 by Chris Bourlet plots the contemporary issues relating to police failures highlighted in the Laming Report. As an insider and formally as a senior member of the Child Protection Command, based at New Scotland Yard, he reveals some of the problems that specifically affected the police organisation locally and strategically and how they coped with them. Using examples taken from the Laming Report the chapter reveals some of the challenges e.g. the handling and sharing of information, professionalising the investigation processes, better partner communication and the change programme. It reveals the changes that have led to the development of proactive methods implemented by the Metropolitan Police Service since 2000. The benefits from better partnership working, enhanced technology and better tools, policies and procedures affording a better chance of success are also examined and explained. It deliberates on the issue of joint case reviews as a means of monitoring progress and as a means of proactive intervention in child protection, and on the need to raise awareness throughout the police service in order to protect children from harm.

Chapter 11 is entitled 'Safeguarding Vulnerable Children and Young People, including those Involved in Prostitution: The Social Work /Child Protection Process' and is written by Nic Hinrichsen and Anthony Goodman. The chapter looks at the statutory child protection/safe-guarding process, from the point of referral to children's social services. It outlines the stages of the statutory social work agency processes in the investigation, and subsequent response-planning in relation to concerns that a child is suffering or is likely to suffer significant harm. The process is set against the Every Child Matters agenda of 'Working Together to Safeguard Children' and is based on the Quality Protects Children's Social Services Core Information Requirements and specifically on the Integrated Children's System (ICS) framework for work-ing with children in need and their families. It is an overview designed to give the reader an understanding of the sequences of events and stages of social work involvement. It is not intended as a comprehensive guide to each of the specific stages. The chapter draws on the problem of child prostitution to illustrate the issues involved when children are at risk of significant harm and when they may not present as 'deserving' victims. This can trigger what has been described as punitive welfarism.

The final chapter, Concluding Themes, by Peter Kennison and Anthony Goodman brings together and develops some of the topics raised in the earlier chapters and draws out the key issues, concerns and what constitutes good practice for the reader. It reveals how child, childhood and child abuse are constructed and what this means in terms of child protection. The impact of different perspectives on child protection is elaborated from the viewpoint of a variety of professionals, including social services, schools, health, police, the religious setting and youth offending teams. It demonstrates how over the years, as disciplines have developed, the search for answers has become more complicated and difficult. This has resulted in the further fragmentation of services and even greater complexity which increases the potential for mistake. In the aftermath of Victoria Climbié and the Children Act 2004, can we be confident that further tragedies will not occur again?

Chapter 1

Constructing childhood and child abuse

Caroline Metcalf and Peter Kennison

Introduction

In order to achieve an understanding of what constitutes abuse, it is necessary to first unpack the debates around what actually constitutes a child, rather than abuse specifically. It is therefore crucial to identify some of the historical, cultural, political, spatial, economical and value-laden doctrines and debates that evidently influence and 'bring life' to the social constructivist perspective of child abuse. This chapter also gives meaning to the social construction of child, childhood, child sexual offenders, and moreover, claims-making activity theory (Spector and Kitsuse, 2001). Socially constructing and interpreting the concepts of child abuse are based on relativism, meaning that these concepts will change in time and space since they are not absolute concepts (Parton and Wattam, 1999). Deconstructing child abuse in this way helps our understanding in relation to degrees of child maltreatment and shows up the lack of societal agreement on child abuse that also means intervention thresholds and associated policy are disputed.

The changing patterns in perceptions of adult–child sexual relationships are also explored in order to help us understand how such relationships came to be viewed as abhorrent and deplorable abuse. The authors raise critical issues that will identify the processes which a claim must go through in order to become an established social problem. It brings in and revives labelling theory (Lemert, 1951; Becker, 1963), and importantly, applies it to the work of professionals involved in managing child abuse and, more particularly, child sexual abuse.

The social construction of child sexual abuse is also raised to show that this phenomenon is made up of a complex matrix of elements. Power lies in the hands of those who define and label child sex offenders in the name of a child-centred approach to child protection policy, which the authors suggest can often be a one-sided debate based on 'fear and risk' rather than the truth.

Deconstructing and understanding the notions of child, childhood and child abuse

As with all social problems, it is important to see how problems are constructed – and labelled – and who is doing the labelling. Social constructivism implies that 'knowing' is linked to 'doing' and that the relationship between understanding and social action is symbiotic. The knowledge of everyday life assigns children to childhood by their parents, guardians and other adults (Berger and Luckmann, 1966), seemingly without choice. This means that child or childhood is associated with and structured by a variety of assumptions, meanings and understandings that relate to that particular social world. They are also concepts which do not stand still in time and space. Therefore whichever way child or childhood is constructed today will continue to change according to what influences are at work on them.

A suitable beginning for any discourse of child abuse must start with defining and arguing the notions of child and childhood. Geographically, these are difficult and disputed concepts which are not only locally, nationally and globally defined, but change according to historical, cultural, social, legal or geographical influences. Theorists may argue that childhood is an objective phenomenon simply because it is highly evident that what constitutes child and child sexual abuse varies not only globally but locally as well.

The concept of childhood is adult-centric and as such parents (and carers) tend to want to preserve the phenomenon by imposing restrictions in the name of protection (Kitzinger, 1997; Parton and Wattam, 1999). The concept of childhood emerged as a focus of renewed interest in the late 1980s and was highlighted by James and Prout (1997) as the new paradigm (Parton and Wattam 1999).

Simplistic value-free dictionary definitions define a child as: 'boy or girl between birth and puberty' and childhood as 'the time or condition of being a child' (CED, 1994). The notion of child is closely linked to childhood, and the status and rights of children are determined by adults. Adults also determine to what extent mistreatment of children takes place (Corby, 2004, p. 9). Statutes determine the notion of child by creating legal principles which not only define when a child or young person becomes sexually mature but also introduces specific offences which regulate sexual activity between adults and children. Legal notions of 'child' suggest that the age of both the child victim and offender are significant. For example, under the Sexual Offences Act 2003, to prove the offence of sexual assault (s 2) if the victim is a child under 13 years old there is no issue of consent to be considered, but where the victim is between the ages of 13 and 16 years old consent must be taken into account.

Even within jurisdictions locally, the notions of child and childhood are contested between practitioners, researchers and academics alike. Furthermore, globally, significance should also be given to the contested nature and the dilemmas of defining and constructing the notion of 'child'. For example, Article 1 of the United Nations Convention on the Rights of the Child defines it as:

> *A child means every human being below the age of 18 years unless, under the law applicable to the child, majority is attained earlier.*

Failing to find common ground through definition also makes researching child-related issues like abuse very difficult. As Russell (1984) has stated:

> researchers and practitioners have reached no consensus on child sex acts that constitute sexual abuse, nor on the age that defines a child.

Even historical notions of child development, maltreatment and childhood are disputed. Differing perspectives range from, on the one hand, non-existence of childhood, with adults perceiving them as detached 'little adults', whilst on the other, showing them to have very close child/adult emotional ties even though this was set against extreme poverty and high infant mortality rates (Corby, 2004, p. 15). Pollack (1983) suggests that the notion of childhood certainly existed throughout the period 1500 to 1900, however the phenomenon changed and developed during this time. A major flaw in any historical analysis has been the way childhood is generalised, since children's experiences must vary even in a particular time and space. For example, children of different classes, genders and races are likely to have widely different experiences in every period of history (Corby, 2004, p. 15).

Definitions change over time, so what may be true today may have been only partly true yesterday and not true at all last week. For example, the smacking and punishment of children was an acceptable part of Victorian society, whereas today there is a far lower tolerance of the physical abuse of children. Explanations of crime directed against children or young people have mainly been rooted in what actually constitutes a child, rather than about the abuse specifically. Thus the constitution of a child is bound also by culture and time periods and, up until the nineteenth century, children were not viewed differently from adults (Howitt, 1995a). Historical understandings are central to grasping the current nature of socially constructing child, childhood, child sexual offenders and economic agendas of the police in tackling offending behaviour against children. A child, then, can be defined in a number of ways legally, socially, politically and culturally.

Jackson and Scott (1999) suggest that childhood is institutionalised through family, education and the state, and further, that these result in children depending on adults and thus becoming excluded from full participation in adult society. Moreover, childhood was constituted through the gaze of social science disciplines (Rose, 1989) and, subsequently, that of social workers, educationalists and others who claimed expertise in monitoring, categorising and managing children. Jackson and Scott argue:

> These expert knowledges have shaped common sense understandings of childhood as a natural state, so that we are all assumed to 'know' what a child is, to be able to comment on what constitutes a 'proper' childhood. (1999, p. 91)

Jackson and Scott (1999) go on to suggest that the process of maturing from child to adult in naturally occurring stages is taken for granted. It assumes that there is a 'right age' at which children should acquire certain freedoms and responsibilities and develop competence. Such ideas about childhood are so widely accepted that they are rarely questioned. Furthermore, they state that the childhood developmental paradigm is at the heart of risk anxiety and risk management in relation to children. Jackson and Scott (1999) also suggest that elements of lost childhood, pressures to develop early maturity and restricted freedom are interconnected. For example, beauty pageants that are seemingly a long-time tradition of American culture are argued to be sexually exploitative and even pornographic. Such arguments are typically cited with the murder of child-pageant star, six-year-old JonBenet Ramsey in Boulder, Colorado on Boxing Day 1996. Jackson and Scott (1999) suggest that the sexualisation of girlhood is not exceptional:

> Many a small girl has been taught that 'in order to be pleasing she must be pretty as a picture' and encouraged to gain attention through 'childish coquetry'. (de Beauvoir 1972, p. 306, cited in Jackson and Scott 1999, p. 99)

Childhood was presented as 'natural, passive, incompetent and incomplete' (James and Prout 1997). However, when applied to child sexual abuse the perpetrator would not only view children as being innocent, ignorant and passive, but also feel that these factors only served to make their victims more attractive to their abuser (Kitzinger, 1997). Furthermore, innocence itself is routinely sexualised (Ennew, 1986; Jackson and Scott,1999; Kitzinger, 1988). Jackson and Scott (1999) propose that sexual risks to children need to be understood as being fundamental to the social construction of childhood and sexuality. Within the current discourse, it is seemingly acceptable for an adult male to be sexually attracted to youth, vulnerability and innocence, provided the subject is not *too* young, too vulnerable and too innocent. A person who breaks this rule earns the condemnation, 'nothing more monstrous than man' (ibid., p. 104).

Child abuse as a social problem

The social construction of child sexual abuse refers to the symbolic activities (Mead, 1934) that determine what behaviours are actually abusive to children and what the nature of intervention should be (Little, 1997). Fullers and Myers (1941, p. 320) identify a social problem as 'a condition which is defined by a considerable number of persons as a deviation from some norm, which they cherish' (cited in Spector and Kitsuse, 2001, p. 74). There tends to be much confusion over the defining of social problems and Spector and Kitsuse (2001) conclude that they are the activities of those who assert the existence of conditions and define them as problems. In an attempt to explore social problems as claims-making activities, Spector and Kitsuse (2001) abandon the notion that social problems are a kind of *condition*, and rather, treat them as an *activity*. Fullers and Myers (1941) argue that value-judgements typically made about a particular topic are premature since such judgements divert attention away from the phenomenon itself.

According to claims-making activity theory, those working with children help in constructing definitions for abuse based on legislation and personal experience (Department of Health, 1995 in Parton and Wattam, 1999). Traditionally, key workers such as teachers, therapists, psychologists and health workers developed their theories of child abuse through discussions with each other (Norman, 1994), and their knowledge and understanding provide new materials for academics to develop the theory of social construction in this setting (Parton et al., 1997). Parton et al., (1997) argues that the objective reality of child sexual abuse is questioned and emphasis is given to the extent that such abuse is in the 'eye of the beholder'. Furthermore, social construction theory relates to the 'emergence, maintenance, history, and conceptualisation of what is defined as child sexual abuse and what is defined as child protection work' (ibid., p. 70).

During the past fifty years there has been a theoretical shift from the focus of analysing the causes of objective social conditions to the processes by which members of society define such conditions as problems (Spector and Kitsuse, 2001). Rubington and Weinberg (1971) have identified labelling theory (Becker, 1963) as one of the five approaches to the study of social problems. However, labelling theory is confronted with problems of logical development that have also plagued value-conflict and other subjectivist approaches to social phenomena. Spector and Kitsuse (2001) note three similarities between the two theoretical perspectives of labelling and value-conflict theory. Firstly, social problems and deviance are envisaged as products of social processes in which members of a group or a community interpret, evaluate and treat behaviours, persons and conditions as problems. Secondly, focus is shifted from the condition to the members of society who conceive a particular issue as a problem. Thirdly, this type of focus requires a theoretical position in order to account for the symbolic processes of such behaviours and conditions.

Understanding child abuse

Child abuse was first used as an official term in Britain in a Government Circular published in 1980 (Corby, 2004, p. 71), and no absolute definition of child abuse exists that satisfies all policy makers, observers and practitioners. A variety of legal and scientific definitions exist in the literature which mostly describes abusive incidents involving beating, sexual interference and neglect of children (DOH, 1995). So what is child abuse and in what settings does it take place?

In 1999 the Department of Health (DOH) issued some formal guidelines to help practitioners that categorised the nature of child abuse in order that practitioners should gain a better understanding, and these are illustrated below. Again, child abuse is a social construct but can be divided into a variety of positive and negative outcomes and actions. Child abuse can include physical, emotional, neglect and sexual abuse of a child by an adult. Because of the difficulties in definition of child abuse the DOH published some useful indicators which deconstructed this phenomenon for reference purposes, such as:

Physical abuse

Can amount to hitting, shaking, throwing, poisoning, burning, scalding, drowning, suffocating or otherwise causing physical harm to a child. (2000, p. 5)

The DOH has warned that practitioners would interpret any behaviour in its context before defining it as abusive in what they describe as phenomenology, e.g. things as they are perceived, as opposed to the study of the nature of things as they are (DOH, 1999). The context within which any of the above takes place is important in interpreting and highlighting any *outcomes* in order to judge whether any form of protective intervention is required. The definition does not offer any guidance as to when any of these types of abusive behaviour becomes serious enough for action to be taken by the child protection agencies (Corby, 2004, p. 71). Other factors to be considered by the practitioner must relate to the seriousness or degree of any injury, the age of the child, the intention of the perpetrator (whether abusive or not), what evidence is available to put before a court, and any other important factors including whether the parent or carer is not necessarily responsible for his/her actions, e.g. Munchhausen's syndrome by proxy. When considering these factors the seriousness of the harm or neglect will range between two ends of the spectrum from minor injury at one end whilst at the other it would be serious injury and/or death. The decision to prosecute means perceiving all the factors together and relating the evidence to legal definitions to see whether a case will succeed. The standard of proof required for professionals will vary since intervention by social workers may be 'on the balance of probabilities' whilst for court proceedings or police purposes the balance of proof must be 'beyond all reasonable doubt'.

Emotional abuse

Is the persistent emotional ill treatment of a child such as to cause persistent effects on a child's emotional development?

This may involve conveying to the children that they are worthless or unloved, inadequate or valued only in-so-far as they meet the needs of another person. It also may be related to age or development, which is inappropriate in terms of expectations placed on the children. Causing them to feel frightened, subjecting them to exploitation, or corrupting them also fall within this category. In all types of ill treatment, children will experience aspects of emotional abuse (DOH, 2000, pp. 5–6). Long-term emotional abuse can have adverse consequences for children's development, especially in terms of a child's mental health, behaviour and self-esteem (DOH, 1999, p. 7). The impact of sustained emotional abuse, particularly during infancy, can be as important as, if not more so than, other more visible forms of abuse. Exposure to such abuse may be more prevalent where there are issues relating to domestic violence, adult mental health problems and parental substance misuse (ibid., p. 7). Research carried out by Garbarino and Gilliam (1980) gave professionals a wide-ranging and broad definition of 'psychological maltreatment' as 'Acts of omission or commission by a parent or guardian that are judged by a mixture of community values and professional expertise to be inappropriate and damaging' (Garbarino and Gilliam, 1980, p. 7, cited in Corby, 2004, p. 81). Corby questions the usefulness of the definition operationally as being too broad, and more specific terms can be found in research carried out by Burnett (1993). Burnett lists nine forms of psychological abuse as follows:

> *confining a child in a small place*
> *severe public humiliation*
> *the 'Cinderella' syndrome*
> *severe verbal abuse*
> *encouraging or coercing a child into delinquency*
> *threatening a child*
> *refusal of psychiatric treatment*
> *not allowing social or emotional growth*
> *not providing a loving, nurturing atmosphere*
> (Burnet, 1993, p. 446, cited in Corby, 2004, p. 81)

Corby asserts that even these situations are disputed, more by professionals than the public, in terms of intervention by the child protection agencies. But the DOH (2000) guidelines, supported by Corby, suggest that emotional abuse which, in theory, is able to take place on its own, will almost certainly be accompanied by other forms of abuse (Corby, 2004, p. 81).

Neglect

Is a persistent failing to act, thus denying basic physical and/or psychological needs, which is likely to result in serious impairment of a child's health or development.

This may occur where a parent, guardian or carer fails or neglects to provide normal care that aids a child's growth and ensures it will thrive. This means a failure to provide food, shelter and/or clothing; failure to protect from serious harm or danger; or failure to ensure access to medical care or treatment. This also means the failure to respond to a child's emotional needs (DOH, 2000, p. 6). Since other aspects of child abuse require a positive action neglect is a negative or failure to do something, meaning that for practitioners it is the most difficult to prove. This aspect of abuse is located within a family setting, so is about parenting and people who are known to the victim and does not involve strangers. Corby highlights the fact that styles of parenting may be brought into question (2004, p. 80) but the DOH suggests that maltreatment occurs in a variety of settings and that the evidence of normal behaviour within families is important in understanding what is abnormal (1995, p. 12). Yet what was normal a generation ago may be abnormal by today's standards. The same can be said socially and culturally. Also what may be socially acceptable by the majority may not necessarily be optimal, for instance, smacking children as a means of control and punishment when they misbehave (ibid, p. 12). What may be typical for some families of certain cultures may not be so for other social groups. Severe forms of neglect can have a major effect on a young child's growth and intellectual development. Persistent forms of neglect can seriously impair a child's health, development, social functioning, relationships and educational progress and, in some extreme cases, can result in death (DOH 1999, p. 7).

Sexual abuse

Involves forcing or enticing a child or young person to take part in sexual activities, whether or not the child is aware of what is happening (DOH, 2000, p. 6)

Guidance here builds on previous DOH advice in 1991, which gave a very broad definition of sexual abuse, as meaning 'actual or likely sexual exploitation of a child or adolescent. The child may be dependent and/or emotionally immature' (DOH, 1991, p. 49). It shows that such activities may involve physical contact, including penetrative (e.g. rape or buggery) and non-penetrative acts. There may also be non-contact activities such as children looking at, or being involved in, the production of pornographic material, or watching activities, or encouraging children to behave in ways which are sexually inappropriate (DOH, 2000, p. 6). Here a distinction is made for the first time in respect of physical sexual contact in what Calder refers to as the 'hands off' sexual crime (2004, p. iv). Corby suggests that the advice does not reflect intra- or extra-familial abuse nor does it raise the issue of the age of the perpetrator (Corby, 2004, p. 78). Corby also suggests that a more appropriate and comprehensive definition comes from the work of Glaser and Frosh (1988) which suggests:

Any child below the age of consent may be deemed to have been sexually abused when a sexually mature person has by design or by neglect of their usual societal or specific responsibilities in relation to a child, engaged or permitted the engagement of that child in any activity of a sexual nature which is intended to lead to the sexual gratification of the sexually mature person. This definition pertains whether or not it involves genital contact, and whether or not there is discernable harming outcome in the short-term. (Glaser and Frosh, 1988, p. 5, cited in Corby, 2004, p. 78)

Child sexual abuse, in whatever form, is considered by child health and welfare professionals to be a very serious form of abuse and a high priority should be given to intervention (Corby, 2004, p. 78). Green (2001) suggests that:

Child sexual abuse is a common manifestation of adult and gendered power, but also that subsequent, typical responses to its detection compound the initial abuse and dis-empower and invalidate children even further. (2001, p. 160)

Green considers the difficulties of research into child sexual abuse and suggests that it is not possible to separate out intra- or extra-familial abuse as many abusers operate both inside and outside their families (MacLeod 1996). Many institutional abusers also target settings and institutions where children reside, such as children's homes, schools, and youth and social groups (Gallagher, 1998).

Moral panic, real or contrived?

Societies appear to be subject, every now and then, to periods of moral panic. A condition, episode, person or group of persons, emerges to become defined as a threat to societal values and interests . . . sometimes the object of the panic is quite novel and at other times it is something which has been in existence long enough but suddenly appears in the limelight. (Cohen, 1972, p. 9, cited in Parton, 1985, p. 70)

The claims-making perspective

Firstly, let us turn to the types of groups involved in making claims with specific reference to the claims made about sex offenders:

Interest Groups This group is typically associated with the media, for they are well known in cynically manipulating values to pursue their own material interest, i.e. selling newspapers. It also comprises that group or those groups making the claims and complaints (Spector and Kitsuse, 2001). It is also possible to situate the police within this group – after all, public reassurance is a key priority on their agenda.

Value Groups This group will typically involve parents and members of the public who could also be situated within the interest group. It will also consist of voluntary organisations.

Disinterested Groups Legislation and non-state agencies. For example, their role is likely to involve responding to the interest and value groups although they themselves are not typically involved in campaigning to document a claim.

These distinctions encourage one to abandon the idea that social problems are developed merely through value-judgements alone. Indeed, some groups are involved to defend vested interests. Moreover, they may adopt value interests as a guise to pragmatically protect their interests (Spector and Kitsuse, 2001). However, it is methodologically difficult to distinguish between those who legitimately belong in the value group and those who do not (ibid.).

Fullers and Myers (1941, cited in Spector and Kituse, 2001, p. 74)) argue that social problems are contained within a natural historical development in which a particular issue must be formulated as a social problem through a set of processes:

> *Social problems do not appear full-blown, commanding community attention, and evoking adequate policies and machinery for their solution. To the contrary, we believe that social problems exhibit a temporal course of development in which different phases or stages may be distinguished. Each stage anticipates its successor in time and each succeeding stage contains new elements which mark it off from its predecessor. A social problem thus conceived as always being in a dynamic stage of 'becoming' passes through the natural history stages of awareness, policy determination, and reform . . . The 'natural history' as we use the term is simply a conceptual tool for the examination of the data which constitute social problems.* (Fullers and Myers 1941, p. 322)

Lemert (1951) refutes Fullers and Myers' (1941) claims that social problems have a natural history. Rather, he focuses on three stages in the development of a social problem, namely, awareness, policy determination and reform. However, Spector and Kitsuse (2001) turn to other commentators who have entitled their studies using the term 'natural history': for example, Clifford Shaw's (1931) *The Natural History of a Delinquent Career*, Lyford Edwards' (1927) *The Natural History of Revolutions*, Louis Wirth's (1927) examination of the natural history of ghettos, and Robert Park's (1955) *The Natural History of the Newspaper*. The application of natural history to such phenomena moved from descriptions of specific cases to generalisations. Moreover, the exploration of sequences of events provides an understanding of how a particular issue develops and unfolds and emerges as a social activity.

Spector and Kitsuse (2001) suggest that official and governmental agencies play a key role in the social problems activities. However, they differ in the natural history perspective with respect to the fate of social problems after some official or governmental response has occurred. For example, Fullers and Myers (1941) and Blumer (1971) seem to view the end of a problem as being once the official response has occurred. Thus, the resolution of social problems remains suspended and unexamined: that is of course, assuming that a resolution (or the cessation of complaints) has taken place. It is evident that this is not quite the case. Neither Fullers and Myers (1941) nor Blumer (1971) have commented on what happens following the implementation of legislation, or once agencies and programmes have been established. Thus arises the confusion of 'when does the social problem cease to exist?' Spector and Kitsuse (2001) address what happens to a social problem following the implementation of policy with the application of a four-stage model. Conversely, it attempts to address the renewed claims and demands born out of the solutions to previous problems.

Stage one – Group(s) attempt to assert the existence of some condition, define it as offensive, harmful or otherwise undesirable, publicise these assertions, stimulate controversy and create a public or political issue over the matter.

Stage two – Recognition of the legitimacy of these group(s) by some official organisation, agency or institution. It could lead to an official investigation, proposals for reform, and the establishment of an agency to respond to those claims and demands.

Stage three – Re-emergence of claims and demands by the original group(s), or by others, expressing dissatisfaction with the established procedures for dealing with the imputed conditions, the bureaucratic handling of complaints, the failure to generate a condition of trust and confidence in the procedures, and the lack of sympathy for the complaints.

Stage four – Rejection by complainant group(s) of the agency's or institution's response or lack of response to their claims and demands, and the development of activities to create alternative, parallel or counter-institutions as responses to the established procedures (Spector and Kitsuse, 2001, p. 142).

Spector and Kitsuse (2001) identify the media as epitomising the process of problem-defining activities. They argue that if stage one of the process does not receive attention from the mass media then the group(s) may be unsuccessful in documenting their claims.

> *The most critical aspect of this beginning stage is the way complaints are raised and the strategies used to press claims, gain publicity, and arouse controversy. The objective seriousness, extent of a condition, or its presumed dysfunctionality may be relatively independent of success or failure for this transformation.* (Spector and Kitsuse, 2001, p. 143)

The four stages cited above illustrate the variables required in order to document a claim successfully. However, it is evident that without the media it is unlikely that claims would be unbeaten, given the visibility the media bestows to certain topics. Moreover, the low visibility would not invite pressure towards the police and Government to deal with the crime puni-tively, in a timely way, and effectively. Importantly, one of the reasons why the claims about sex offenders are so strong is because nobody dares to refute them. The claims do not come from one group alone – they come from several groups and to rebuff such claims would no doubt bring unpleasant consequences to the opposing person or group.

Cultural variations in notions of legal concepts

In western culture, there is little controversy about defining, for example, photographic images of sexual activity involving children as constituting child abuse. Historically, the collection of abusive images has mostly been socially constructed as unacceptable (Jenkins, 1998), perhaps because the images were not easy to obtain and it was assumed that the perpetrator must have a strong sexual interest in children. In contemporary society, however, obtaining these images is not so challenging and so the socially constructed view of what constitutes a 'paedophile' is problematic and increasingly difficult to pinpoint; therefore it is possible that some individuals are being unfairly labelled and defined.

Child sexual abuse is generally conceptualised differently from emotional and physical abuse. Firstly, the history of sexuality unfolds as an entity of its own, and indeed sexual relationships between adults and children have not always been considered abusive. However, physical and emotional abuse characterises the history of punishment and, moreover, its negative connotations were associated with forms of entertainment, particularly in the Middle Ages. Secondly, the definition of child sexual abuse is difficult to unpack on a global scale. Jackson and Scott (1999) argue that the social construction of childhood and sexuality are culturally specific. For example, anxieties about the risk to children in the UK and the USA are not so evident in Scandinavian and Nordic countries. Although child sexual abuse is arguably a global phenomenon, some of its manifestations are culturally specific. The sexual exploitation of children in Asia is rooted in social relations that differ from those underpinning even organised abuse in wealthy countries (ibid.). As previously mentioned, Fullers and Myers (1941) have utilised the concept of values in their account of the definitional process in which a claim must penetrate. However, Bott (1968) has argued that the use of values and culture as an independent variable is unreliable since there is a tautology between the values and the behaviour it is meant to explain:

> *To say that people behave differently, or have different expectations because they belong to different cultures (i.e. have different values), amounts to no more than saying that they behave differently because they behave differently, or that cultures are different because they are different.* (Bott 1968, p. 219, cited in Spector and Kitsuse 2001, p. 86)

In essence, Bott (1968) is arguing that citing values as a reason for why people define conditions as social problems is avoiding the important issue: how and by what process do values produce such effects?

Time is another factor party to socially constructing child sexual abuse. Standards of how abuse is labelled changes considerably over time, not only within the same cultures but also between people within the same culture.

> *Child abuse is thus a social construction whose meaning arises from the value structure of a social group and the ways in which these values are interpreted and negotiated in real situations.* (Taylor, 1989, p. 46, cited in Parton, 1997, p. 71)

Gibbons et al. (1995) surmise:

> *Child maltreatment is not the same sort of phenomenon as whooping cough: it cannot be diagnosed with scientific measuring instruments. It is more like pornography, a socially constructed phenomenon that reflects values and opinions of particular times.* (Gibbons et al., 1995, p. 12, cited in Parton, 1997, p. 221)

The investigation of child sexual abuse has always been typically problematic given the lack of overt signs. Thus, importance is placed on the context in which the events occurred in order to construct definitions. Conversely, public attitudes and perceptions on child sexual abuse have fluctuated and varied widely. It was once the opinion that people with a sexual interest in children were just confused individuals and were unlikely to cause any harm – but this has now swung to the other extreme, namely the belief that they are 'monsters' incapable of change (Jenkins, 1998).

The social construction perspective provides a systematic argument that the world in which we live does not consist of total objective phenomena. Indeed, it is constructed by a whole range of social arrangements and practices (Berger and Luckmann, 1966, in Potter, 1996). Some commentators may argue that the social construction perspective is meaningless because if everything is a social construction then surely nothing really exists; rather, it is simply how we label something (Parton, 1997). However, the authors argue that it is unnecessary to take such an extreme social constructivist stance, and that is important to acknowledge the place of objective reality, and then recognise the role of how one socially constructs such objective realities. For example, firstly, we are well aware that sexual relations between adults and children occur and, to our knowledge, have always occurred. That is an objective reality. Secondly, we also understand that the majority of children who are involved in sexual relations with adults suffer some psychological effects, particularly in later life. This is also an objective reality. Thirdly, how we understand and interpret messages of such sexual relations and construct meanings to the perpetrator and recipient of such relations is dependent upon our social construction standpoint. Moreover, it is quite evident that social construction standpoints are contingent upon notions of culture, time and even professional occupations.

Controversies about sexuality surely have evolved from the alterations in patterns of work, family organisation and gender relations that have been the driving force behind the continuing struggles over 'appropriate' sexual behaviour for women and men.

Currently the lowest age of consent in a western country is 13 years, in Spain. The lowest age worldwide is 12, in Argentina, Colombia, Mexico and Peru. Sex between same sex partners is typically illegal across most religions in Algeria, India, Malaysia, Saudi Arabia, Singapore and Tanzania. Alabama is the only state that makes homosexuality illegal (Age of Consent Online 2005). Indeed, the framing of sex-crime lay in the backdrop of the reshaping of western thought in the latter half of the nineteenth century.

During this era, when neo-classicist ideas became outdated positivist criminology assumed that deviant acts resulted from medical or biological influences. This revolution in criminology is, for example, manifested in the observation of an English psychiatrist, Henry Maudsley, during the 1870s, when he argued, 'Crime is on the borderline of insanity'. The phenomenon of child sexual abuse remained a political concern, particularly while the women's movement in America was enjoying success between 1918 and 1920, although shortly afterwards political feminism fragmented, social reform for children halted and, suddenly, labelling certain behaviours, like smacking, as cruel now became seen as 'middle-class busybodyism' (Jenkins, 1998). A journal article by Jacob and Rosamond Goldberg in 1935 (ibid.) discussed child rape and molestation, but despite this, public interest in this topic remained patchy. It is thought that other criminal activity was more newsworthy during the early 1930s (ibid.). However, in the progressive era in the aftermath of the Second World War, the sex offender became known as the 'predator'. During this time sex fiends were not entirely differentiated from the psychopath murderer (ibid.).

Then came the sexual revolution of the 1950s after the publication of Kinsey et al.'s (1948) research on human sexuality, which sanctioned hitherto stigmatised behaviour, and the hysteria over sexual deviancy dramatically decreased. This 'apathy' continued into the next two decades and child sexual abuse became virtually an invisible activity and crime thereafter. The way in which theories of child sexual abuse have changed has been particularly non-linear. Opinion amongst the public has been fickle in nature and agencies managing cases of child sexual abuse have varying degrees of expectations. Even today, it remains difficult for many to accept that intra-familial sexual abuse (abuse that takes place within the family) is a common fact in our lives. Knowledge of child sexual abuse reached new heights following the events of Cleveland in 1987 when a hospital in Middlesbrough appeared to have an extensive problem of suspected cases of child sexual abuse. Public concern grew strongly and the Cleveland Report of 1988 by Lady Butler-Sloss capitalised on the public mood; since then the mass media and legislators have followed suit. It was recommended in the report that social workers and the police share responsibility for the control of child sexual abuse. The social construction of deviancy as described above was perhaps the biggest factor in opening the pathway for legislation to be reinforced and this continued as Internet offences came to light. Despite legislative responses, child sexual abuse had remained an invisible crime, and was thought to be a rarity.

Sex offending is a crime particularly significant and useful in offering explanations of the social construction phenomenon, given that ideologies of sex can change and are perceived differently according to time and cultural values. In many ways, liberalism and late modernity have granted the freedom of sexual expression, and yet almost paradoxically, there have been attempts to increase surveillance and state sovereign control of the domestic sphere.

This brings us to the requirements of today's Sex Offender Register and the Sex Offender Orders, which were implemented as part of the Crime and Disorder Act 1998. Registers of offenders compound the idea of 'knowing' that there are convicted or cautioned sex offenders living within the community. In turn, this possibly alters the social construction phenomenon, in that the public must accept that there are sex offenders living nearby, perhaps 'around the corner' even. It may not be the image of a paedophile that is altered as much as the social construction of the 'threat' existing in the community. Despite the threat of a registered sex offender living in the community, there is also the reassurance that the offender is being monitored, although there is a misconception on both parts to be addressed. Silverman and Wilson (2002) reflect on a study of victim surveys by Grubin (1998), in which the conclusion has profound implications for understanding the prevalence of child sexual abuse. Grubin (1998) notes that the annual number of victims of child sexual abuse in England and Wales can be estimated at anywhere between 3,500 and 72,600. Indeed, statistical analysis is unreliable and assumptions cannot be made, 'let alone sensible policy-making' (Silverman and Wilson, 2002, p. 21). In other words, it is not the ex-offenders living in the community that pose the widest threat, rather, it is the unconvicted offenders that have not yet been caught, and perhaps never will.

Silverman and Wilson rightly point out:

> *Thus the belief (held by the News of the World and others), that by focusing on one narrow measure of sexual crime – the Sex Offender Register – we are contributing to child protection, is ludicrously wrong-headed.* (2002, p. 21)

The Sex Offender Register created under the Sex Offenders Act 1997 is subject to heavy criticism, firstly because it is not 'retrospective', so offenders are only registered if the offences were committed after 1 September 1997 when the idea was first introduced. Secondly, there is debate about how the register actually protects the public (Silverman and Wilson 2002). However, the register is particularly useful for the concept of multi-agency initiatives and information-sharing also brought alive by the Crime and Disorder Act 1998. The regular meetings of Multi-Agency Public Protection Panels (MAPPPs) comprise the relevant professionals to discuss a 'case' and assess the risk of a registered offender. Indeed, it may be a future trend that volunteers involved in the Circles of Support and Accountability project will attend these meetings, thus compounding some of the positive and useful aspects of the Sex Offenders Register.

Conclusion

This chapter has outlined the main theoretical propositions that have helped to make sense of child abuse. Deconstructing the notions of child and childhood and relating them to abuse using historical, cultural, legal, political, economical, media and moral influences has helped in our understanding that has identified certain structural imbalances. These imbalances include the moral dilemma of where there is a new liberalism to sexual activity at one level yet on another there is a greater state surveillance of the private sphere. It shows a lack of public and professional agreement on what constitutes a child, child abuse and child sex offending. Moreover, child protection guidance has been dependent on how policy makers interpret the risk and actual threat. Also, heightened fears of child maltreatment by child sexual offenders when added to media exposure emphasises and exacerbates the problem, and the moral panic that reinforces itself creates even more predicaments. For example, increased statistics of child sexual abuse will continue to reinforce the problem by creating increased resources that uncover further offending which then supports a view that policies should become increasingly punitive. Having children and living nearby to a convicted sex offender will often contribute towards the moral panic. Public concerns about the danger to their children and extra familial risk misrepresent and over-state the actual fear of crime and risk rather than the real issue of crime control.

As this chapter has demonstrated, the social construction of child sexual offenders is contingent upon many components. When exploring this debate, it is both helpful and necessary to account for the motivations of those constructing child sexual abuses. For example, are their motivations based on value and moral or political doctrines? Thus, it is necessary to move away from the extreme end of social constructivism and adopt a realist perspective.

WEBSITES

Age of Consent Online 2005. www.encyclopedia.com/doc/1E1-ageconse.html. Visited 6 December 2007.

Chapter 2

The wrong kind of victim?

Children, young people and street crime

David Porteous

Introduction

As Nils Christie puts it, 'crime does not exist. Crime is created. First there are acts. Then follows a long process of giving meaning to these acts' (1998, p. 121). What is defined as crime, in law, in official statistics and in the everyday interactions of the public and the criminal justice system, is not fixed but contingent and changeable. Acts that in the past would have been treated as crimes no longer count as such. Behaviours previously deemed troublesome or a nuisance become formally 'anti-social' and subject to orders. When I was first asked to write this chapter, it was perfectly legal to walk into a pub in England and light up. By the time it is published, smoking in public spaces will have been outlawed, even in the recently approved (but already subject to review) 'super-casinos'. Elsewhere in the world, it is permissible to smoke but not gamble. The laws of society, unlike the laws of nature, reflect prevailing ideologies. They are not and never have been universal.

As with crime, so with offenders and victims. In an essay entitled 'The Ideal Victim' (1986), Christie observes that some people in some circumstances are much more readily ascribed the status of victim than others. To exemplify the point, he compares two imaginary victims, a 'little old lady' mugged by a large male stranger on her way home from caring for her sick sister and a young man hit on the head and stolen from by an acquaintance in a bar. The former matches the profile of an 'ideal victim' because she is weak, engaged in a 'respectable project', cannot be blamed for being on the street at the time and has fallen prey to someone big, bad and unknown. By contrast, sympathy for the young man is likely to be qualified by his relative strength and the fact that he was drinking and knew the assailant. The status of victims (ideal or otherwise) changes with time. As Christie observes:

> Today we can see the witches (of medieval Europe) as victims of oppression. But that is four hundred years too late. At the time of the witch-hunt, their torture was a matter of course and their burning a part of the public entertainment. (1986, p. 22, parentheses added)

Christie's notion of the ideal victim is used in this chapter as a starting point for analysing children and young people's experiences as victims of street crime, a phenomenon which reality television shows have translated into a contemporary form of public entertainment. Whereas in other contexts, for example in relation to paedophilia, human trafficking or Internet pornography, children more readily meet his ideal type criteria, as victims of crimes such as robbery and assault, they have, at least until quite recently, represented something of a blind spot with the gaze of politicians, the media, criminologists and the public at large more or less fixed upon the young offender (Brown 2005; Jubb 2003). To begin with, the chapter reviews the growing evidence from police records and self-report surveys that children and young people are more likely than adults to be victimised 'on the street', that they are, as Hartless et al. (1995) put it, 'more sinned against than sinning'. The chapter continues by examining what research tells us about the distribution of this kind of victimisation and about the characteristics of victims. Drawing on qualitative research, the chapter then discusses the problem of street crime from the perspective of young people involved and suggests that the statistics probably underestimate the scale of the problem in certain areas. The policy implications of this focus on victimisation in public spaces are discussed by way of conclusion.

Defining and measuring the problem

First, however, it is necessary to stipulate what is meant by 'street crime'. Researchers (e.g. Fitzgerald et al., 2003; Hallsworth, 2005; Smith, 2003) have tended to use the legal definition employed by the police whereby street crime describes offences of robbery, attempted robbery and snatch theft from the person. The advantages of restricting the meaning of the term in this way are that it simplifies analysis of official statistics, specifies a particular kind of offence with features and dynamics very different to other 'street crimes' and 'because it avoids other unfortunate connotations with which (street crime) is too often associated' (Hallsworth, 2005, p. 5), notably 'mugging', the term favoured by the popular press. The disadvantages with this narrowing of focus are that it inevitably overlooks numerous criminal offences, not to mention 'anti-social behaviour' to which children and young people fall victim (as well as commit) in public spaces and that it means excluding a wide range of sources which do reveal other forms of victimisation. As one of the main objectives of this chapter is to highlight the disproportionate victimisation of children and young people, I shall attempt to get the best of both worlds by reviewing the available data on street robbery in the first instance and then turning to research encompassing a wider set of crimes experienced by children and young people in public spaces.

Until recently, data on children and young people's victimisation has been limited because official bodies, in part due to the ethical issues associated with doing research with children, have tended not to collect it. The age of victims is not routinely included in the police recorded crime statistics published by the Home Office whilst the British Crime Survey (BCS) has on all but one occasion (Aye Maung, 1995) included only young people aged 16–17 years. A major strength of Smith's (2003) study of street robbery, therefore, which involved analysing over 2,000 police reports and witness statements in seven police force areas, is that it provides empirical evidence of children and young people's exposure to this particular crime problem. Thus, 11–15 year olds were the victim in 22 per cent and 16–20 year olds in

23 per cent of cases and school children accounted for 55 per cent of all victims under 20 years of age. Whilst street robbery, alongside other forms of violence, accounts for only a small per centage of overall crime – 4 per cent of BCS crime and 2 per cent of police recorded crime in 2005/6 (Walker et al., 2006) – the facts suggest that children and young people are the victim in up to a third of all known such incidents and this in spite of the fact that they are less likely to report crimes against them to the police than adults (Aye Maung, 1995; Finkelhor, et al. 2001, and see below).

Official statistics also suggest that street robbery is bucking the downward trend in overall crime in England and Wales (and many other countries) having increased 14 per cent between 1981 and 2000 against a drop of 10 per cent across all BCS offences in the same period (Kershaw et al., 2000, cited in Hallsworth, 2005) and from approximately 56,000 to just under 90,000 police recorded offences between 1998/99 and 2005/6 (Walker et al., 2006). By way of caution it should be noted that the number of recorded street robberies actually peaked in 2001/2 since when there has been a 19 per cent decline (ibid.) and that the surge of robberies in the mid-1990s is explained in large part by the growth in mobile phone ownership (Harrington and Mayhew, 2001). Nevertheless, for now we can say that these figures suggest an overall growth in the recorded number of young victims of street robbery over time, a trend, for London at least, reaffirmed by Smith (see also Fitzgerald et al., 2003):

> Over the last ten years there has been a pronounced shift towards the victimisation of younger age groups. Metropolitan Police Service data on personal robbery show that the number of 11–15 year-old victims has increased threefold (by 320 percent and 296 percent, respectively) since 1993. Overall, the number of victims increased by 121 percent during this period. These increases have been most dramatic since 1998. One in four of all victims in the Metropolitan Police Service are now aged between 11 and 15 years; 16–20 year-olds now account for 22 percent of victims. By contrast, in 1993 these two age groups accounted for 12 percent and 13 percent of all victims respectively. (2003, p. 20)

As noted already, street robbery is a relatively rare form of victimisation. According to the 2005 Offending, Crime and Justice Survey (OC&JS), the third in a panel series of surveys of just under 5,000 10- to 25-year-olds, between two and three per cent of 10- to 17-year-olds reported being robbed in the previous twelve months whereas over a quarter (27 per cent) of young people had been the victim of some form of personal crime in the last 12 months, most commonly assault without injury (11 per cent) and other personal thefts (9 per cent) (Wilson et al., 2006). Across this wider range of offences, the survey, as with previous attempts to measure the criminal victimisation of children and young people (andAye Maung, 1995; Hartless et al., 1995; Morgan and Zedner, 1992; Smith et al., 2001) found rates of personal and violent crime to be high relative to that within the adult population and especially so amongst younger children. Wilson et al. report that 10- to 15-year-olds were more likely to have been victimised than 16- to 25-year-olds and that there is a drop in the victimisation rate from the age of 22 upwards.

Although many of the incidents reported by children and young people in such surveys will have occurred in school or college, a significant proportion of the more serious offences take place on the street. In the OC&JS a majority of robberies and around one in four assaults had occurred in public places whilst in the 2003 youth survey conducted by MORI for the Youth Justice Board (2003b), a significantly higher proportion of young people reported being a victim outside of rather than inside school. Overall, just under a half of children and getting on for two-thirds of excluded children in the MORI survey reported having been a victim of crime within the past year. Whilst bullying, for those in mainstream school at least, was mostly experienced inside school, a majority of physical attacks and mobile phone thefts and a significant proportion of other incidents occurred either in the area where the child lived, on the way to or from school or elsewhere outside of school. Both excluded children and those in mainstream school reported higher levels of concern about incidents they face outside of school. Although in the majority of cases and for most offence types, victims identified the offender as being someone aged under 18, up to a third of physical attacks, over a half of mobile phone thefts and two-thirds of racial attacks were said to have been committed by adults.

The characteristics of victims and the distribution of victimisation

In the same way that youth crime researchers have investigated those risk factors which increase the likelihood of offending amongst children and young people (Farrington 2007; Wikstrom and Butterworth 2006; Youth Justice Board, 2001b), factors which best predict victimisation (Finkelhor and Asdigian, 1996; Smith et al., 2001) have also been identified. Taking more or less fixed personal characteristics first, Smith's analysis of street robbery, the OC&JS and the MORI Youth Survey are consistent in finding significant differences by age and gender, with older males the most at risk of offences such as robbery and physical assault. The importance of ethnicity is less clear. Smith reports that members of ethnic minorities are more likely to report being a victim in some areas but less likely to do so in others whilst Wood writes that 'white groups were more likely than black and minority ethnic groups to be victims of assaults and less likely to be victims of robbery' (2005, p. 6). Other research (e.g. Porteous, 1998) points more conclusively to the disproportionate victimisation of children and young people from minority groups, a finding which as Jubb (2003) observes, conforms with the national picture for adults according to successive sweeps of the BCS (see also Bowling and Philips 2002).

Turning to more changeable factors, the key variables identified by Wood in his analysis (2005) of the 2004 OC&JS data are as follows:

- Living in a financially troubled household

- Living in an area where three or more types of anti-social behaviour are common

- Attending a school perceived as being disorderly

- Having been temporarily or permanently excluded from and/or having truanted from school

- Having a 'negative parental relationship'

- Having friends who have been in trouble with the police

- Not being brought up by both natural parents

- Having taken any (illegal) drug in the last year

- Having committed a criminal offence in the last year

- Having felt drunk once a month or more

- Having engaged in anti-social behaviour in the last year

Further analysis reveals that 'the underlying factor most strongly predictive of victimisation among young people was criminal offending by the victim', in fact an offender is more than twice as likely to be a victim than a non-offender. For Wood, the most likely explanation for this overlap is that the young people involved lead 'lifestyles that constitute risks for both offending and victimisation' (2005, p. 6). The victim, this seems to suggest, has only him or herself to blame.

According to Wood, 'the area, in terms of relative deprivation or whether urban or not, was not a significant predictor of personal crime victimisation' (2005, p. 5). Other research points to a very different conclusion. Fitzgerald et al. (2003), for example, found a clear, if imperfect, correlation between levels of deprivation and the number of street robberies committed in the 32 boroughs of London in 2001/2. A glance at the Metropolitan Police website (www.met.police.uk/crimefigures) suggests that not much has changed. In the twelve months to August 2007, there were 1,838 personal robberies recorded in the most deprived borough (Tower Hamlets), 1,598 more than that recorded in the least deprived (Kingston upon Thames) in the same period. A concentration of inter-personal violence is also graphically illustrated in Dorling's (2005) analysis of 13,410 homicides in England, Scotland and Wales between 1981 and 2000. This reveals a stark inequality in murder rates, one that has widened noticeably in the 20-year period in question. Young men were most likely to be murdered, Dorling found, but the strongest statistical determinant of who was murdered was poverty.

The apparent discrepancy between these sets of findings, one seeming to suggest that it is what young victims of crime do that determines whether or not they become a victim, the other that the key factor is where they live, can be resolved by accepting that lifestyle is shaped and constrained by socio-economic circumstances. Within areas scoring high on measures of deprivation, other factors to do with age, gender, ethnicity, life-style, family circumstances, peer groups and performance at school place some children and young people at greater risk than others. Yet over time the continuing concentration of crime and disorder in certain areas and amongst the poorest people is what resonates:

> When the cobwebs of historical myth are cleared away, then we can begin to see that the real and enduring problem that faces us is not moral decay, or declining parental responsibility, or undutiful working mothers, or the unparalleled debasement of popular amusements – or any other symptom of spiritual degeneration amongst the British people. Rather, it is a material problem. The inescapable reality of the social reproduction of an underclass of the most poor and dispossessed is the material foundation to these hooligan continuities. (Pearson, 1983, p. 236)

Although Pearson's concern is to record the perennial habit of politicians, journalists and others of invoking a crime-free golden age when diagnosing the current causes of offending behaviour, the same tendency to overlook the rather stressed-out-looking elephant in the room afflicts the present-day search for risk factors associated with children and young people's victimisation. Following Pearson, this is not to say that poverty causes children and young people to be victims of street crime, merely that the fact that it is from amongst the less well-off that victims (as well as offenders) are usually found is unlikely to be a coincidence (which is precisely what an absence of statistical significance implies). From a historical perspective, the material facts of relative socio-economic disadvantage – youth unemployment, low pay, overcrowding, lack of money and debt, limited access to leisure facilities and opportunities etc. – are also 'risk-factors', ones which have endured over time and which have witnessed any number of individual lifestyle choices, the decision as to whether or not to wear a hoodie, for example, simply being one of the more recent.

At the same time, it is important to note that much violent crime on the streets occurs not in residential neighbourhoods but in town and city centres at night-time when each week millions of young people, including many officially under-age, binge themselves silly on alcohol. Neither poverty nor a particularly unusual lifestyle can explain this form of street crime. A combination of peer and beer pressure and an insatiable appetite for young consumers amongst large corporations seem the more *potent* risk factors here. How much of this kind of crime involves those aged under 18 is not possible to discern from the statistics. According to Winlow and Hall (2006), only a fraction of the violence of the night-time economy is likely to come to the attention of the police so despite being subject to public viewing via CCTV, television and the Internet, much of this form of crime escapes official notice or sanction.

The issue of under-reporting

That much street crime goes unrecorded is unsurprising. It is well known that less than a half of all crimes are reported to the police (Walker et al. 2006) and evidence suggests that young people are less likely than adults to do so. Wilson et al.'s (2006) report on OC&JS data for example records that 28 per cent of robbery victims aged 10–25 had had their case brought to police attention (by themselves or others) whereas in the BCS, 49 per cent of robbery victims aged 16 and above had done so. The same pattern holds for assaults with or without injury except that overall reporting rates for this more common crime are even lower. The OC&JS indicates that the younger children in its cohort were less likely than older young people to report incidents: 11 per cent of 10–15-year-olds, for example, reported an assault with injury compared with 33 per cent of 16–25-year-olds. The evidence from the MORI surveys of 11–16-year-olds for the YJB repeats the general pattern with one in eight offences having been reported to the police.

A common reason given by young people for not reporting incidents is that they did not consider it a crime and/or felt it was too trivial an offence to report and this seems to be truer of younger children. 84 per cent of 10–15-year-olds who reported in the OC&JS that they had been injured in an assault said either that it was 'wrong but not a crime' or simply 'something that happens' whereas 50 per cent of 16–25-year-olds described these kinds of incidents as a crime (Wilson et al., 2006, p. 84). But young people may also not report through a desire for or fear of retribution, through pressure from peers not to 'tell', or because they are embarrassed or ashamed. A further reason for under-reporting is that in many cases the decision to formally notify the police may not be the child's but that of their parents or another adult (teachers, police officers themselves) who effectively gate-keep access to the criminal justice system and who make judgements on behalf of children and young people subject to their own emotional, practical, legal and material concerns as well as those of the 'victim' (Finkelhor et al., 2001). Given that access to formal justice is mediated by adults, it is not so surprising if young people sometimes choose to 'sort it out' amongst themselves.

Although it is as a result of surveys that light is shone upon the 'dark figure' of under-reported crime, they have their own limitations. One problem concerns sampling error or bias. The OC&JS for example excludes any young person currently resident in a Young Offender's Institution, whereas we know, ironically from the survey itself, that young offenders are disproportionately likely to have been victims themselves, so discounting their experiences will lead to an overall underestimation of victimisation. A strength of the MORI surveys is that they include a sub-sample of children and young people excluded from school who, as we have seen, report higher levels of victimisation than their counterparts in mainstream school. The bigger problem with this survey is that it is based on self-completion questionnaires, a method where it is difficult to control against respondents misunderstanding questions, exaggerating or downplaying incidents, forgetting relevant details and so on. Even if such problems are minimised by careful wording of questions and clear instructions, there is no escaping the bigger issue that survey research involves defining the problem at hand in the researchers' own terms. Since the survey method inevitably brackets what could be very different subjective meanings of an act into a form amenable to statistical analysis, the validity of results – the extent to which they accurately convey what is going on – is always subject to doubt.

Findings from qualitative research

With this in mind, I want to briefly turn to three recent qualitative studies of crime involving young people which seem to bear out the picture painted so far but also to complicate it. Martin et al.'s (2007) research into young people's experiences of street crime in an East London borough, Young et al.'s (National Youth Agency, 2006) study of 'knives, guns and gangs' for the Youth Justice Board and Winlow and Hall's (2006) ethnographic account of 'violent night(s)' in the North East of England, whilst very different in focus, have in common that they sought through interviews to understand the experience of crime from the perspective and through the words of young people themselves.

The East London study was undertaken in a borough which, according to the Index of Multiple Deprivation 2000, was at that time the third most deprived area in England with 64 per cent of children estimated to be living in poverty. Within the borough, police youth crime data show considerable variation in the extent of victimisation between wards and amongst different sub-groups of the population – 85 per cent of all young victims of robbery are male for example. Nonetheless, for all young people, robbery and violent assault were the most common forms of crime reported. In this context, and given that the researchers purposely sampled 11–16-year-olds known to have experienced crime and anti-social behaviour, fear of crime might well be expected. However, the predominant sentiment was not so much fear as an almost casual acceptance of crime as an everyday feature of life. Thus one interviewee commented:

> *There has been a few murders in my area. It does not really make me feel safe in my area anymore but I have lived there my whole life so you just get used to it.* (15-year-old female cited in Porteous et al., 2007)

This feeling of having to 'get used to it' was very strong across the sample. Responding to the question 'Is there a lot of crime where you live?' another respondent told the researchers 'The area I live is just based on crime', whilst a third, reflecting on what might improve matters commented 'The police can't change anything. What will happen will happen.'

A similar sentiment is found in Young et al.'s interviews with young people involved in gang-related violence:

> *Yeah it's violence everywhere, ain't it. I mean you see it everywhere . . . on TV, on games, ruckin' on the streets. It's what happens . . . what people use . . . to sort things out . . . . and get things done. At some point you have to get involved. It's the way it is.* (14-year-old male, cited in Young et al., 2007, p. 106)

Young et al. comment that 'it was commonplace to find that violence and aggression were a constant backdrop' in the everyday lives of the young people they spoke with; 'all had varying accounts of how they had been either directly involved in violence, been the victim of violent abuse, knew someone who had been, or had observed it up close' (ibid.)

Moreover, whilst this familiarity with violent crime might be expected in a study of gang members, the fact that it is echoed in the East London research amongst a younger and more 'ordinary' sample of children suggests that the familiarity, in high-crime neighbourhoods at least, goes beyond individuals caught up in group-related conflicts and patterns the lives of many secondary school aged children, affecting the journeys they take, the places visit and stay, the things they carry and so on.

The same sense of the ubiquity of public violence is also present in Winlow and Hall's research where the context is the town or city centre at night-time and where all that links respondents, for the most part, is that they enjoy an evening out. The researchers observe:

> *Most of our respondents started 'going out' around the ages of fifteen or sixteen and had seen a significant amount of violence over the years. They regarded its constant presence in a rather fatalistic manner: violence was, to them, an effect of alcohol consumption and therefore . . . quite unavoidable.* (2007, p. 96)

The feeling that being a victim is always a possibility, that the threat of violence is never far away, links all three studies, confirming in a sense the 'facts' about young victims of street crime discussed already, including that many incidents go unrecorded. At the same time, the very different focus of the studies draws attention to the problem of generalisation. In the East London research, victims were clearly identifiable as such, a number for example having been robbed by a group of older males whilst alone. But in the two other studies, the distinction between offender and victim is much less obvious. The sort of violence described by Winlow and Hall's respondents typically involves two or more protagonists squaring up to each other after an argument, whereas Young et al.'s gang members define a lot of their experiences of crime as a product of ongoing conflicts with other groups. The apparent paradox thrown up by risk factor studies that offenders are more likely to be victims than non-offenders ceases to be strange on a reading of *Violent Night* where 'common assault' appears common indeed and the use of violence by men is deeply embedded in a youth and young adult culture so generously catered for by the night-time market. Similarly, the young people interviewed by Young et al. conform with the profile of the young person equally at risk of being an offender and a victim. Their lifestyles are inherently risky, they inhabit risky worlds.

Conclusion and policy implications

Youth crime is not a new problem and, notwithstanding that official statistics suggest that children and young people may be more prone to becoming a victim of street crime than they were in the past, it seems unlikely that there was a time when this kind of violence and theft were not perpetrated against (as well as by) them. However, the long-standing equation of youth crime with youth offending has served to distract public and political attention from the other side of the coin. Whilst the history of youth justice is one of balancing concern for the welfare (needs) of young people with concern about their behaviour (deeds), the focus has remained for the most part on the young offender and even though it has been long understood that the most frequent offenders are themselves very likely to have been victims, of family violence and child abuse as well as of crimes in public spaces, still the emphasis has been on to what extent this excuses and explains their offending.

Yet as the evidence presented in this chapter shows, children and young people are as, if not slightly more, likely to be a victim of a street crime, broadly defined so as to include inter-personal violence and thefts occurring in public spaces (outside of the home and not in school/college), than adults. Amongst the under-18 population, street crime victimisation is not evenly distributed. Children and young people living in inner city neighbourhoods characterised by relative social and economic disadvantage are exposed to higher levels of street crime in general, and in all neighbourhoods, including town and city centres, older boys, particularly ones who have offended themselves, are most at risk. Qualitative research with young people concerning their experience of street crime would seem to confirm the findings from quantitative research and that statistics probably underestimate the scale of victimisation. Across different studies there emerges from children and young people a shared a sense of the inevitability of crime, a sort of casual fatalism – 'shit will happen' – from which follows the notion that whether one becomes a victim or not is as much a matter of luck as of anything – the risk is built into the environment rather than the individual.

The very simple message then is of the need to take young people's victimisation in public spaces seriously and to develop policies which are geared towards the protection and safety of all children and young people in public spaces. In this regard, whilst the government's 'Every Child Matters Outcomes Framework', which identifies staying safe as one of five objectives to be achieved by children's services, is a positive development, it is not yet clear how this objective is to be realised 'on the street'. Existing research (Martin et al., 2007; Newburn, 2007; Pain, 2003) suggests that children and young people in public spaces feel over-policed and under-protected, viewed with suspicion rather than care. The challenge for government and society is to explore and promote ways of reversing this perception.

Chapter 3

Parental use of alcohol and illicit drugs

A critical review of recent research

Caroline Chatwin

Introduction

The only purpose for which power can be rightfully exercised over any member of a civilized community, against his will, is to prevent harm to others. His own good, either physical or moral, is not sufficient warrant. (John Stuart Mill, *On Liberty*, 1859)

The argument cited above has been used to justify, even to an excessive level, the use of alcohol and, more recently, illicit drugs. If the only harm caused is to the users themselves then what right does the state have to intervene? Increasingly however, research shows that the families and dependents of problem-substance users are also subjected to harm. Children, in particular, have been highlighted as the innocent victims of excessive substance use by their parents. This chapter seeks to critically evaluate the literature in this area, both the earlier work focusing on physical and medical developmental problems and the later qualitative work exploring the social and psychological problems that the children face. It also assesses the impact of this research on policy in the UK and suggests how the lives of children whose parents who are problem-substance users could be improved.

In this chapter the terms 'substance use' and 'drug use' refer to the use of illicit drugs and of alcohol, the legal drug. The problems experienced by the children of parents who use either are so strikingly similar that to separate them seems obtuse. Problem-substance use refers to the heavy and dependent nature of the use of these substances. Studies cited throughout the chapter have been predominantly concerned with the use of alcohol, cocaine and opiates, and are always referring to instances where use has become problematic in its nature, as far as problematic use can be described as a stable behaviour. It is not suggested that drug and/or alcohol use have negative effects *per se* on the parenting of children.

Prevalence

Statistical evidence shows that numbers of drinkers and drug users are at a relatively high level in British society. Roe and Man (2006), using findings taken from the British Crime Survey 2005/06, report that 34. per cent, or some 11 million people aged 16–59, have tried illegal drugs at least once in their life time and that this figure rises to 45.1 per cent of those aged 16–24. Of course, not all of these have reached a problematic level of abuse. The Department of Health (2004) estimates that there are 360,811 problem-drug users in the UK and that 123,498 of these are intravenous drug users. In relation to alcohol, the Prime Minister's Strategy Unit (2004) recorded 6 million people who are drinking at levels above recommended guidelines and 2 million who are drinking at harmful levels. It must also be appreciated that, due to the secretive nature of excessive drinking and illicit drug-taking (Kroll and Taylor, 2003), these figures are likely to represent serious underestimations of the numbers of people affected.

In 2003 the Advisory Council on the Misuse of Drugs (ACMD) produced an influential report on the number of children affected by parental problem-drug misuse and the needs of those children. They estimated that between 250,000 and 350,000 children of problem-drug users existed, or about 1 for every problem-drug user. They further reported that about 1 per cent of all newborn deliveries were to drug users, which amounted to about 6,000 births per year. The Alcohol Harm Reduction Strategy (Prime Minister's Strategy Unit, 2004) has estimated that 1.3 million or 1 in 11 children are affected by parental alcohol misuse. Again these figures are highly likely to underestimate the problem. Most of the figures provided here exclude those who have not made contact with either social services, the criminal justice system or treatment programmes, for whatever reason.

Given that heavy and dependent drug and alcohol users tend to be 'ordinary people doing ordinary things' (Kearney and Ibbetson, 1991, p. 106) it is hardly surprising that so many of them give birth to children. Many problem-substance abusers are of a young, child-bearing age and Klee et al. (1997) have reported a rise in babies born to drug-using women throughout the 1980s and 1990s. The number of children affected by this problem is therefore likely to be high As such it is essential to understand the nature of the problems these children will face, as well as any strategies employed, in order to prevent or limit the negative consequences for the children as victims.

Political context and policy

Since the devastating case of the torture and brutal murder by her carers of Victoria Climbié, a young girl living in North London, rocked British society in 2000, the Labour government has embarked on a programme of change, seeking to bring the agencies working to safeguard children closer together, which is outlined in the Governmental Green Paper *Every Child Matters: Change for Children* (Department for Education and Skills, 2004a). While the use of drugs and alcohol were not implicated in Victoria's death, the consequences of the case have been wide-ranging, and policy-making has touched upon the issue discussed here, for example in the Government's publication *Every Child Matters: Change for Children – Young People and Drugs* (Department for Education and Skills, the Home Office and the

Department for Health, 2005). Problem-substance use by parents is an area of increasing research interest, evidenced by the surge in UK-based qualitative studies produced in the last decade, but how far has this research interest permeated actual policy-making?

In 1992, Famularo et al. (p. 457), working in the US, declared that 'child maltreatment and substance abuse have both emerged as critical issues for public policy and clinical practice'. Since then, the number of problem drinkers and illicit drug-takers has risen, the number of research studies has at least doubled, and the results are beginning to filter through to a level at which they can inform UK policy-making. In 2002 the Home Office published its *Updated Drug Strategy*, with the key aim of reducing 'the harm that drugs cause to society – communities, individuals and their families'. Within this document calls have also been made for more support to be given to parents, carers and families especially for increased access to advice, help, counselling and mutual support.

Beyond this, however, progress, in the form of identifying particular issues for the children of problem-substance users and developing specific strategies to allow them to overcome these difficulties, has been limited. In 2003, the ACMD produced its aforementioned report *Hidden Harm: Responding to the Needs of Children of Drug Users*, which sought to identify the difficulties that the children of problem-substance users experience and to plan responses to those difficulties, informed by the testimony of the children themselves. *Hidden Harm* is a comprehensive and informative document, illuminating many of the problems faced and the solutions applied, yet there is little evidence so far to suggest that it has impacted significantly on British policy-making in this area.

A later update on the situation, *Hidden Harm: Three Years On* (ACMD, 2007, p. 14), discusses the desire to 'embed the recommendations of *Hidden Harm* in the emerging *Every Child Matters: change for children* agenda' but is disappointingly only able to report 'some' (ibid.) progress in this area. Improvements have largely surrounded the issue of recognising parental problem-substance use as a possible negative influence on their children, compromising their safety and well-being. Clearly then, there is still a considerable way to go in prioritising this issue. More recent qualitative studies, however, that have included interviews with parents who are problem-substance users and their children, allow us to gain a useful insight into both the nature of the problems faced and the strategies employed by those involved to overcome these problems. The question now is, will the government continue to take notice of the knowledge uncovered by academic research and transform it into effective policy practice?

Medical, physiological and developmental effect on children

A relatively large body of research has been developed on the way children are affected by the problematic substance use of their parents; however, a large proportion of the work is selective in its nature. Many studies, in particular the earlier ones, have focused on the medical and developmental progress of these children and research has largely targeted neonates (newborn babies) and infants rather than older children. The studies are predominantly concerned with the effects of cocaine, opiate or alcohol addiction at the expense of other drugs and much of the work has been conducted in America. Studies have not always included a control group of children not born to alcohol or drug-addicted parents and the experimental population has been almost exclusively drawn from parents attending treatment programmes or who are in touch with the social services.

Overlooking, for the moment, these methodological problems, drawing general conclusions from the research remains difficult. The dangers associated with smoking tobacco and drinking alcohol during pregnancy have permeated the public consciousness, yet, even at this level, the consequences of using illicit drugs during pregnancy are less comprehensively understood and less unambiguously proven. While some of the studies cited below undeniably show the children of problem-substance users to be disadvantaged on specific criteria, not all do so, and many more of the studies show mixed results. Studies of children beyond infancy are rare, but show similarly mixed results.

The children of problem-substance users first became a research priority in the 1970s and some of the earliest studies in this area reflect the ongoing difficulty in determining the specific consequences of having a substance-using parent. Nichtern (1973) and Fanshel (1975) both studied groups of American children who had been removed from parental care due to heavy parental substance use, yet reported very different results. Nichtern (1973) found that these children had more developmental problems and socialisation issues than children removed from parents for other reasons while Fanshel (1975) found that the children of substance users had no significant problems in comparison to children removed from their parents for other reasons. Since these early studies, results have remained very much mixed and inconclusive.

Perhaps one of the most widely investigated areas of research is on the effects of problematic substance use on foetuses. The effects of tobacco (Abel, 1984) and alcohol (The Royal College of Physicians, 1995) on the foetus are well-documented and have perhaps provided an incentive for the study of the effect of illicit drugs on the unborn baby. Several key studies have linked cocaine and opiate use with physiological deficits, namely reduced birth weight and head size (Bateman and Chiriboga, 2000; Drucker, 1990; Eiden et al., 2006; Schuetze and Eiden, 2006), and others have highlighted the risk of contracting the HIV virus in the womb (Hogan, 1998) and coping with withdrawal symptoms at birth (Williams, 1983). Beyond this however, little concrete evidence of further substance-related damage is evident.

> *Even cocaine used in high doses during pregnancy is not unequivocally linked to any foetal defect other than low birthweight and small size. The vast majority of infants born to drug-using mothers are as 'healthy' as other infants born in poverty.* (Drucker, 1990, p. 11)

Various other studies have failed to show any significant differences in the neonates of problem-substance users in comparison to a control group, other than in birth weight and head size (Burns et al., 1996; Hurt et al., 1995; Leopold and Steffan, 1997, p. 9; Ornoy et al., 1996). In a review of the research evidence produced for the Council of Europe, they have declared therefore the effects of substance abuse on neonates to be 'not as great as expected'.

Moving beyond the study of neonates and the effects of substance misuse on the foetus, one of the most serious allegations levied at parents with problem-substance use is that they neglect or abuse their children. In addition to the studies discussed above on the medical and developmental effects of problematic substance use on children, many studies have focused on this issue as well. These have encompassed areas such as 'medical neglect, failure to provide adequate food, clothing, accommodation, and protection from harm' (Alison, 2000, p. 12) as well as more traditionally defined forms of abuse. One of the earliest studies in this area was conducted by Black and Meyer (1980) who investigated 200 families where one or more of the parents was a problem-drug user and concluded that there was some evidence of neglect in all of the families. Since then many studies have found evidence to support this key finding that the children of problem-substance users are more likely to be subjected to abuse or neglect than other children (Behling, 1979; Famularo et al., 1986' Forrester, 2000; Jaudes et al., 1995, Stone, 1998; Wasserman and Leventhal, 1993). Famularo et al. (1986, p. 483), however, caution that this does not reflect a causal relationship between problem-substance use and child abuse or neglect, but rather suggests that there is a 'statistical association', and Kroll and Taylor (2003, p. 32) echo this by rejecting the conclusion that substance misuse leads to child abuse and/or neglect, instead they simply cite 'evidence of coexistence'.

The other relatively conclusively found difference in the children of problem-substance users, in comparison with other children, is their propensity to experiment with, and/or become dependent on, alcohol and illicit drugs at a relatively early age. Many studies have found them to be at greater risk of developing these behaviours than children whose parents have not been problematic drug and/or alcohol users themselves (Fawzy et al., 1983; Kumpfer, 1999; Kumpfer and DeMarsh, 1985; Turning Point, 2006; Velleman and Orford, 1999; and White et al., 2000)). The experimentation of children with drugs and alcohol, together with their likelihood of experiencing some form of abuse or neglect, stand out in the research as areas where comparative agreement has been reached. Numerous studies report a range of developmental deficiencies, but these are inconclusively evidenced and have been contradicted by other research.

Researchers have noted, for example, control problems and behavioural issues (Kandel, 1990. Kolar et al., 1994) such as: anti-social trends (Herjanic et al., 1979, Kumpfer and DeMarsh, 1985; Nichtern, 1973); lower achievement at school (Moss et al., 1995; Sowder and Burt, 1980); motor development problems (Arendt et al., 1999; Bernstein et al., 1984; House-holder et al., 1982); depression and anxiety (Johnson et al., 1991); developmental delay (Singer et al., 2002); and tension and irritability (Bauman and Levine, 1986; Bernstein et al., 1984) in the children of parents who are problem-substance users. Many of these findings, however, are contradicted by other studies and are therefore not as established as the associations with child abuse and/or neglect by the parents and drug and/or alcohol use in the children. Some studies have found no significant difference between the children of problem-substance users and the children of parents who do not use substances (Hurt et al., 1995; Ornoy et al., 1996). Others have reported mixed results with deficiencies noted in some areas but not found in others: Fanshal (1975) found no differences in levels of adjust-ment, Bauman and Levine (1986) found no differences in intelligence levels, Burns et al. (1996) found no difference in developmental progress and Bernstein et al. (1984) found no differences in either cognitive or social functioning. A limited number of studies, atypically focussing on fathers, have found positive parenting results. Kandel (1990) reported an increase in positive parenting amongst substance-using fathers and Tarter et al. (2001) found that children of dependent substance-using fathers showed fewer deficiencies than children whose fathers were absent from the family home.

A comprehensive trawl of the relevant research literature therefore provides a very small degree of certainty on the physical and developmental effects on children of problem-substance use in their parents, leading Hogan (1998) to suggest, in reference to the research, that:

> There is little of it, it lacks direction and cohesion, and the findings are at best inconclusive, at worst contradictory. It is almost impossible, therefore, to point with certainty to the kinds of difficulties experienced by children of drug users, and the degree to which those problems are experienced across different family situations. (p. 614)

If we combine the confusion and contradiction seen here with the methodological problems briefly outlined at the beginning of this section, it becomes very difficult to draw reliable conclusions about the effects on children of parental problem- substance use. In addition to much of the research originating from the USA, where the drug problem is significantly different from the UK and being predominantly focused on the cognitive, physiological and motor development of children, there are other considerable methodological issues not yet discussed. Hogan (1998) further states that the literature:

> provides no information about children who have not been hospitalised, whose parents have not been referred to the courts on charges of abuse, or who are not in care outside the home. (p. 612)

This is an important oversight, as researchers may be missing an entire population of substance-using parents who are not connecting with the state, either because their lives are too chaotic for intervention or because they have not displayed any problems which bring them to the attention of the authorities. An appreciation of this failing led Lester et al. (1997, p. 487) to comment on the 'compromised' nature of research in this area.

In addition to these sampling problems, the relevance of factors other than problem-substance use is an issue that many have addressed. In a significant number of the studies cited above, researchers are attributing developmental problems to the excessive use of substances, yet it can be difficult to be certain that problems displayed are definitively connected to substance use rather than to an array of other factors present in the child's environment. For example, Singer (1999) suggested that it is difficult to separate the effects of problem-substance use from the effects of various factors such as belonging to a minority race, receiving poor prenatal and/or antenatal care, having a single marital status, having a lower level of education and having a larger number of siblings. In other studies, poor maternal nutrition and health, exposure to violence (ACMD, 2003), the relatively young age of the mothers (Cassado-Flores et al., 1990) and the heavy use of tobacco in addition to other substances (Dempsey and Benowitz, 2001; Eiden et al. 2006) have all proved difficult to disentangle from the effects of heavy substance use.

Overwhelmingly however, researchers have found that it is difficult, if not impossible, to separate the effects of growing up with problem-substance users as parents from the effects of being born into a family of low socio-economic status (ACMD, 2003; Elliott and Watson,

2000; Fals-Stewart et al., 2003; Hogan, 1998; Kearney and Ibbetson, 1991; Kroll and Taylor, 2003; Luthar and Cushing, 1999; Ornoy et al., 1996; Templeton et al., 2006).

The problems in this area are summed up by Derren (1986), who stated that:

> *drug abuse does not exist as an independent factor. It is usually associated with a host of characteristics . . . separation of the contribution of these factors has not been accomplished.* (p. 86)

While the studies discussed so far have been beset by methodological problems and are marred by their limited focus, in more recent times several qualitative studies have been undertaken. Through interviews with parents who are problem-substance users and the children of those parents, more in-depth information has been collated on the potential consequences for children of parental problem-substance use. The results of these studies, many of which originate in the UK, will be discussed in the next section.

Social and psychological effects on children

These qualitative studies seek to explore the social and psychological effects of parental problem-substance use on children, and glean information from the testimonies of those directly involved – both the children themselves and their parents. They still tend to use families where the parent is involved in treatment or the family is in contact with social services. However, many are UK-based and all are considerably wider in their scope in seeking to represent the problems as 'seen through the eyes of children' (Barnard and Barlow, 2002, p. 45), allowing them to have a chance both to express themselves and inform policy as to their urgent requirements. Generally speaking, these studies focus on the social context of the lives of children of problem-substance users which have been described by Bancroft et al. (2004, p. 9) as 'disrupted and difficult', and to shed light on the pressure put on parents 'between the time and lifestyle demands of their drug problem and their children's needs for care and attention' (Hogan and Higgens, 2001, p. 30). Out of these recent qualitative studies has come a series of commonly agreed-upon factors impacting on the lives and experiences of the children of problem-substance users, which can presumably be used to reliably inform policy in this area, and which will now be discussed in further detail.

Resources

The excessive consumption of any substance, legal or illegal, places strain on the economies of a household – particularly where that household already holds a low socio-economic status. Studies have consistently shown (Bancroft et al., 2004; Barnard, 2007; Bays, 1990; McKegany et al., 2002; Taylor, 1993) that not only are financial resources in the homes of problem-substance users being spent predominantly on drugs and alcohol, in some cases over and above the needs of children, but also that time and emotional resources are being used up in the acquisition and taking of the drugs themselves. This is a point that is recognised by both parents and children.

> *The children were really starving and, instead of running about trying to get them food, I was running about trying to get my drugs.* (parent cited in McKegany et al., 2002, p. 237)

When I was about 15, she was smoking . . . £105 a week it was costing her. She was only getting £115 in benefits. (child cited in Bancroft et al., 2004, p. 17)

Child's role as carer

Researchers have also consistently found that the children of problem-substance users tend to have 'foreshortened-childhood[s]' (Bancroft et al., 2004, p. 9) caused by taking on household responsibilities and caring roles at a very early age, either for themselves or for other siblings.

> *Rebecca doesn't go to school. She stays at home to look after Julie and Christophe . . . She cleans up in the house. She has to mind them.* (case worker cited in Liverpool Health Authority, 2001, p. 17)

This reversal of the traditional roles has resulted in children feeling 'stigmatised and undervalued . . . [and being] left to cope alone' (ACMD, 2003, p. 40). Over and above the difficulties associated with taking on inappropriate levels of responsibility for themselves and their siblings, Bancroft et al. (2004, p. 20) report that 'several described their parents as emotionally dependent on them', placing further strain on their ability to experience a normal childhood. Turning Point (2006) has also commented on the likelihood that the taking on of such adult roles would have a negative impact on school attendance and achievement.

Absence and neglect

Some researchers have also pointed to the frequent absence of parental substance users from the family home, whether because of illness, death or imprisonment related to their substance use, or because they were attending treatment programmes, were busy trying to obtain drugs or had disappeared on a drug-taking binge (Hogan, 1998; Turning Point, 2006). Such behaviour left children to cope on their own, contributed to their acquisition of caring roles within the family and left parents open to accusations of neglect. Neglect has predominantly been found to be of 'material, medical and physical needs' (Barnard, 2007, p. 99), as demonstrated by Klee et al.'s (1997) work with drug-using parents.

> *I wasn't hitting them or battering them, nothing like that, I was just neglecting them. I wasn't feeding them regular. I wasn't washing them regular.* (parent cited in Klee et al., 1997, p. 14)

Such behaviour did not go unnoticed by the children themselves: Barnard and Barlow (2002, p. 52) refer to their feelings that 'drugs were more important than themselves to their mothers and/or fathers', and the hurt and rejection that this caused them.

Secrecy

> *I've always wanted to tell one of (my friends) about my Dad being an alcoholic. I just find it dead hard to keep it inside me, but I feel it's something I want to keep within my family.* (child cited in Hill et al., 1996, p. 164)

The sentiments recorded here by Hill et al., in their study which interviewed parents, children and young adults about the effects on the family of parental problem-drinking, are echoed by other researchers who have noted the general reluctance in the children of problem-substance users to discuss the situation with others. Where these substances are illegal the need for concealment is only intensified, leading Barnard and Barlow (2002, p. 54) to describe a 'careful nurturing of the family secret' and to suppose that life for these children must be 'like a world of mirrors where nothing is as it seems'. In their consultation with children and parents about the impact of parental drug use across ten Liverpool-based organisations, Liverpool Health Authority (2001) further suggested that this general air of secrecy pervading the children's lives could lead to increased feelings of isolation.

Witnessing inappropriate behaviours

Finally, researchers have commented on the propensity of parental drug use to expose children to a criminal and deviant lifestyle not normally experienced at such a young age. Some researchers have commented on the likelihood of parents being involved in criminal activity connected with their drug use (Bays, 1990; Hogan, 1998; McKegany et al., 2002), and therefore exposing their children to a criminal lifestyle. Others have focused on the effect on children of witnessing deviant behaviours such as the injecting of illicit drugs, even where this is at a very young age (Barnard and Barlow, 2002; Hogan and Higgens, 2001)

> I did use in front of her when she was younger, thinking she didn't cop but she did . . . When she was about 3 or 4, she put a piece of string around her arm and started tapping her arm, mimicking me. (parent cited in Hogan and Higgens, 2001, p. 15)

Positive effects on parenting

While the majority of information gathered in these studies is concerned with the negative influences of problem-substance use on parenting, it is noteworthy that several of the studies also touched on the perception that substance-using parents could sometimes bring positive benefits to their children. In the main, these 'positive effects' were cited where drugs were thought to give the parent more energy to keep up with the housework and childcare and/or put them in a better and more loveable mood so they could enjoy spending time with their children (Bates et al., 1999; Klee et al., 1997; Richter and Bammer, 2000).

> I have the time and the energy and just the inclination inside of me, and the patience to do anything at her level, at her time, at her speed, in her pace – much better. (parent cited in Richter and Bammer, 2000, p. 408)

Taylor (1993, p. 108), in her ethnography of a female injecting community, noted that mothers who are also problem-substance users shared the same concerns about their children's safety and welfare and the same desire to be as 'good mothers' as women who were not problem-substance users. Finally, Barnard (2007) has suggested that having children may provide an important catalyst for change in the life of a substance-using parent.

Stereotyping

While the testimonies of parents and children taken from the studies cited above do overwhelmingly show the effects of problem-substance use on parenting in a bad light, most of the researchers involved are quick to caution that we should not stereotype drug-using parents and that each individual case must be treated on its own merits. Klee and Jackson (1998, p. 45) had described the stereotypical substance-using mother as a:

> *devious manipulator, aggressive troublemaker, weak willed, victim, prostitute, unwashed, self-neglecting junky and, worst of all, someone who put her own self-gratification before the care of her children.*

Such stereotypes must have an impact on substance-using parents and the social stigma they experience can only add to the difficulties of maintaining their habit while attempting to care for their young children. Where professionals are shown also to hold to these stereotypes (Taylor, 1993), substance-using parents are left in a very isolated position.

Instead, researchers such as Richter and Bammer (2000) suggest that the impact of problem-substance use on parenting is in constant flux. Not only can the level of drug use change but independent factors, such as the presence of a non-substance-using partner or the support of the extended family (McKegany et al., 2002) can temper the effects on parenting practices. Evidence from the research seems overwhelmingly to deny the possibility of a 'single stand-alone method' (Liverpool Health Authority, 2001, p. 6) or 'blanket-policy' (McKegany et al., 2002, p. 242) to solve this complex problem that we are only beginning to understand. Rather, we must seek to evaluate the strategies employed by parents, children and social services to make headway in this area.

Coping strategies

Several of the research studies in this area have also tried to identify processes employed by either substance-using parents or their children to temper the effect of parental substance use on their offspring. The ACMD (2003, p. 46), in their investigation into the needs of the children of problem-substance users, have suggested that we need to 'shift away from focusing on negative factors and move towards identifying factors which promote resilience' in order to make an impact on the lives of these children. Some of these positive factors to have come out of the research are discussed below.

Resilience

Some studies have shown evidence of certain children being resilient to the negative consequences of parental problem-substance use (Gilligan, 2000; Gorin, 2004). Bancroft et al. (2004, p. 11) define resilience as 'a series of choices made and strategies adopted by children to help them "get by" in their lives'. In a study of adults who were the children of problem-drinkers, Velleman and Orford (1999) found that, although their research team encountered some negative differences in the lives of the very young children, in many of the older adults they interviewed no obvious consequences of these early differences existed.

> *It was not the case that offspring had generally poorer mental health as young adults, or specifically reported greater anxiety, or a greater dissatisfaction with life. Nor, overall, were they leading lives that were less stable than comparisons in terms of home, close relationships, friendships, work or education.* (Velleman and Orford, 1999, p. 187)

That certain children are better able to deal with the negative effects of having a parent with problem-substance use is evident from the research, but our understanding of the nature of this resilience or how to promote it remains incomplete. Templeton et al. (2006) question how we can use this information to inform policy, and Newman (2004) envisions it as forming an important part of a broader strategy including agencies, institutions, communities and individuals, yet without a fuller understanding of what helps children to be resilient we cannot adequately utilise this valuable resource.

Parenting strategies

I think they (social workers) panic a bit . . . they think your kids are bound to be at risk if you take drugs . . . there's plenty of ways you can make sure they're not going to be at risk. (parent cited in Bates et al., 1999, p. 77)

Across the studies cited here parents have referred to the strategies which they employ to lessen the negative effects on their children of their problem-substance use. Richter and Bammer (2000), in their work with twenty-two Australian substance-using mothers, have listed some of these: stopping using; going into treatment; maintaining a stable, low-level habit; shielding children from drug-related activities; keeping the home environment stable, safe and secure; staying out of prison; and placing children with a trusted caregiver while maintaining as active a role as a parent as possible under the circumstances. Again, further exploration of the nature and success of these strategies would allow us to capitalise on a potentially valuable resource.

Social support networks

Other than strategies that could be employed by either the parents or children themselves, studies also suggested that the single most important external factor that could help to alleviate the problems associated with parental problem-substance usage was the existence of a strong social support network (Bancroft et al., 2004; Hogan, 1998 The roles taken on by friends and neighbours and, in particular, grandmothers (Bancroft et al., 2004; Hogan and Higgens, 2001) were highlighted, although, worryingly, Bancroft et al. (2004, p. 31) point out that out of the thirty-eight children of drug and alcohol users that they interviewed in their report for the Joseph Rowntree Foundation, 'only a minority had any long-term, unconditionally supportive relationships'. Barnard (2003) suggests that there may also be dangers in relying too closely on family networks as the parents themselves risk becoming isolated from their children. The willingness of others to step in and take responsibility may encourage parents to continue in their substance dependency and/or the problem-substance users may have faced experiences in their own childhoods that have left them reluctant to leave their own children in the care of their grandparents.

Conclusions

I'm too frightened of asking anyone for help, I would do but I'm just too frightened about me kids, if they take me kids because that's all I've got left. (parent cited in Klee et al., 1997, p. 26)

As seen in the previous section, the recent wealth of qualitative literature on the impact of parental problem-substance use has provided much insight into the problems experienced by children, and has identified some of the processes which may be able to minimise the negative effects of these problems. However, one of the greatest difficulties facing those seeking to implement policy in this area is the initial reluctance of problem-substance users with children to come forward and identify themselves as such (Bancroft et al., 2004; Coleman and Cassell, 1995; Klee and Jackson, 1998; Klee et al., 1997; Liverpool Health Authority, 2001; Macrory and Harbin, 2000; Templeton et al., 2006; Turning Point, 2006). The main parental fear surrounds the issue of having their children removed from their care if they are judged to be unfit parents. The social stigma of being a substance-using parent has been discussed in the previous section, alongside the possibility that negative stereotypes are prevalent, not only among the general public, but also among professionals in this area. The report produced by Turning Point (2006), based on interviews and focus groups with parents who drink alcohol to excess and their children, has suggested that not only is this fear strong among substance-using parents but that their children are also reluctant to come forward and talk about their problems due to the fear of being removed from their parents, therefore resulting in an inclination to 'suffer in silence' (ibid., p. 23). Evidence suggests that the desire for treatment among problem-substance-using parents is strong (Templeton et al., 2006), but the fear of making contact with authorities has been described as an 'insurmountable barrier (Liverpool Health Authority, 2001, p. 5). The first task then must be to implement policies and processes that encourage drug-using parents to come forward and 'assure them of support rather than punishment' (Klee and Jackson, 1998, p. 439).

Evidence further suggests that getting parents who are problem-substance users into treatment can provide the most effective way to solve the problems, or at least minimise their consequences for children (ACMD, 2003; Richter and Bammer, 2000). Over and above the reluctance to come forward for treatment as discussed above, important gaps in the provision of services in this area have been identified. Templeton et al. (2006) suggest that there is a separation between child and adult services in this area which allows the problems of the children of dependent substance-users to slip through the net. Brisby et al. (1997) further report that many of the treatment services directed at adult substance-users exclude the needs of young children from their provision. Instead, 'a policy response that operates at the level of the child, family, wider kin and community' (Bancroft et al., 2004, p. 49) is suggested. Research also suggests that services should aim to meet the needs of parents as well as children if they are to be able to adopt responsible care-giving roles (Commission for Social Care Inspection, 2006). This finding was strongly supported by the testimony of children themselves who argued for their parents to be 'given a second chance' (ibid., p. 27) and 'not to be given up on' (ibid.).

Studies where specific interventions with problem-substance-using parents have been evaluated are rare and tend to be American in origin, but the results do show that they have a strong potential for success where they are directly organised around the needs of children. Day et al. (2003) investigated a specialist service for pregnant drug users implemented to help them with the additional problem of child care that they would face as dependent drug users. The study demonstrates that participation in the programme led to 'significant improvements in key outcome measures' (ibid,, p. 99) and led the researchers to conclude that 'pregnancy may be a crucial point for potential change in a career of drug use' (ibid.).

Similarly, in a study conducted by Catalano et al. (2002), an intensive family intervention, Focus on Families, for substance-using parents was favourably evaluated as alleviating the problems experienced by their children. This important information that treatment programmes have the power to effect positive change, combined with the indication that many substance-using parents may be reluctant to come forward for treatment because of the feared removal of their children, strongly suggests that the improvement of treatment services and of access to them should be a key issue for policy implementation. While abstinence from substances may remain an ultimate goal, treatment providers must aim not to alienate those who continue to use drugs and alcohol to excess, but instead must reach out to and seek to engage as wide a range of parent problem-substance users as possible. Only in this way can we hope to fully address our responsibilities to the children of problem-substance users and begin to implement a policy and practice that will make a difference.

WEBSITES

Home Office (2002) *Updated Drug Strategy*. www.drugs.gov.uk/publication-search/drug-strategy/updated-drug-strategy–2002.pdf?view=Binary.

Chapter 4

Making sense of sex offender risk and the Internet

Caroline Metcalf

Discovering how, over time, children have become socially constructed as victims and in what way they become victimised is important in our understanding of sex offending. This is not to take away the importance of children as victims, but appreciating the context of sex offending in this way allows us not only to critically review policies and practices but also to see whether they are effective enough under the circumstances. The legal and criminal justice processes involved in shaping child sexual abuse as the crime are also considered. This chapter is specifically concerned with children as victims in relation to sexual abuse and the Internet. It identifies the historical, cultural, legal, political, economical, media and value-laden doctrines that evidently influence and 'bring life' to the social constructivist perspective. For the purpose of this chapter I draw specifically on the current political debates about child sex offender risk and, furthermore, about the media impact on understanding Internet sexual offending and the subsequent legal and political changes and interventions. The ever-growing aim to protect children highlights significantly the determination of our culture to protect them from becoming victims.

Firstly, it presents the current political debates about child sex offender risk and, in particular, its underpinning in conservative neo-liberal rhetoric that New Labour have perpetuated in similar fashion. It draws on the impacts of recent events, namely the Soham murders and Operation Ore, which have directly influenced the political agenda regarding the way sex offenders are managed in the community. In particular, I refer to one community project funded by the Home Office, Circles of Support and Accountability, which neatly illustrates the current attempt to reintegrate sex offenders into their local area by directly involving members of the same community. Furthermore, it examines the political debates surrounding the demand to 'name and shame' registered sex offenders. Despite the growing trend to give victims of crime a 'voice' by focusing primarily on their welfare needs, the Government reaction to sex offenders residing in the community is very much reflective of 'offender focuses'. The impact on understandings of 'paedophile' risk may be marked by public knowledge of such offenders inhabiting the community and this section seeks to address the ongoing phenomenon of 'stranger danger'.

Our understanding of child abuse images and the impact of the computer has been generated mostly through the media. Thus it is fair to suggest that the media have impacted substantially upon the social construction of child sexual abuse. The ways in which the Internet can facilitate child sexual offenders have become high-profile phenomena, particularly following the media coverage on the murder of schoolgirl Sarah Payne in July 2000. Kennison and Read argue:

> *A number of highly publicised murders of children in recent years have further heightened media speculation that the Internet has contributed in some way to their deaths.* (2003, p. 20)

It has raised social tension in terms of children, sexuality, gender roles and the function of families (Norman, 1994). In other words, more emphasis is placed upon the welfare and safety of children and the understanding of the dynamics of sexuality together with the importance given to gender roles in the maintenance of a child's well-being. This section draws on how this shift emphasises the way that such offences are viewed and then bound by social, political and ideological influences, and in addition, the overwhelming impact that this has had on public attitudes (Jenkins, 1998).

Importantly, this chapter also reviews the Sex Offenders Act 1997 as an approach to risk management of those offenders in the community. It can be seen that although such approaches echo neo-liberal stratagems by enforcing and tightening up the monitoring process, the mere fact that many sex offenders are subject to community orders (note that the word 'rehabilitation' has been removed) clearly equates with welfare policies.

The political debate

The political debate is rather paradoxical in which child sexual abusers have become subjects of social exclusion rather than re-integration back into normal life following the 1987 events in Cleveland. Indeed, one only has to look at a sex offender's licence in order to understand such exclusionary processes. Under the Crime and Disorder Act 1998 the sex offender order restricts the offender's access to certain places, namely schools and other institutions in which children are likely to be present, and therefore it becomes increasingly difficult for sex offenders to obtain employment. The political climate, increasingly characterised by fear, conveys the message: 'It's too dangerous to not see them as dangerous'. Such fears are further entrenched by the disastrous consequences of the 'lazy' monitoring of Ian Huntley who was responsible for the Soham murders in August 2002. Despite having a string of allegations for sex offences, he worked as a caretaker at the school of the victims and his employment was never questioned. Consequently, Humberside police were fiercely blamed, leaving the Home Secretary to enforce the Chief Constable's resignation.[1]

There are two factors that have called for a wider understanding of child sexual offending risk: firstly, the growing knowledge about the prevalence of child sexual abuse, and secondly, the swelling prison population of the twenty-first century. Consequently, managing sex offenders in the community is increasingly common. Indeed, in support of community strategies there has been a growth of surveillance in a bid to reduce opportunity to commit crime and, moreover, a growth in the use of risk-based technologies to assess a person's risk of re-offending. The fear of paedophile crime is arguably at an 'all time high', particularly as the occurrence of Internet sex offending continues to rise, as has previously been mentioned. On the one hand, sex offenders residing in the community are becoming increasingly accepted, and community projects such as Circles of Support and Accountability and community treatment programmes are illustrative of this. On the other hand, ideas about 'dangerous people walking around' are common rhetoric in western culture. Circles of Support and Accountability became operational in the Thames Valley in April 2002. The programme is rooted in a restorative justice approach and is aimed at providing a comple-mentary alternative to traditional approaches of managing sex offenders in their local com-munity. Very simply, the volunteers and core member (the offender) meet once a week for approximately 90 minutes and assist the core member in developing community ties, which in turn encourage the offender either to take up education or to build confidence by engaging in social activities within the local area (Ricks 2005). Ricks (a treatment manager for a sex offender group work programme) suggests that circle members provide a stepping-stone between the formal support of agencies and informal support, such as that from family and friends. This, she argues, creates a heightened sense of self-value for the core members because they then realise that the volunteers are not being paid to spend time with them. Essentially, the principal aim is to enhance treatment supervision, the individual's ability to self-manage, and work to support long-term maintenance of the core member's risk management plan (ibid.). The rationale of Circles of Support and Accountability is underpinned by the fact that sex offenders tend to experience emotional loneliness, isolation and low-self esteem. Ricks surmises:

> *Humans usually turn to others to help them alleviate these factors and manage stress. However, it is not uncommon for these men to have poor social support. This may be due to a number of reasons; individuals may become estranged from their family and friends, perhaps as a direct result of the individual's sexual offending or due to the offender's own shame and embarrassment.* (2005, p. 16)

This aptly demonstrates how risk is perceived amongst professionals, and how such concepts of risk are utilised through the management of sex offenders. Such a community initiative is not aimed at 'curing' sex offenders. Rather, it endeavours to interfere with the pattern of offending and reduce risks by helping the offender to implement strategies and increase the motivation to avoid situations that are likely to increase the danger of re-offending. In the last three years fifteen circles have been established in the Thames Valley and have included twenty high-risk sex offenders. Chris Wilson (2005), project manager for Circles of Support and Accountability, suggests that the expected rates of recidivism have thus far been reduced with three men being recalled on licence but none having committed a further *sexual* offence. This equates with the experience of the Canadian 'circle' recidivist rates evaluated over a ten-year period (ibid.). A recall occurs when a volunteer reports 'risky' behaviour of the offender, thus preventing further victimisation. This community project is illustrative of the changing perceptions of sex offender risk and what can be done to reduce it. It seems that almost for the first time sex offenders are understood as community members who are complex individuals and who should not necessarily be demonised and who, moreover, do not necessarily pose the imminent threat that the media would have us believe.

However, the fear of 'stranger danger' remains well documented. Thus, it is useful here to illustrate some known facts surrounding the dangers posed to children. Jackson and Scott (1999) state that despite the lack of evidence of 'stranger danger' a heightened awareness of sexual and fatal risk emerged in the UK during the late 1990s. The children most in danger of being murdered are infants under the age of one: the group least likely to be exposed to people unknown to them. Children aged five to fifteen are, of all members of society, the least likely to be victims of homicide. It is children over the age of fifteen or sixteen that become exposed to the danger of strangers (CSO, 1994, in Jackson and Scott 1999, p. 92). Here in the UK, up to February 1996 (prior to the killings in Dunblane) fewer than six children under fourteen had been killed by strangers each year since 1984. Approximately 600 children die in accidents per year (CSO, 1994, in Jackson and Scott, 1999) yet typical media coverage would suggest a reverse order of danger (Jackson and Scott, 1999). A Home Office campaign launched in Leeds in 1988 warned children against strangers when the 'stranger-danger' programmes were carried out through police visits to primary schools and then spread throughout the country. As an eight-year-old child during this period I witnessed such programmes but school visits were somewhat periodic (certainly at my school at least) and the warnings of 'stranger-danger' were ever-present among teachers, parents and children alike. Although such oratory is thought to have instilled fear and panic among parents, Jackson and Scott (1999) rightly point out that it is quite likely that parents were aware that the chances of their child being abducted and murdered by a stranger was highly unlikely. Nonetheless, the fact that it happens at all is enough to instil such fear with deeply embedded pessimistic phrases such as 'never say never', 'you never know', and 'it could be you'. The recent abduction of four-year-old Madeleine McCann in the Algarve certainly illustrates this point. The consequences of this moral panic (Cohen, 1972) were the increasing limitations on children's freedom. For example, 80 per cent of seven and eight-year-olds in the UK went to school on their own in 1971, and by 1990, only nine per cent were doing so (Hillman et al., 1990, in Jackson and Scott, 1999). Jackson and Scott recognise other factors for such a decline including the increase in car ownership, although the statistics remain indicative of the decreasing opportunities for children to develop autonomy and self-reliance. Therefore anxieties generated by risks to children are rooted in the social construction of childhood at an age of innocence and vulnerability. The central concern given to crime control appears to be rooted in public concerns about fear and risk (Stenson, 1999).

Central to debates about the changing forms of paedophile risk is the recent debate on community notification of the residence of sex offenders. This arose in the wake of the murder of eight-year-old Sarah Payne on 1 July 2000. The argument for a UK public sex offender register became amplified following the news that Roy Whiting, the man convicted of Sarah's murder, had a previous sexual conviction (Thomas, 2003). The campaign for community notification was modelled on the US 'Megan's Law', passed in 1996, following the abduction and murder of seven-year-old Megan Kanka by a man who also had previous sexual convictions. The Home Office refused the public right of access to the sex offender register in accordance with the Sex Offenders Act 1997 Part I. Attempts to amend the Bill as it went through Parliament were lost (ibid.). The rationale for refusal is located in the threat of vigilantism and driving sex offenders underground. At the Labour Party Conference 2002 the then Home Secretary David Blunkett stated:

We cannot open the Sex Offenders Register to the vigilantes who do not understand the difference between paediatricians and paedophiles. ('Blunkett pledges to target sex offenders', *The Guardian*, 2 October 2002, cited in Thomas, 2003, p. 218)

Blunkett (2002) was referring to an incident where vigilantes confused the two and vandalised the home of a paediatrician (Thomas, 2003). Although the Home Office restricts the police in disseminating confidential information to other agencies, e.g. housing officials, schools and social services, there have been some exceptions to the rule. One such, for example, is the case law cited to support 'controlled disclosure' of police information in the case of *R v Devon County Council ex parte L*, which upheld the right of social workers to notify a woman with children that her new co-habitué was suspected of assaulting children (*R v Devon County Council ex parte L* [1991] 2 FLR 541, in Thomas, 2003). There was also the North Wales decision where courts upheld the right of the police to notify immediate neighbours that two people with previous child abuse convictions had moved into their immediate neighbourhood (*R v North Wales Police ex parte AB and CD* (1997), *The Times*, 14 July; *R v North Wales Police ex parte Thorpe* (1998), *The Times*, 23 March). The North Wales decision was based on the premise that notification should only occur where there is specific risk of re-offending. This led to the police jointly assessing risk with other relevant agencies and making decisions about disclosing 'controlled' information (see Maguire et al., 2001, in Thomas, 2003).

The case against public access to the sex offender register stems from the lack of research and evidence to suggest that it acts as an investigative and preventative tool (Hebenton and Thomas, 1997). Moreover, access to the US registers emerged from community uproar over a few highly publicised sex crimes against children, as opposed to being dictated by any hard research evidence (Small, 1999).

The key message then is the fact that if extreme threats to children exist at all then it is seemingly enough to justify the moral panic and heightened awareness of paedophile risk. Furthermore, when a child is murdered we are very quickly informed by the inescapable presence of the mass media which clearly has a well-established influence over public perceptions.

Children as victims: the impact of the media

Garland (2001) argues that the public and media play an active role in policy-making including policy on punishment. Such processes are based on fear and righteous anger, particularly upon media reporting of offenders being released into the community and, moreover, media reporting on re-offending. Consequences of such media reporting and neo-liberal doctrines include vigilantism, which was discussed earlier in this chapter. MacVean (2000) refers to the complex links between the media and the Government. The *Sun* newspaper, MacVean and Spindler (2003) suggest, has been a powerful conveyor of conservative principles and supports the neo-liberal rhetoric. The *Sun* used editorials to relay conservative understandings of crime and crime control (MacVean, 2000; Skidmore, 1995). Soloski (1989) argues that news stories contain hidden morals, but the media is more powerful than merely conveying morals. Skidmore (1995) argues that the media have the ability to change or maintain the structures of power in society by being primary definers and agenda setters (MacVean,

2000). This has been demonstrated on numerous occasions by representations of sex offenders that convey a very clear message: your children are not safe until this person is locked up again. Furthermore, when news breaks of a sex offender being sentenced, the media draws out the inadequacies of Government legislation and policy (MacVean, 2000). Cohen and Young (1973) describe the sensational and exaggerated style of the media as a 'deviance amplification spiral'. Hall et al. (1978) claim that the media are powerful institutions that are primary definers and, in particular, they have played a significant role in redefining child abuse as a criminal rather than a medical or welfare issue (MacVean, 2000).

Media templates are notorious for augmenting and sensationalising the most serious sex crimes rather than the typical (Greer, 2003). The term 'paedophile' has been constructed through media templates to give meaning to the words like 'beast', 'monster' and 'depraved', the purpose being for the public to make sense of the threat paedophiles appear to pose. As Kitzinger (1999) suggests, the word 'paedophile' is burdened with assumptions that restrict and narrow thinking and ideas. As recently as a decade ago child sexual offenders were generally believed to be homosexuals, and portrayed as such in an attempt to further separate them from the rest of society. By producing a catalogue of words and terms that automatically equalise fear and disgust at these individuals, a social construction was gradually built so that we have come to know and associate 'paedophiles' as the 'unknown other' (Greer, 2003). This is by no means a modern phenomenon. During the early twentieth century in New York City it became a popular belief that those committing sex crimes were not a part of the community and they were most likely identifiable by a 'scruffy' appearance that separated them from the rest of society (Jenkins, 1998).

So far as children are concerned, child sexual abuse, whatever the nature, is a crime that will never become socially accepted in western society. It is somehow 'set apart' from other forms of criminality because the dynamics of it are very difficult to understand and emphasise the notion of 'otherness' (Greer, 2003). How child sexual offenders are socially constructed is difficult to understand. It is not just how media templates, police and social workers interpret these individuals and eventually convey these constructions to the public audience. It is already deeply rooted in people's tendency to be appalled by the concept of children as sexual beings or objects. It is argued that how the media have defined terms for sex offenders has resulted in the escalation of people's fears and preconceptions of child sexual offenders as outcast fiends as opposed to ordinary people within the community (Kitzinger, 1996; Soothill and Walby, 1991, in Greer 2003; Soothill et al., 1998; Thomas, 2000; Websdale, 1999). Despite this, Greer (2003) found that these terms used in newspaper tabloids were the source of complaint amongst practitioners and some journalists who participated in the research. This point highlights some potential benefits for the general public in presenting well-informed articles about some of the real issues related to sexual offending. For example, the use of a demographic analysis that emphasises links between learning theory and sexual offending as opposed to unhelpful beliefs that insinuate 'they can't change'. This is especially important in relation to individuals who download child sexual abuse images from the Internet. This old crime through a new medium is at a critical stage for social construction theory. This is because little is known about the Internet sex offender, i.e. one who looks at child sexual abuse images on the Internet. Very little is known about the kind of risk that is posed and to what degree. Calder (2004) describes these as 'hands off' sexual offenders and highlights the difficulty faced by practitioners in managing the cross-over to 'hands on' offending.

Those seen as 'lookers' at child abuse images have been recast by the media as potential child killers, in the light of the murder investigation of two ten-year-old school girls, Holly Wells and Jessica Chapman, in August 2002. DC Brian Stevens,[2] the family liaison officer for Jessica Chapman's family, was a suspect in Operation Ore, compounding fears of 'guilt by association' among the public that downloading child sexual abuse images off the Internet is somehow related to child killings. These shifts in wider cultural meanings, represented in media accounts, change the climate within which policy and criminal justice processes operate.

Although victim issues have generally been downplayed since stories of child abuse on the Internet have emerged in the media, the locations of where images are produced are sometimes mentioned. However, notwithstanding such media reports, scientific and reliable data in this area is as yet unavailable. Issues of child sexual abuse in the media have broadly centred on the risks of children using chat-rooms, as there have been significant numbers of individuals 'grooming' children online for the purposes of sexual gratification. However, the manner in which the media and British legislation have responded to Internet sexual offending would suggest that the children in the images are real victims of those viewing the images and they deserve as much justice as any other child victim.

Perhaps the most startling aspect of the Internet offending phenomenon arises in those arrests of famous icons, namely Gary Glitter and more recently Pete Townshend (The Who). Glitter was arrested when a company repairing his PC found more than 4,000 indecent images of children and he was sentenced to four months' imprisonment (Krone, 2005). The effect was profound among the public because famous icons are familiar and are somehow viewed as 'trusted' figures. Suddenly, the once solid social construction of the child sexual offender began to fragment. Historically, the 'paedophile' label has been reserved for a small minority of individuals who fit a demonised stereotype usually portrayed by the media. The fears and concerns which Operation Ore and other investigations have produced are well founded in real cases although a rational perspective needs to be discovered if there is hope of reducing the whipped-up hysteria resulting in moral panic (Cohen, 1972). It is possible that collectors (if indeed they are) of illegal images are perhaps fundamentally different to child molesters. There is insufficient knowledge about Internet sex offenders to make assumptions about the nature of their crimes and their intentions.

The legal agenda

Laws on sexual offences have generally been considered out of date, given that the Sexual Offences Act was forty-six years old and consisted of consolidated laws from the nineteenth century. Commentators usually refer to the murder of eight-year-old Sarah Payne as a reason for legislative alterations and indeed, some highly publicised paedophile crimes have put the Government under pressure to 'do something'. A review was published in 2002, 'Setting the Boundaries' together with a White Paper, 'Protecting the Public', in which were set out recommendations for specific changes on the existing law. David Blunkett himself commented that the proposed reforms reflect changes in social attitudes (Batty, 2002), particularly the laws on gay sex and child sexual abuse. Reviewing the proposed changes reveals a dominant theme typically surrounding the concept of consent. For example, offences of gross indecency, buggery and soliciting are now decriminalised and so it is legal for homosexual acts to take place consensually in private when there are more than two people taking part or are present 'as it is a victimless crime' (Batty, 2002). It remains an offence to engage in homosexual activity in a public lavatory. The reform includes increased penalties for drug rape and new offences for victims with learning disabilities or mental illness. Again, this reflects a socially constructed definition centred on consent. This is mirrored further in new child abuse laws that close the loophole that previously enabled those accused of child rape to claim that the alleged victim consented. The new law states that sexual intercourse with a child under twelve years of age will be considered as rape. Persuading children to undress is now regarded as a non-contact (hands-off) offence carrying sentences of up to ten years. Interestingly, bestiality, necrophilia and voyeurism have all been introduced as new offences and such activities have been brought to attention as a direct result of sex crime via the Internet. All three activities expose themselves as 'real' social problems, mostly because the Internet reveals the nature and scope of the crime and means the material is more readily available. The problem of child abuse images on the Internet does not throw up any more challenges for legislation as images are images – whether on the Internet or not. However, the Home Office recognises that sexual approaches towards children are increasing, with more than a dozen recorded cases involving sexual abuse and rape. The Act includes a new offence of 'grooming', which makes it illegal to befriend a child on the Internet with the intention of abusing them. The Act also extends to prohibit inappropriate conversations of a sexual nature between adults and children through Internet chat-rooms.

The Sex Offenders Act was implemented on 1 September 1997 and requires an offender who is cautioned, convicted or found not guilty by reason of insanity to supply details to the police of his/her name, date of birth, address and any later changes to them. A series of amendments were made through the Criminal Justice and Court Services Act 2000 and four changes were made for the initial notification:

1. Initial notification is required within a period of three days, not fourteen.
2. Initial notification must be made in person.
3. A new power for the police to take fingerprints and photographs of the offender. Upon initial notification:
4. Notification of relevant information on first visit.

The Act also introduced new provisions to strengthen court and police powers:

> *An increase in the maximum penalty for a failure to comply with the Act's requirements.*
> *A new power for courts to impose a restraining order upon convicting an offender.*
> *Offenders must notify their Public Protection Officer of an intention to leave the United Kingdom and of their return (HOC 20/2001).*

The Sex Offenders Act 1997 was introduced as a strategy for managing risk, and the police, in partnership with the probation service, measure an offender's risk using the specifically designed technology of Matrix 2000. There are many elements that can be drawn from the Sex Offenders Act and its recent amendments. Firstly, the provisions of the Act reflect the fashion of the current criminal justice trend in which offenders residing in the community are continuously measured by their 'risk', both according to their risk assessment formulae and their observed behaviour by both police and probation officers. The Act has also paved the way for new Community Rehabilitation Orders and strikes a balance between meeting the needs of the offender as well as the community, and reflects the agenda of 'reassurance policing'. It may be argued that any form of contact with the offender, whether it is with probation, police or volunteers of the community, is a form of social control (Hirschi, 1969). Outside help is likely to influence the offender in positive ways, for example, solutions to accommodation and employment needs that are quite likely to reduce their risk of re-offending. Secondly, it is becoming increasingly documented that knowledge of existing risks carries the danger of creating new risks, and the amendments of the Sex Offenders Act support this view. For example, the amendment concerning the notification of intention to travel abroad is twofold. Offenders have previously been able to claim that they were abroad if they were found to be absent from their home, and remain within legal boundaries. Also, it is important to understand the dynamics of the social construction variation across the water; the amendment is designed to ensure that sex offenders from the UK do not target children in countries where the law is considerably more lenient (HOC 20/2001). This grants power to the police and they may pass on relevant information to another jurisdiction if they consider the offender to pose a sufficient risk. The new power of restraining orders is also symbolic of the Act in revealing 'new' risks. The restraining order is imposed at the point of sentence and perhaps under the recommendation of a pre-sentence report. It is designed to place restrictions on the offender's behaviour; for example, prohibiting close proximity to schools or other high-risk areas. Finally, the key amendments in the Sex Offenders Act can be situated in the context of social construction. The re-introduction of 'ticket of leave' concepts, rehabilitation, identifying risks and new risks all lie in the back-drop of a greater phenomenon, which are initiatives created on knowledge, perception and a response to the public's reaction. Importantly, these initiatives mirror British and western culture and are indicative of a mixture of neo-liberal concepts and elements of the welfare state. Rehabilitation places the offender in a somewhat advantageous position as it implies that the offender is somehow able to 'fix' his problem and therefore his character may become redeemable.

In 2005 it emerged that plans had been published suggesting outlawing possession of pornography depicting bestiality, necrophilia and serious sexual violence, and bringing them into line with offences of possessing and making images of child sexual abuse. It was suggested that the Home Office will recommend sentences of up to three years for possession (*The Independent*, 30 August 2005).

This section has defined the macro setting of defining child sexual abuse, and such new offences just outlined characterise the maintenance of the neo-liberal agenda and the 'tightening up' of acceptable sexual behaviour. The following section continues the process of definition by exploring the meso setting, that is, the role of criminal justice and policy processes.

Criminal justice and policy processes

It is rather surprising that the social construction of child sexual abuse through the criminal justice process has generally been ignored. Police discretion is typically considered a negative yet unavoidable part of everyday police work. Reiner (1991, p. 276) argues that discretion is the 'art of suiting action to particular circumstances'. This is especially relevant to the policing of sex offenders in the community when a great deal of judgement regarding risk is supported by the 'role of the hunch', which is produced from personal contact with the offenders. Police discretion is increasingly significant in light of non-contact offenders, where contact offences are unknown or have not been committed. An understanding of how sex offender officers construct meaning about such offences and offenders in the context of cultural realities is essential for this purpose. Importantly, the same difficulties that arise in the social construction of contact offences also exist within the virtual world. For example, the High Tech Crime Unit organises images into 'categories' according to levels of seriousness. It is the general consensus that suspects will be charged on a maximum of sixteen counts to include the most serious of images. The categories of paedophile images are as follows:

Level One: Images that depict erotic posing without sexual activity.

Level Two: Sexual activity between children, or solo masturbation by a child.

Level Three: Non-penetrative sexual activity between adults and children.

Level Four: Penetrative sexual activity between children and adults.

Level Five: Sadism or bestiality.

(As set out in the Court of Appeal by Lord Justice Rose in *R* v *Oliver, Hartrey and Baldwin*).

This categorisation is a key element in the social construction of levels of penalty. Police officers may dispute the applicability of the categorisation because levels may seem to be blurred in practice. Some officers or members of the High Tech Crime Unit may not differentiate between level three and level four when processing cases through the criminal justice system. Indeed, the categorisation process should account for the age of the victim. For example, what if a level one image is an image of a baby? This factor might not be considered in court as it is technically classed as no more than a level one image. This particular characteristic of dealing with Internet offences is just one significant example of the role and importance of the social construction of sex offences through the criminal justice process. This is a significant example that may give an indication of how the policy of the categories may not reflect the reality. Policy documentation is a significant source in bringing social constructivism to life. That is, the guidelines written in simple black and white allow for a clear understanding of how criminal justice professionals might interpret them differently to each other.

Conclusion

This chapter has highlighted how children have come to be understood and viewed as vulnerable and, moreover, how ideas of what constitutes child sexual abuse have been constructed. It is evident that the political climate alters accordingly when media reporting about child sex offender risk is heightened, and this could not be more evident when we think about the reporting of Internet sexual offending. Arguably, the political agenda focuses on the needs of offenders; an argument most significantly illustrated with the Circles of Support and Accountability project. However, it is important that one maintains a logical understanding of the underpinnings of the project's rationale, i.e. to reduce re-offending and thus retain the notion that it is children who are the potential victims, not the perpetrators. This is not where the political paradox lies however. Projects are supported and funded to re-integrate the offender into the community and are based on long-standing research that supports the view that decreasing socio-affective deficits, such as emotional loneliness, reduces the risk of re-offending. At the same time however, there are ideas being driven forward to introduce the 'name and shame' campaign. Paradoxically, this is yet another attempt to reassure the public, but the campaign runs the risk of driving individuals underground and *increasing* their emotional loneliness and entrenching other socio-affective deficits, e.g. poor self-esteem. Such notifications will include Internet sex offenders also, and we do not currently have an established understanding of their risk of harm to the public. Moreover, sex offenders are a heterogeneous group and misconceptions of them might lead to a gross over-estimation of risk amongst the lay public without offering any really helpful solutions in protecting children from becoming victims.

This chapter demonstrates how complex it is to understand child sexual abuse, sexual offenders and, indeed, the risk of abuse occurring. Politicians and criminal justice workers have become real 'people pleasers' when it comes to tightening up sex offender legislation and performance targets. The rise in Internet crime has only served to validate the current climate in which such workers operate. As this chapter conveys, however, the protection of children is not a straightforward argument. We need to focus on the criminogenic needs of the offender if we have any chance of protecting children. One thing is clear, however: children are vulnerable members of society who require protecting. This chapter illustrates that there are a number of different ideas and ways in which this may be done.

Notes

1 See Chapter 10 for further details regarding the consequences for the handling of information and intelligence by police, including the concerns raised in the Bichard Report, the public inquiry called in the light of the Soham murders (Editor's note).

2 Brian Stevens was cleared of three counts of indecent assault against two females, three counts of distributing indecent photographs of children and five counts of possessing indecent photographs of children. He was cleared due to lack of evidence. Anthony Goodridge, an exhibits officer in the Soham case, was given a six-month sentence in March 2003 after pleading guilty to the possession of 330 indecent images of children (*The Guardian*, 20 August 2003).

WEBSITES

Anon. (20.08.03) 'Soham officer cleared of charges', *Guardian*. www.guardian.co.uk/crime/article / 0,2763,1023820,00.htm. Visited 1 September 2005.

Batty, D. (20.11.02) 'Questions and answers: Sex Offenders Bill', *Guardian*. http://politics.guardian.co.uk/.

Home Office Circular (20/2001) Criminal Justice and Court Services Act 2000: Amendments to the Sex Offenders Act 1997. www.homeoffice.gov.uk. Visited 29 December 2004.

Krone, D. (2005) 'International police operations against online child pornography', *Trends and Issues in Crime and Criminal Justice*. Australian Institute of Criminology, 296. www.aic.gov.au/topics/cybercrime/publications.html. Visited 27 September 2005.

Norman, C.A. (1994) 'Not in families like us: the social construction of child abuse in America', paper presented at Emerging Theories/Merging Practices in Gender Studies, The Ninth National Graduate Women's Studies Conference. University of California at San Diego: April 14–17.

Case law

R v *Devon County Council ex parte L* [1991] 2 FLR 541. Concerns disclosure of information relating to paedophiles, Art. 8 of ECHR.

R v *North Wales Police ex parte AB and CD* [1997] 4 All ER 691, DC. Concerns the release of police information about offenders to third parties in order to prevent crime or to alert members of the public to an apprehended danger.

R v *North Wales Police ex parte Thorpe* [1998] 3 WLR 57. Concerns the release of information by social workers concerning offenders to third parties in order to prevent crime or to alert members of the public to an apprehended danger.

R v *Oliver, Hartrey and Baldwin* (2002) Court of Appeal, Lord Justice Rose, August. Concerns the analysis of increasing seriousness by reference to five different levels of activity derived from the COPINE Project's description of images.

Chapter 5
Children as victims of crime

Sally Angus

Introduction

In recent years, the role of the victim has migrated from the periphery of the criminal justice system to (virtual) centre stage. The Crime and Disorder Act 1998 and the Youth Justice and Criminal Evidence Act 1999 introduced, for the first time in English law, criminal justice interventions based on restorative justice principles. These principles seek to enable victims to engage more fully in 'their' crimes and maximise offender responsibility.

This chapter will consider the role of children as victims of crime and how the criminal justice system in England and Wales (particularly the youth justice system) responds to their victimisation. For the purposes of this chapter the term 'child' and 'children' mean people under the age of eighteen. This includes mid to late teenagers, usually referred to as 'young people'. Following an historical overview of the victim and the criminal justice system this chapter will consider the concept of restorative justice and its application to victims in the youth justice system, illustrating this with reference to research undertaken in three youth offending teams (Angus, unpublished PhD Thesis) which considers the role of youth offending teams (YOT) and how they respond to children and young people who are victims of crime perpetrated by other young people.

Victims in the criminal justice system

Whilst this chapter focuses specifically on children as victims of crime, it is important to understand the role of the victim in the criminal justice system and how this has developed over time.

Prior to the mid nineteenth century, victims of crime were responsible for taking their own cases to court. This situation had advantages and disadvantages but enabled victims to retain ownership of the decision to prosecute. This changed during the latter half of the nineteenth century when the state incrementally appropriated responsibility for prosecuting offenders. This was ostensibly to protect victims from retribution and provide objectivity regarding the decision to prosecute, focusing on public rather than individual interests (Christie, 1977).

In practice, this resulted in victims losing their stake in the case and reducing their role to providers of testimony on behalf of the state in what Nils Christie refers to as the victim's 'conflict' which has been stolen by the state. In this seminal text Christie states:

> *We have focused on the offender, made him an object for study, manipulation and control. We have added to all those forces that have reduced victims to a nonentity and the offender to a thing. The victim has lost participation in his own case. It is the Crown that describes the losses, not the victim. It is the Crown that gets the chance to talk to the offender. The victim is left outside of the case, angry, maybe humiliated through cross examination in court, without any human contact with the offender. He has no alternative. He will use all the classical stereotypes around the criminal to get a grasp on the whole thing.* (Christie, 1977)

The notion of victim participation was virtually absent from the criminal justice system until the mid twentieth century when state recognition of the victim as a stakeholder in criminal justice started to emerge. One tangible example was the introduction of Criminal Injuries Compensation in 1964, where state compensation was offered to victims as legitimate (injured) parties (Miers, 1977).

The 1970s saw a number of convergent factors which precipitated the rise of the victimology, one of which was the rise of the women's movement and the active campaigning for women who were fleeing domestic and sexual violence. Women's Aid and Rape Crisis are just two examples of agencies directly supporting female victims in the aftermath of crime.

The same period saw the rehabilitative model of working with offenders, an increase in crime, and public outrage at the apparent movement towards excessively lenient criminal justice outcomes. The Government at the time was under increasing pressure due to the escalating fiscal, economic and political cost of crime.

The last two decades have seen unprecedented governmental attention to victims of crime. Victim Support (the national charity supporting victims, witnesses and their families in the aftermath of crime) is a prime example of the growth of the victim 'industry'. Starting in the early 1970s it has grown, year on year, with increased Government funding. Funding from the Home Office in recent years has amounted to approximately £30 million, although this sum, combined with that paid out by the Criminal Injuries Compensation Authority, is still only 2 per cent of the whole criminal justice budget. From victims being largely ignored by the state, they emerged as a useful political commodity. Some commentators have criticised the Government's attention to victims as being putative, accusing it of using victims to deflect attention away from its failure to tackle offending (Newburn, 1995; Williams, 1999).

The introduction of the Victim's Charter in 1990 (Home Office, 1990) was a significant milestone in state acknowledgement of the needs of victims and the legitimacy of their involvement in the criminal justice system.

Since 1997 the Government has produced a raft of legislation to meet the needs of both victims and witnesses and to involve them in the criminal justice system. The now familiar rhetoric 'putting the victims at the heart of the criminal justice system' (Home Office, 2007) can be evidenced in two key Government policy documents; 'Speaking up for Justice' (Home Office, 1998b) and 'Justice for All' (Home Office, 2002a). The concept of the victim as a 'consumer' of the criminal justice service is highlighted by Miers (2004), who points out the value to the state in engaging with victims to ensure they continue to act as 'suppliers' of information. This acknowledges the danger of victims withdrawing from criminal justice processes resulting in important cases failing to be successfully prosecuted.

Analysis suggests that two drivers have coalesced to increase the state's commitment to victims. Firstly, it was keen to avoid the accusation that it was 'placating victims [as] a political manoeuvre designed to divert attention away from successive governments' failure to reduce the incidence of crime' (Williams, 1999, p. 38). Secondly, the importance of engaging the victim in terms of suppliers of information is evident in the Government's own research where it was found that during 2001 in excess of 30,000 criminal cases were abandoned because witnesses and victims failed to attend court or to give evidence (Home Office, 2002a, p. 36). The Government was quick to realise the implications of victims not engaging in the criminal justice process – its crucial role being to bring offenders to justice.

Children as offenders

In twenty-first-century Britain the involvement of young people with the criminal justice system is understood more in terms of their offending behaviour than as victims of crime. Children's propensity to offend is not new. However, in the last decade the Government and the media have paid significant attention to youth crime and its antecedent, anti-social behaviour. The present Government, New Labour, has chosen this as a prime area to display its determination to tackle crime and disorder. By so doing, and with media assistance, the public are encouraged to regard youth crime as a growing problem requiring new and tougher measures.

New Labour's programme of changes to the youth justice system came in the aftermath of the murder of James Bulger by two ten-year-old boys. The public outcry was unprecedented and, sensing the need to retain a robust approach to youth crime, the Government pledged to 'be tough on crime and tough on the causes of crime' (Home Office, 1997, p. 3). The abolition of *doli incapax* [incapable of crime] is perhaps seen as one of the most radical changes. New Labour abolished this doctrine, which had been enshrined in law since the fourteenth century, on the basis that '10–13 year olds were plainly capable of differentiating between right and wrong' (s. 34, Crime and Disorder Act 1998).

The Government's determination to hold both young offenders and, to some extent, their parents responsible for their offending behaviour has marked a change from safeguarding the welfare of children from dealing with them outside of the criminal justice system to tackling their offending behaviour as a priority from within. The principal aim of the new youth justice system is to 'prevent offending by young people' (Home Office, 1997, p. 7).

Pearson (1983) saw concern over the putative recent surge in youth crime as a demonstration of 'extraordinary historical amnesia' whilst reminding us that 'youth crime has always been present in western society and youth crime and misconduct is part of the social landscape' (1983, p. 70).

Certainly the reforms of the youth justice system have received a mixed response. Whilst victim groups welcome the reforms in terms of acknowledging the needs and the role of the victim, many of those working within the field of youth justice, and in academia, have raised concerns about drawing more and more children into the criminal justice system.

The reforms, taken together, portray a dichotomous policy approach to children's issues. On the one hand the Children Act 1989 prioritises the welfare of children within the care and child protection systems whilst, on the other hand, children who offend are dealt with robustly by the youth justice system which (ostensibly) holds them accountable for their actions.

The 'children first, offenders second' philosophy is intrinsic to the culture and ideology of practitioners working in the youth justice system (Cross et al., 2003). However, in practice, youth justice practitioners struggle to deliver services that promote this perspective. An example of this can be found in the Government's pledge to 'speed up' the youth justice system and reduce the time from arrest to sentencing (Home Office, 1997). Pitts argues that policies such as these are about 'managing crime and its aftermath' rather than addressing young offenders 'social or psychological needs' (2005, p. 4).

Children as victims

Here the focus is almost exclusively on children who are victims of abuse, usually by an adult parent or carer. The past twenty-five years have seen a number of high profile child abuse cases, the most significant being the murder of Victoria Climbié in 2000 (see also Chapter 7).

The public inquiry that followed provided impetus to the Government intention to develop a preventative agenda for children which spanned the fields of child protection and youth justice through the 2004 Children Act and associated policy guidance issued under 'Every Child Matters: Change for Children' (DfES, 2004a). In this context, children as victims are visible and endowed with the right to expect help to achieve five critical outcomes; be healthy, stay safe, enjoy and achieve, make a positive contribution, and achieve economic well-being.

Government reforms have also taken account of children as indirect victims of crime such as domestic abuse perpetrated in the family home. The Domestic Violence and Victims Act 2004 acknowledges the harmful impact that seeing or hearing domestic violence has on children. It is now considered a child safeguarding issue, as per the revised definition of emotional abuse in *Working Together* (DfES, 2006b).

Some commentators see the focus on children as victims of abuse as obscuring the needs of children who have been the victims of 'ordinary' crimes (Morgan and Zedner, 1992, p. 80). Other than demonstrating an interest in the veracity and reliability of children's testimony, academic and state interest in children as victims of other types of crime is almost non-existent. Prior to Morgan and Zedner's work there had been no research looking solely at children as victims of crime.

Responding to this challenge, subsequent research has been undertaken on children's experience of crime and the criminal justice system. Some of this research deliberately focuses on victimisation (Anderson et al., 1994; Graham and Bowling, 1995; Harrington and Mayhew, 2001). However, much of this research is quantitative and a qualitative extrapolation of children's experiences of victimisation, whilst potentially very informative, is difficult to obtain. Morgan and Zedner's research focused on children as both direct and indirect victims. They looked at children as indirect victims of burglary as well as being victims of direct crimes such as robbery and assault and concluded that children's access to justice was dependent on (their) significant adults both acknowledging their victimisation and interpreting the event as a crime; they identified a strong tendency for such events to be minimised and interpreted as youth on youth activity. Only when supportive adults recognise such activities as criminal acts are children enabled to seek a criminal justice resolution.

Due to ethical and privacy imperatives, obtaining data on crimes against children is usually prohibitive, particularly with self-reporting surveys. The British Crime Survey, for example, does not seek data on crimes against children below the age of sixteen years. Anderson et al. (1994) suggest that this is a serious omission as young people are one of the most vulnerable groups in society. An exception was made in the 1992 British Crime Survey which surveyed a small sample of young people and discovered that those aged between twelve and fifteen were more likely to be victims of theft and assault than adults (Maung, 1995).

Subsequent research, both Government-commissioned and independent, shows that crimes against children are increasing and these are often perpetrated by peers (Home Office, 2005a; Home Office, 2005b; Victim Support, 2003; Youth Justice Board, 2004). A Home Office study (2005a) revealed that 71 per cent of assaults committed by ten to fifteen-year-olds were against people known to them, of whom 49 per cent were peers. Interestingly, other research commissioned by the Government (which was not specifically victim-focused, but rather investigated what motivates young people to offend) led to recommendations that Government consider strategies to reduce offending by young people that 'pay as much attention to young people as victims of crime as it does to them as offenders' (Fitzgerald et al., 2003, p. 71).

Research from Edinburgh confirms a correlation between victimisation and subsequent offending. David Smith, in a longitudinal study of 4,300 young people, explored the relationship between victimisation and offending by young people, which revealed a strong link between victimisation and offending behaviour and concluded that 'the more often victimization is repeated, the more strongly it predicts delinquency' (Smith, 2004, p. 3).

Restorative justice

Restorative justice, by definition, involves all parties to a crime. It may be useful at this point to look at the commonly accepted definition developed by Marshall (1999):

> *Restorative Justice is a process whereby parties with a stake in a specific offence collectively resolve how to deal with the aftermath of the offence and its implications for the future.* (1999: 5)

There has been much debate over this definition (see Braithwaite, 2002; Dignan, 2005; Morris and Maxwell, 2001), a discourse which deserves more detailed analysis than this chapter allows. However, in summary the debate centres on the nature of restorative justice; is it a process, a paradigm shift, or an approach to crime? What is beyond debate is that the 'parties' include the offender, the community and the victim. The extent of the involvement of each party is to some degree determined by the underlying ethos, or aims of the restorative justice project, and 'how' it is delivered. A fundamental precursor to delivering a restorative justice outcome is that the offender admits guilt. Unless or until the perpetrator admits wrongdoing and accepts responsibility, the process cannot move forward.

Restorative justice delivery is multifaceted and reflects the vagaries of the definition. Proponents argue that in order for restorative justice to be meaningful, it needs to be voluntary on all sides (McCold, 1999). Here lies the problem, as sceptics argue that restorative justice cannot meet this imperative when it is delivered within a criminal justice system, due the coercion that is intrinsic to the system (Haines, 1998). In an attempt to circumvent this conundrum others suggest that restorative justice needs to be more flexible than the purist position allows, pointing out that if it is only offered as a model of voluntary settlement between the three parties, and based on free agreements, then it will be 'condemned to stay as some kind of ornament at the margin of the hard-core criminal justice system, reserved for "soft" problems' (Walgrave, 1998, p. 13). Historically, restorative justice has been delivered outside of the formal criminal justice system, primarily by indigenous communities in Australia, Africa and New Zealand. However, in New Zealand it became formalised into their youth justice system in 1989 through the Children, Young Persons and Families Act.

Most restorative justice models focus on young offenders. One of the reasons for this is that for much of the last century the juvenile justice system, both here in England and Wales as well as abroad, has vacillated between welfare and justice credentials, gloriously failing to fit 'exclusively into either one of the categories' (Alder and Wundersitz, 1994, p. 3). This theoretical homelessness is therefore partially resolved by the advent of a practical framework which purports to span both camps.

Whilst there are a number of different methods of delivering restorative justice, including mediation and peace circles, the Family Group Conference (FGC), which has its roots in New Zealand, remains the dominant model. The conference involves members of the young offender's family, the victim and their family, as well as professionals such as teachers, social workers and the wider community representatives, and is facilitated by an independent person. The purpose of the conference is to draw up a contract, considering the needs of the offender and those of the victim.

Restorative justice in England and Wales

Earlier restorative justice initiatives in England and Wales were often delivered on a 'take-it-or-leave-it philosophy' (Sherman and Strang, 2007, p. 23). A small number of mediation projects were delivered by the Probation Service in the early 1980s but were not successful in terms of satisfaction rates (see Umbreit, 2001 for a more detailed analysis). Since 1998 the concept and principles of restorative justice have underpinned youth justice legislation in England and Wales by borrowing from the Australian and New Zealand models.

For the first time in English law 'restoration', 'responsibility' and 'reintegration', the three driving principles of restorative justice, have found their way into statute (Home Office, 1997). Government reforms place restorative justice formally within a legislative framework and provide an alternative to 'more traditional punitive measures, which must be made available to the courts in order to protect the public' (ibid., p. 34).

Working to these principles, the Youth Justice Board promotes the development of services that provide opportunities:

> *For those directly affected by an offence – victim, offender and members of the community – to communicate and agree how to deal with the offence and its consequences.*
> (YJB, 2006)

The Crime and Disorder Act 1998 introduced a number of Orders, including the Reparation Order, Action Plan Order and Supervision Order, all of which require the young offender to make reparation to the victim, the community or both.

The Youth Justice and Criminal Evidence Act 1999 make provision for the most restorative of all orders, the Referral Order. This order is primarily aimed at young people who have pleaded guilty to a first offence and is used in over 29 per cent of all disposals at the Youth Court (YJB, 2007).

The Government's reformed youth justice policies demonstrate a redoubtable commitment to restorative justice. Whilst the primary aim of the new youth justice system is to 'prevent offending and re-offending by children and young people' (YJB, 2007), when it comes to restorative justice the YJB states:

> . . . *unlike other interventions within youth justice, the prevention of offending is not the central aim of restorative justice. The repair of harm, including harm to relationships, is what matters most.* (YJB, 2003, p. 7)

However, whilst the rhetoric of restorative justice is invoked, both in the legislation and underpinning policy documents, service delivery remains offender-focused, leaving the other two sides of the restorative justice triangle, in policy implementation terms, relatively deprived (Goodey, 2005). The evaluation of pilot youth offending teams (Holdaway et al., 2001) and Referral Orders (Newburn et al., 2001) lends support to this analysis. Holdaway et al. point out that YOT members seem relatively oblivious of 'the significant change of philosophy contained in the Crime and Disorder Act 1998' (2001, p. 14).

Victims and restorative justice

Evaluating restorative justice interventions is notoriously difficult, including evaluating victims' experiences of restorative processes (Haines, 1998; Johnstone, 2002). Whilst Sherman and Strang assert that 'evidence consistently suggests that victims benefit, on average, from face to face restorative conferences' (2007, p. 8), for Johnstone there are too many variables to determine how satisfied people are. An example of this can be found in the evaluation of the restorative justice projects funded by the YJB (Wilcox and Hoyle, 2004) which looked at restorative justice interventions. It reported that the attrition rate was very high. Within a population of over six thousand young participants, fewer than 14 per cent of interventions involved direct meetings with victims.

Getting some sense of who the victims of restorative justice are is also difficult. As Young so aptly puts it:

> *In much of the restorative justice literature, victims appear as ageless, colourless, genderless, classless individuals. In other words they are presented as an undifferentiated homogenised mass.* (Young, 2002, p. 146).

Standard data collection methods make it almost impossible to establish how many victims are children. Attempts to do so include eliminating crimes that are adult-specific in relation to victims by crime type. For example, victims of burglary and car theft/car damage are more likely to be adult, whereas victims of assault and robbery may well be children or young people.

One small study commissioned by Trafford Youth Offending Team and victim support scheme sought feedback from children who had been victims of crimes perpetrated by other young people. Although over five hundred questionnaires were sent out, the response rate was very low, generating just sixty-nine responses. In this small sample, over a third of young victims knew their offender, and many reported feeling reluctant to meet the offender and were apparently content to communicate their feelings through the YOT practitioner (Wilkinson, 2002). Evidence suggests that victim engagement in restorative justice has been piecemeal. Those victims that choose to engage in restorative justice initiatives are generally pleased with both the process and the outcome (Umbreit, 2001). However, many victims choose not to engage, saying that the crime was too trivial to bother with, whilst others state they were never asked or, when asked, it was not a convenient time (Morris and Maxwell, 2001).

How, and to what extent, victims engage in restorative justice is dependent on a number of factors including agencies' primary client groups, their funding arrangements, and the 'degree of cultural resistance on the part of some of the agencies involved' (Dignan, 2005. p. 166). Bazemore and O'Brien note that many restorative justice projects have a strong offender bias where projects tend 'to lean toward pursuit of offender-orientated objectives' simply because 'policymakers fund programmes largely based on the promise of reduced recidivism' (2002, p. 31). Offender-driven organisations tend to lose sight of the victim within the restorative process. Barton typifies many restorative justice proponents who question the legitimacy of restorative interventions where 'one or more of the primary stakeholders is silenced, marginalised and disempowered in processes that are intended to be restorative' (Barton, 2003, p. 29).

Factors that militate against the delivery of sound restorative justice are varied but include organisational allegiances to offenders and lack of practitioner understanding of restorative principles. These specific factors can perpetuate a tendency to view restorative justice as an adjunct to existing rehabilitative packages of support to offenders and conspire against bringing the offenders and victims together in a positively restorative way (Johnstone, 2002, p. 5).

Victims, restorative justice and youth offending teams

As mentioned earlier, many, but not all, YOTs have struggled to find a way of working successfully with victims of crime. Holdaway et al., in their evaluation of the pilot YOTs, suggest that 'the unequivocal adoption of a victim-focused approach represents one of the most important and far reaching cultural changes required by the Crime and Disorder Act 1998' (2001, p. 36). The evaluation team came across open resistance by some YOT practitioners to engage in victim consultation. The National Association for Youth Justice (NAYJ), whose membership largely comprises YOT practitioners, recommends that whilst

> *enhancing children's awareness of the effects of their offending on others may be beneficial, victims of crime should have their needs met separately.* (YJB, 2006)

Although there is evidence to suggest a philosophical 'resistance' on the part of some YOT practitioners, it is important to recognise the procedural constraints facing practitioners in their contact with victims of crime.

Part of New Labour's agenda on youth crime was to speed up the youth justice system and thus reduce the time from arrest to conviction. An inevitable consequence of this has been the imposition of strict time limits for contact with victims. An example of this can be found in Referral Orders, the most restorative of all the orders, as it involves the community (in the form of panel members), the victim (who may be invited to the panel) and the young offender. Once issued, a Referral Order requires the offender to attend a Youth Offender Panel within twenty days. Whilst Referral Orders are specifically designed to provide an opportunity for victims to attend Offender Panels and say how the crime has affected them, the tight time-frame provides very little time to contact, discuss and prepare the victim to engage in restorative justice.

The use of Referral Orders is significant. In 2003 the YJB estimated that youth courts issued approximately 27,000 Referral Orders, accounting for 29 per cent of all court disposals for young people (YJB, 2003a). Despite the substantial use of this Order research has shown that victim participation is exceptionally low. Newburn et al. collected data on 274 Panels and found that in only 27 Panels did the victim or victim representative attend (2001). In spite of newly constructed legislative framework, policy missives and targets, restorative justice delivery involving victim participation is prone to circumvention. This is due, in part, to the inclusion of considerable procedural latitude. Section 7(4)(a) of the Youth Justice and Criminal Evidence Act 1999 states that the panel 'may allow any person who appears to the panel to be a victim of, or affected by, the offence . . .'. The victim does not have a right to attend, but may be allowed to do so at the discretion of the YOT practitioner.

Guidance issued to YOTs on Referral Orders in April 2000 recognises that there may be occasions where, in spite of victims' desire to participate, 'the YOT is forced to exclude them' (Home Office and YJB, 2000, p. 23). The guidance allows this in circumstances where victims 'may pose a threat to the offender, or it may be considered that he or she is likely to be obstructive to the panel process' (2000, p. 23). Whilst it is difficult to confirm with any certainty that the incidence of child victims engaging in restorative justice is proportionally small, the number of children who are victims of crime perpetrated by other children is not.

Given the above, it would seem logical that young offenders who are given a Referral Order for a crime committed against another young person would come before a youth offender panel. However, this is not the case and, as I will highlight below, the issue of child victim visibility is a contentious one.

Restorative justice, child victims and the youth justice system

The application of restorative justice principles within the current youth justice in England and Wales is compromised for a number of reasons already highlighted. Additionally, in findings from research undertaken by the author, there appears to be systemic reluctance in youth justice processes to apportion responsibility for criminal behaviour perpetrated by the child offenders against child victims. The author examined ninety case files where young offenders were issued Referral Orders for crimes perpetrated against young people. The crimes included assaults (of varying degrees of seriousness) and robberies. Of the ninety cases, only one young victim attended a youth offender panel.

As mentioned earlier, the research from Trafford YOT and the local Victim Support Scheme revealed that there was a one in three chance that the parties will be known to one another (Wilkinson, 2002). In the research undertaken by the author, 28 per cent of cases involved victims and offenders that were known to one another, slightly less than the Trafford research.

Evidence from research tells us that child victims are reluctant to meet offenders (Hoyle and Young, 2002; Wilkinson, 2002), with key causal indicators being fear of retaliation and a desire to communicate their feelings indirectly through the YOT practitioner. However the author's research challenges inferences that these factors are significantly causal as, in the majority of cases examined by the writer, practitioners considered it inappropriate for the child victim to attend (Angus, 2001).

This judgement appears to be based on the belief that restorative justice processes, from an 'offender' perspective, would be compromised by 'victim' participation. Whether, or to what extent, parties are known to each other can increase complexity when assigning labels to 'victim' and 'offender'. Dignan views the designation of young people engaged in offending behaviour with each other as either victims or offenders as problematic, particularly as research tells us that many young offenders have also been victims of crime (Home Office, 2005b). This can create situations where 'it is often a matter of chance who is charged as the "assailant" and whose testimony will be sought as the "victim"' (Dignan, 2005, p. 163).

Whilst the findings from the author's research are preliminary, and require further analysis, a number of themes are emerging in relation to the absence of child victims attending youth offender panels.

Mixed messages

There appears to be a lack of synchronicity between Government policy and restorative justice delivery and this deserves closer scrutiny. Guidance issued to the courts, YOTs and youth offender panels set out four main tasks for YOT staff in relation to youth offender panels:

- assessing young offenders and producing reports for the youth offender panel;
- engaging with victims;

- participating in the panel: and

- monitoring the compliance of the young offender with the contract drawn up by the panel (Home Office, 2002a).

Official guidance states very clearly that youth offender panels should 'operate on restorative justice principles' (Home Office/Lord Chancellors Department/YJB, 2002, section 6.1); victims should always be given the opportunity, if they so wish, to participate in the resolution of the offence and its consequences and victims may ask questions, receive an explanation and an apology.

Furthermore. Government is keen to promote restorative justice within the youth justice system. In a report published by the YJB in 2001 they set a target for 'restorative procedures' to be used in 80 per cent of YOT 'interventions' by 2004 (YJB, 2001a, p. 4).

Cultural resistance

The philosophical shift from focusing on 'offender' to 'offence' has been painful and problematic (Bailey and Williams, 2000; Crawford and Newburn, 2003; Dignan, 2005). It could be argued that it is unrealistic to expect offender-orientated organisations to work with victims and communities in a restorative way when the primary aim of such organisations is to prevent re-offending. Haines and Drakeford ask: 'Is it justifiable for youth justice workers to take the victims' perspective and to base one's intervention with the offender on what will be the best for the victim?' (1998, p. 231). Forthright in their views, they add 'it seems to us to be morally unacceptable to promote victims' interests at the expense of the child's. Children have rights too' (ibid.). Their position is clearly problematic as it is based on the assumption that whilst offenders are children, victims aren't.

Decisions to prioritise the needs of offenders over victims or communities in restorative justice programmes seem more justifiable when the offender is a child or young person. This is very much linked with the welfare and justice debate; practitioners often see the offender as a victim of circumstance, assisting offenders to adopt a responsibly 'neutral' position (Matza and Sykes, 1957).

Apart from retaliation (offending as a response to perceived victimisation), young people's belief in their socio-economic victimisation or 'relative deprivation' (Taylor et al, 1973) may contribute to their proclivity (or decision) to offend. Whilst research shows that many offenders have been the victim of violence or abuse by an adult (Pitts and Bateman, 2005), the seriousness is often mitigated by claims to deterministic factors such as poor housing, education and mental health issues. Zehr however, believes that young people's perceptions of themselves as victims 'does not absolve responsibility for offending behaviour' and needs to be challenged (2002. p. 30).

Six of one and half a dozen of the other

The author's research reveals not only cultural resistance to working with victims and a child-first philosophy, but also a perception of victim precipitation; the majority of respondents interviewed (over thirty in total) felt that child victims were often complicit and offenders were not entirely responsible for their actions (Angus, 2001). Practitioner perceptions on responsibility are based primarily on discussions with offenders (although some practitioners also said they had looked at the Crown Prosecution Service papers) and were rarely informed by direct work with victims or the reading of victim impact statements. Here lies the problem: the final decision as to whether victims attend panels is with the YOT practitioner who is expected to make a professional judgement. This is done based on the appropriateness of victims attending panels without the benefit of an objective review of victims' involvement in the circumstances of the offence or their current attitude.

There is no formal assessment of the victim in terms of their suitability to attend a panel. Back in 2001 the YJB introduced a new 'restorative justice assessment tool' to be used with young offenders and victims (YJB, 2001a). The tool was piloted in five YOTs which resulted in a recommendation 'that it would be available to YOTs on a "non-compulsory" basis in late 2004 or early 2005' (Cullen, 2004). However, in further correspondence in February 2005, Cullen commented thus:

> *The RJ Assessment Tool materials in fact produced a mixed response when piloted with four youth offending teams and there is no current plans for publication.* (Cullen, 2005)

Assessing victim suitability will remain problematic whilst the tools to achieve this objectivity and consistency have no official mandate.

Conclusion

Smith's (2004) findings raise important questions about the way society treats victims and supports the intuitive notion that positive treatment at an early stage of victimisation may prevent victims becoming perpetrators of crime. This is entirely consistent with the author's own research and literature review which leads inexorably to the conclusion that better treatment of victims by the youth justice system, and in particular restorative justice processes, would result in more positive engagement of victims and leave them feeling that justice had been done.

For young victims, current youth justice processes cannot mitigate, and may sustain, the correlation between victimisation and subsequent criminal activity. Ironically, restorative processes can actually exacerbate feelings of exclusion from the processes of justice and leave victims with unchallenged perceptions that offenders are systemically excused.

Restorative justice, as currently delivered, tends to deter young victim participation due to a number of factors, not least cultural-professional attitudes that implicitly minimise offender responsibility through the attribution of some responsibility for the event to peer victims. The need for independent scrutiny of the attribution of responsibility is clear, as is the need for restorative justice practitioners to improve their understanding of, and commitment to, restorative principles. YOT managers could do more to promote victim participation and this should be supported through stronger policy missives and victim-oriented performance measures.

Chapter 6

Child abuse in the religious context

The abuse of trust

Peter Kennison

Introduction

During the last thirty years or so the pernicious effects of child abuse have surfaced in the religious setting the world over. Religious institutions (RIs) and some members of their clergy have participated in physical and sexual abuse of minors, children and young people. For many years inflicting physical harm as a means of punishment against a child or young person, especially in an institutional setting, e.g. school or children's home, was an acceptable part of everyday society. It was commonplace for a variety of persons *in loco parentis* to administer a smack to a naughty child. including not only parents or guardians, but also teachers, police officers, nuns and other members of RIs.

Today, the attitude is that to inflict physical violence against anyone is no longer tolerated. There is also some empirical evidence to suggest that a number of RIs have shown violence towards children and some of these institutions which still advocate this have been and are particularly cruel, severe and brutal – a matter which is of serious public concern. This chapter shows that when child abuse has been discovered, in a religious setting, RIs have dealt with the matter no differently than any other institution which had a duty of care towards children in their care. Child abuse is an under-publicised crime, hampered by the lack of reporting and because of the secrecy surrounding many circumstances. Sexual abuse of children takes place in situations where the conditions are present and ripe for further exploitation.

RIs are similar to other institutions and, in some cases, mirror them since they will share common characteristics which allow child abuse and, more particularly, child sexual abuse. These institutions are by their nature closed to all but its members (Gallagher, 1999, p. 201). These characteristics are about power, authority and control over the child by an adult, usually by a dominant male. Such power within a closed, secret or hidden institution means that those in charge are able to deny malpractice. Detection in the institutional setting requires the abuse to be followed up and confronted: factors which create a daunting challenge to child protection (Gallagher, 1999).

Some RIs appear to be changing, due in part to the negative effects of offending clergy who abuse children. The watershed in Britain appears to have come about in 2000 when the Roman Catholic Church, in co-operation with a number of other RIs, set up a Committee of Inquiry to consider child protection in the religious setting. This was a significant and positive first step in ensuring the safety of children in their care. Since then the Committee has made a number of positive recommendations which other RIs have also adopted. Many of these other RIs have yet to adopt or sign up to any form of child protection, and they remain secretive and insular, since these measures are not statutory and remain voluntary. These RIs will continue to be open to criticism and controversy.

Media reports and research involving the Roman Catholic Church and other RIs are used in this chapter as examples, not only to illustrate the abuse of children in their care but also explain why it has occurred. Child abuse is also endemic in many other RIs. There have been a number of high-profile court cases involving witchcraft, ritual practices and child abuse in the church and the peculiar features under which these take place will also be considered.

Children in the religious setting in Britain

The influence of RIs today is still quite marked. In Britain children participate in religious life on a daily basis by being members of a congregation, attending boarding and day faith-based schools and clubs or play groups run by church authorities. Large numbers of children and young people come into contact with the church in one form or another on a day-to-day basis. To show the scale of contact, there are 7,000 faith-based schools (589 secondary and 6,384 primary schools) in England out of a total of 25,000. There are 40 non-Christian with 32 being Jewish (Economist, 2006b). For example, the Diocese of Westminster alone is responsible for 223 Catholic schools and 92,264 children. In addition, the Church of England deals with school visits to its churches, cathedrals etc., and these account for 300,000 pupils each year.

There are 1 in 4 primary schools and 1 in 16 secondary schools totalling 4,700 which are Church of England schools. Just under 1 million children are being educated in a Church of England School.[1] For Muslims in Britain there are 140 Muslim schools, 7 of which are funded by the state. There are also around 700 or so Madrasas (mosque schools) that teaches basic Islam (not full-time education) to pupils of school ages who attend after normal school hours. Some Madrasas have over 500 children attending (Siddiqui, 2006).

Defining and understanding the religious setting

Religion has always played a dominant yet consistent part of every day life in multi cultural Britain.[2] Generic terms like 'religion' and 'church' have meaning to individuals and church-goers, yet these notions are contested – not easily agreed or defined. Equally these raise a whole set of beliefs, assumptions, meanings and understandings in our minds. Perhaps such difficulty arises because of the multitude of religious organisations that exist today in a variety of human cultures, making it hard to categorise them in any real sense (McNeill and Townley, 1993). However, in the West most religions are rooted in Christianity and trying to understand the religious setting in this way is essential. In sociological terms Christian religious organisations are located across a broad continuum, with the church located at one end and the notion of sect positioned at the other. In between there are denominations, cults, new religious movements, ecclesiastical orders and new age movements. The 'church' is defined as:

> *a formal organisation with a hierarchy and bureaucracy of paid officials. Its beliefs and values are widely accepted and tends to have a close relationship with the state and Monarchy.* (Chapman, 2004)

This is certainly true in the UK with reference to the Anglican Church, but abroad a variety of differing religious organisations add to the diversity of religion. Not all religions, especially the non-Christian versions, have or relate to the notion of 'church', so for the purposes of this chapter all religious organisations will be expressed as RIs. The term 'clergy' is also used and is defined as:

> *all those who owe a professional and fiduciary obligation to their parishioners (and followers) in their role as a member of the clergy.* (Gonsiorek, 1999)

Determining the role of the clergy is difficult, since with the variety of religions these functions will change. The functions will involve a range of liturgical activities, spiritual direction, pastoral and other counselling, fund-raising, group leadership and social activities usually with the same group of worshippers or parishioners (Gonsiorek, 1999, p. 37). The clergy hold a unique position in their individual communities and their function seems to attract a certain status. Their role can be exceedingly onerous, unique and very responsible – it is a function not performed by any other individual. Here the meaning of clergy, their role, functions and institutional context has been highlighted and defined.

Settling the account – compensating for the abuse of trust

Appreciation of the contemporary history of religious child abuse is an essential starting point in our understanding of churches and religious orders. It will show how, over a number decades, individuals at all levels within RIs have ignored their duty of care and trust with respect to children and young people who have been victims of clergy abuse. This situation has not occurred only in Great Britain but abroad as well. RIs also share similarities with other institutional settings involving children and young people. Like those where child abuse and child sexual abuse take place, the strategy also includes apparently hiding and denying its very existence. There is very little written on the subject in Britain and even less research has been carried out into child abuse by the clergy. Empirical evidence or research into clergy abuse or sexual abuse in the USA is small (Plante, 1999). Obtaining access to RIs for the purposes of research has been problematic, with denial being the safest option. Since the mid 1990s sensational media speculation has raised the spectre of clergy abuse and, more particularly, of sexual abuse of children to a level akin to a moral panic. It is essential in the first instance to investigate the perpetrators as a means of understanding child abuse in its various forms, situations and how it affects its victims.

In recent years there were a number of high-profile court cases and financial settlements both at home and abroad, which gave cause for concern and even moral panic in respect of clergy abuse. Clergy abuse in the Roman Catholic Church first came to light in the USA in the mid-1980s, although the sexual behaviour of priests with consenting adults and minors has been the subject of media documentation for centuries (Plante, 1999). In fact, clergy sexual abuse in the USA first surfaced in 1985 (Bryant, 1999) but the same did not occur in Britain until about ten years later, in the mid 1990s. Events in the USA were being anxiously and closely watched by clerics from many religious groups in the UK and around the world.

Vast sums of money have been paid out to claimants by a variety of Catholic dioceses and other RIs not only in the USA but also other countries.[3] The Catholic Church was in serious crisis as the vast number of sexual abuse allegations against the clergy was threatening to engulf them. Publication of an 880-page file documenting the sexual abuse of children by Friar Paul Shanley going back to 1977 was particularly damaging for them (Rennie, 2002).

Donations by loyal supporters also began to dry up and were being deliberately withheld (Johnson and Petre, 2002). Perhaps this sign above all else focused the mind of church authorities and forced them into taking action. These cases became the catalyst for change, as case after case exposed Roman Catholic clergy who had been particularly involved in sexual abuse of children over a lengthy period of time. Some 194 separate dioceses have been affected by claims, with Boston and Cardinal Law, the most powerful US Catholic cleric, being accused of covering up these crimes. Cardinal Law later resigned. His reluctant resignation sent shock waves around the world because it was exceedingly rare for a bishop of the Catholic faith to resign at all. News also began to leak out that tens of millions of dollars had been secretly spent over the years to settle child abuse claims involving dozens of priests. As one Boston lawyer Bob Sherman stated at the time:

> The firm of Greenberg Traurig has won more than 150 settlements against the Boston Arch Diocese in the last decade, involving 30–40 priests. Each was covered by a confidentiality agreement. (Rennie, 2002)

Confidentiality agreements were imposed by lawyers for the defence as a condition of settlement, which effectively restrained anyone in the case from discussing or reporting matters, especially to the media. This agreement maintained the cloak of secrecy.

Claims of child abuse, and particularly child sexual abuse, were not restricted to the USA, with religious orders in Ireland being particularly concerned about claims. Where church and state are inextricably linked (and have been for years) in terms of education, social work, child care provision, health care and welfare, there have been particularly serious problems. So serious was the situation that in 2002 three separate Catholic RIs set up a fund containing £86m (a figure which the Irish Government then trebled) to compensate the victims of child abuse. There are considerable numbers of claims each year from this fund which do not find their way into the courts, as liability is accepted from the outset.

The Hare Krishna church or International Society for Krishna consciousness (ISKCON) was ordered by a court to pay $9.5m to ninety students who endured physical, sexual and emotional abuse in the 1970s and 1980s (Garden, 2004). A prestigious private Anglican boarding school at Groton, Massachusetts, in the USA was accused of child abuse and cover-up in 2004 when they failed to report sexual assault and bullying on male pupils to the authorities (Warren, 2004).

Even in the UK the leading Catholic cleric Cardinal Cormac Murphy-O'Connor who had introduced measures to combat child abuse by the clergy in 2001 was being called upon to resign by the media following pressure concerning personal involvement regarding a member of the clergy. This involved the case of Father Michael Hill who had been kept in office even though his own bishop (now the head of the Catholic Church in the UK) had been aware that Hill was a paedophile. Yet even where religious child abuse has properly been reported to the appropriate authorities a cover-up is still likely: some would say in the public interest, or to minimise the damage to the church or for various legal reasons.

An institutional cover-up occurred in Newfoundland, Canada, for example, in the mid 1970s, when the police investigation into 100 allegations of child sexual abuse by a Roman Catholic Christian Brotherhood was ordered to be kept secret. The report was withheld for eleven months once the trials of five Christian Brothers, a lay order, and three former members were completed. In 1976 the investigating officers were even ordered to rewrite their reports without reference to sexual abuse or ill treatment by the brothers. This illustrates how in times of trouble even other institutions rally to help religious orders save their reputation. This situation is not unusual as Sipe (1999) points out, since both church and judicial author-ities at times disavow their own responsibilities, further perpetuating abuse by striking a compassionate and repentant pose (p. 121).

More recently, in May 2007 Peter Halliday, aged 61, from Farnborough in Hampshire was jailed for thirty months after admitting a number of sex offences in the 1980s and 1990s when he was choir master at St. Peter's Church. After voluntarily removing himself from the church following allegations of abuse he later surfaced to become a singer in the Royal School of Music, where he continued abusing choristers as young as ten years old during individual singing tuition, choir trips and in their dormitories at night.[4]

From Buenos Aires to Boston, Hong Kong to Sydney, and Dublin to Rome, there is clear evidence of clerical cover-up following incidents of child sex abuse by the clergy. The Roman Catholic Church realised their reputation was at stake following disturbing findings after an internal investigation in Brazil in 2005. They decided to publish these findings in the media, which contended that in Brazil, where there were 125 million Catholics, some 10 per cent of its clergy (1,700 priests) were sex offenders (Phillips and Hooper, 2005).

There is still a long way for religious institutions to go, but admitting a potential problem is a good first step to change. There are cases of child abuse reported against a variety of churches and religious orders so it is impossible to assert that any one religious institution and its clergy are more guilty of sexual abuse of minors than any other. The legacy portrayed by the media makes shocking reading, but how do we gauge the risk factors that lead to clergy abuse?

Setting the moral code for us

There is a widely held belief that RIs set day-to-day standards for us to follow and the assumption is that the clergy obey their own religious, legal, ethical and moral standards.

High-profile court cases of child abuse in the church in this country and abroad have tended to demonstrate that a small minority of the clergy do not follow their own teaching. The issue of clergy sexual abuse of children has become a matter of national attention, but in terms of the number of cases this is secondary to the numbers of civil and criminal cases against the clergy who have breached normative sexual boundaries and engaged in seemingly deviant sexual relations with adult parishioners (Berry, 1992; Burkett and Bruni, 1993; Sipe 1990, 1995). Church authorities find this a very difficult topic indeed, since initially they may not want to believe that something as terrible as sexual abuse could be perpetrated by a member of their own church, especially since they hold themselves to 'higher' levels of moral conduct (Manuel, 1999). However as Lothstein argues:

> For many of us it is unthinkable that individuals in the public trust who are well educated, involved in caring, educational, and spiritual professions, would betray a basic trust with a child (or adult) and molest, sexually assault, or rape. (1999, p. 65)

Researchers into clergy abuse have shown that priests, among many others, have not always honoured their presumably freely chosen values, which is something that is hardly news (Loftus, 1989, 1994) but amongst church-goers there is astonishment, surprise and even disbelief at religious infractions. They believe that religious pastors are different and live to a higher standard, making them somehow closer to god (Loftus, 1999). What also makes Roman Catholic clergy different and unlike others is that their employment as priests requires them to be celibate, e.g. to remain unmarried.

What celibacy actually means, in a classical moral Roman Catholic sense, to the church and the individual priest is a matter of considerable debate and controversy. Suffice to say that the assumption of celibacy in terms of sexual purity is misplaced and they can no longer be said to be celibate in any strict sense of the word (Loftus, 1999). One licensed psychologist went further by suggesting that he had reported on a number of priests who do not view having sex with men or boys as breaching their vow of celibacy (Lothstein, 1991).

The clergy hold a responsibility over their parishioners to behave appropriately and any breach of trust through the abuse of children has three distinct levels. Firstly at the moral level it is sinful, secondly at a legal level it is against the law and lastly at the level of the church it is a breach of the individual's fiduciary responsibility. This responsibility of the clergy, as Sipe (1999) suggests, 'concerns behaviour essentially incompatible with one's identity, mission and responsibility' (p. 121). When these criteria are breached by them, it seems that their whole position as clerics is seriously compromised, making the situation untenable. Yet the reaction within most religious organisations ranges from doing nothing to treatment of the deviant clergy in some form then re-assignment to another location. In the case of the Roman Catholic Church this occasionally meant a transfer for treatment to Rome and the Vatican City.

Denial, by leaders of institutions dealing with children, that any child abuse problem exists is also often used within these settings. The same tactic is also a common feature within closed RIs and faith communities and may well hinder any progress over child protection matters. An example is given in respect of the Muslim community by Siddiqui (2006), who sums up the situation eloquently when he says:

The Muslim community are in denial – denial of the fact that child abuse takes place in places of worship including in mosques, madrasas (mosque schools) and families. It's a taboo subject. There is very little discussion taking place in the community on the subject at any level. Hence when such a crime is committed, the victim knows no one to turn to and the abusers are answerable to no one. This protects the abuser and ostracizes the victim. The victims of child abuse on growing up often become abusers themselves, taking their revenge on others. Taboo perpetuates the situation. (p. 1)

The faith community also needs to accept these difficult matters in order to make progress towards change. Community understanding in accepting rather than denying is critical in developing appropriate policies that help to create a safer environment for children.

But denial is not only institutional and community-based – there is an individual responsibility as well. This is a critical dimension since perpetrators, including those from the clergy, are often in denial and will invite others to join them to verify the denial (Plante et al., 1996). Colluding and conspiring in the denial seeks to reinforce the power of the establishment or institution, leading the victim to rethink and question the validity of his or her accusation. Reaction by parents, officials and friends may also question the legitimacy of the victim's claim which is likely to result in pressure on the victim to withdraw the allegation or allow the RI to resolve matters internally. One researcher of clergy abuse has suggested that the institutional abuse of power by the Roman Catholic Church is demonstrated when:

The weak and vulnerable are targeted by the predators, and then trivialised and scorned by the institution in protecting the predators, to a level that sometimes seems like class war. (Sipe, 1995)

Despite the fact that RIs should have been ensuring a safe environment for children, their primary aim has been to protect their own interests and not that of the victim. Reporting after a notorious case in the USA in the mid 1980s[5] it was suggested that the church was more interested in protecting the reputation of the institution and the clerical profession than it was in safeguarding its own children (Bryant, 1999, p. 88).

RIs are vitally concerned with preventing their members from further transgressions yet, according to one leading researcher in this area, there are a number of features which obstruct the development of a prevention plan that involves the clergy or the religious (Sipe, 1999, p. 111). These are:

1. Lack of methods for *screening* out potential sex offenders from joining the priesthood.

2. Widespread *denial* by church authorities and lay Catholics who employ tactics of rationalisation, avoidance and the shifting of blame.

3. *Preservation and protection* of abusing clergy involved in child sexual abuse.

4. Lack of any *ethical standards* regarding sexual behaviour of the priesthood.

5. Lastly, that internal processes, policies and procedures may obstruct natural justice.

   This is evidenced by religious leaders hiding behind a facade of openness whilst at the same time undermining the relative merits of any allegation with the object of discouraging any further participation.

In terms of screening, traditionally it has been the responsibility of seminaries to educate and train priests ensuring that each training system counted on itself to weed out the inept and to form the remainder into observant priests. Ensuring fitness for the candidate's final attestation of ordination and ministry was the responsibility of the senior community members, seminary rector and ordaining bishop (Kauffman. 1988). There is no doubt about this, as Sipe suggests that:

> *Some priests who abuse children enter seminary training with a history of, or a known proclivity for, sex with minors. But only some of these priests act out their sexual preference. There are a number of priests whose sexual preference for children [will] develop, or is discovered during religious training; others have a fantasy life that does not disappear, but they never act on their fantasies or desires [temptations].* (Sipe, 1999, p. 112)

Some clergy will act out their fantasies, and priests who commit such crimes are viewed by insiders as having fooled the screening system by deliberately and covertly manipulating the strictures barriers to successful acceptance into the priesthood.

According to Sipe (1999), the characteristic of denial in religious organisations has nine levels, facets or characteristics. Sipe suggests that denial is:

> *An unconscious mental mechanism that allows one (an individual or organisation) to reject facts that are experienced as overwhelming or a threat to one's integrity or homeostasis.* (1999, p. 113)

Denial is the normal response when faced with such incredible facts, a response which, under certain conditions, does not require an explanation by an accuser. Denial that exploits this statement, *'there is no problem because it just can't be true'*, is one such example. This tactic has been used in the past and this level of denial can be highly organised and institutionalised. The pattern of institutional denial is very revealing and becomes clear when court documents or civil court settlement papers are viewed. Institutional cover-up, conspiracy and fraud matters are all part of the denial process (Sipe, 1999, p. 114), much of which borders on the criminal.

Another sub-facet to denial focuses on the issue of *'abuse by priests may exist, but it is very rare'*. The denial that a problem exists in the first place fails to acknowledge a number of difficulties and it affects the reputation and therefore the public image (McIlroy, 2004) which RIs view as media distortion.

The next sub-facet is *'the media distorts everything'*, making the story untrue in a literal sense. A reputation for honesty and proper ethical standards is essential for any church organisation. Denial under these circumstances has a negative side since it also dents reputation. Repeated allegations of child abuse create a media feast but not a media distortion, because this form of denial effectively portrays the church as harbouring abusive clergy. It leaves images in the minds of readers which tend to negatively stereotype clergy, when the image the religious institution wishes to portray is one based on reputation, honesty and transparency. Reputation can be undermined or damaged under these circumstances and in some cases irretrievably so. Paedophilic clergy are therefore by association dishonest. Sexual clergy abuse is set within an atmosphere of secrecy, victim powerlessness, denial and a lack of accountability in order for this behaviour to flourish (Demarest, 1999, p. x).

Another denial feature suggests that *'the problem is no worse than other religious groups or in the general population'* and presents a positive spin on a negative situation. It suggests not only the humanity of offending clergy as an excuse for misdeeds but also plays down its seriousness. This explanation seeks to lessen the impact of the offence by reducing the severity to the level of normative behaviour.

'They wanted it – they liked it' is another denial characteristic, which is defensive by nature and is a common excuse of paedophiles in explaining their offending behaviour. This excuse deflects the blame from the abuser to the abused. Attacking the sexual integrity of the victim in this way and also suggesting a lack of vigilance on the part of the victim's parents are tactics employed by solicitors in their defence of offending clergy (Sipe, 1999).

The next characteristic suggests the *'Abusers are sick'* and therefore by inference treatable in some medical way. This concept is based on the psychological premise of sexual deprivation, which before 1995 was recognised as a situational issue by the American Psychiatric Association, whereby some sexually adapted males could illegally seek sex with children (Sipe, 1999).

'The consequences were not dire and the victim was sick anyway', represents another level of denial that supports two factors. Numerous studies and surveys show that the sexual abuse of minors is common, 20–50 per cent of women and 6–19 per cent of men report being abused as children (Hopper, 1997). Here, trivialising misdeeds and somehow connecting these to the alleged sickness deflects the blame back to the victim.

'Father is only human' (Burkett and Bruni, 1993) is an appeal to fallen human nature. This explanation not only suggests a certain inevitability of abusive conduct but also covertly alludes to saving mankind by forgiveness as we see next.

'Forgive and forget' is another facet of denial. The Roman Catholic Church advocates forgiveness as a venerable religious ideal and is a basic tenet upon which the Catholic faith is grounded. A plea for forgiveness may be interpreted as a public relations response to a public outcry or legal reversals. Rossetti (1995) suggests the sexual abuse of a minor by a priest, no matter how horrendous, is not the un-forgivable sin of the gospel. Forgiving may be one thing but forgetting such sin is of course another issue.

Sykes and Matza (1957) refers to these facets as 'techniques of neutralisation' in what they describe as the deviant's attempt to justify the behaviour and lessen social control. They further suggest that such imperatives seek to make any violations acceptable if not right in an apologetic way, with the purpose of weakening the moral bond of law abiding society. Sykes and Matza's work attempts to explain the relationship between belief and action and how delinquency is basically the translation of both. For some time techniques which attempt to reduce the effect of deviant or illegal behaviour on the part of individual clergy involved in child abuse has been a common feature of RIs and particularly the Roman Catholic church.

The official religious institutional response to allegations of child sexual abuse mirrors the reaction of other institutions, like residential homes, etc. This institutional response does not necessarily operate in the best interests of the child (Gallagher, 1999). How church leaders react is fundamental in our understanding of religious institutional power relations.

Appreciating under what circumstances institutional child abuse is allowed to take place is an important issue. The introduction of preventive interventions is based on investigation and evidence so that it is not allowed to happen again. There were no preventive interventions, just a problem after child abuse had occurred. Perhaps further insight can be gained by examining the organisational or institutional nature that is the ecclesiastical structure.

Guarding children from the religious institution

Child abusers differ in their relationships with children, and the power of individuals within the religious setting increases the likelihood of coercive behaviour towards the victim, due in part to the clergy's status, authority and position in society. When considering the power relations in any environment the dominant and traditional approaches to child protection fail to understand, or even appreciate, the importance of the abuse when confined in an institutional or structural setting (Parton, 1991). 'Institutional abuse' occurs in those places where adults work with children, and the problem has been brought to the fore because of the number of investigations into child sexual abuse in children's homes (Gallagher, 1999).

Gallagher expands the traditional notion of institutional abuse by suggesting that child sexual abuse occurs not only in children's residential homes but also in all institutional settings, including day schools, nurseries, Scouts, sports clubs and religious organisations (p. 197). Because there seems to be a certain protection for child abusers in the religious institutional environment it affords situations that can be manipulated not only prior to the abuse taking place but also after it has happened. Its closed secret setting affords greater privacy, thereby concealing child abuse and perhaps allowing child abuse to carry on for years.

Corby (2000) subdivides institutional abuse into four distinct categories. Two such categories relate to 1. neglect and 2. peer bullying whilst Wardhaugh and Wilding (1993) identified two further measures as 3. *control* involving psychological cruelty or physically abusive practices, and 4. sexual abuse that was perpetrated by those who exploited the *power* opportunities afforded them according to the positions they held within the institution. Whilst these were originally related to children's homes the same features pertain to the religious institutional setting as well.

Convicted sex offenders often turn to religion whilst in prison and there is a great effort by RIs to encourage offenders to find spiritual awareness in an effort to prevent further crimes. Consequently, it should come as no surprise that apparently rehabilitated sex offenders are present not only in their congregations, but also to a certain extent in the clergy as well. Research by an independent Government-backed charity in 2005 supports this fact and it raised concerns about paedophiles who convert to Christianity in prison and join RIs on their release. The Churches' Child Protection Advisory Service alerted church members to be on their guard as the church was being ruthlessly exploited by sex offenders who have 'found god' on an evangelical 'Alpha course' in jail. Some five churches a week are requesting help because of the risk to young worshippers from sex offenders on leaving prison (Petre, 2005b). They argue:

> The fact is that some offenders are simply too dangerous to be allowed anywhere near

children and therefore it may not be appropriate for them to be part of some churches. (Petre, 2005b)

Changing times – out with the old in with the new

Past practice and policy of the Roman Catholic Church in dealing with offending clergy has been shrouded in secrecy, certainly well into the 1990s, and the aim of the policy paper was to 'preserve the dignity of the offending adult'. This document was seen by many critics as protecting paedophiles after being discovered accidentally by a Texan lawyer, Daniel Shea, in 2003 while working in the Vatican archives (Bowcott, 2003). Vatican policy, promulgated on 16 March 1964 by Pope John XXIII, in part explains the behaviour of the Roman Catholic Church.

This 69-page policy document written by Cardinal Alfredo[6] entitled 'On the Manner of Proceeding in Cases of Crime and Solicitation' was marked 'confidential' and formed the foundation on which offending clergy were dealt with. Distributed to senior clerics world-wide, it threatened excommunication to those who spoke out about child abuse and voiced allegations against clerics. All clerics were sworn to observe the strictest secrecy and not to discuss matters even among themselves. Contained within the document was a section which defined the offence of solicitation:

When a priest tempts a penitent, whoever that person is [where] . . . the object of this temptation is to solicit or provoke [the penitent] towards impure and obscene matters, whether by words or signs or nods of the head, whether by touch or by writing, whether then or after or whether he has had with the penitent prohibited or improper speech or activity with reckless daring. (Ottaviani, 1964, p. 1)

Another section focused on the 'worst crime' which was defined as 'any external deed, gravely sinful' carried out by a church member 'with a person of their own sex' (Bowcott, 2003). It clearly placed a responsibility on the 'ordinaries of the place' like a bishop, abbot or prelate, the administrator, any vicar or prefect apostolic and a range of others, to become the judge and investigate the matter. This required the judge to:

admonish and correct [punish] and if the case demands it to transfer him to another [assignment], unless the ordinary of the place has forbidden it because he has already accepted the denunciation and has begun the inquisition. (ibid., p. 2)

Sometimes these procedures prevented the reporting of abuse by the victims or other adults because those involved had to swear an oath of secrecy before God. The oath required the keeping of 'the secret' and was applicable to all those concerned including the accusers, witnesses and the accused. It became the discretion of the 'the ordinary' to decide whether the matter should be brought to the attention of the authorities (p. 3), or the police for the matter to be dealt with according to state law. Of course, the Roman Catholic Church practices forgiveness in its teachings as a venerable religious ideal, and this policy allows for this as Rossetti points out:

Some victims cry for blood and banishment, while some priest clinicians argue for prolonged supervision and reassignment in pastoral positions that do not involve contact with minors. (1995, in Sipe, 1999)

This is a disputed document, a fact which the Roman Catholic Church accepts, and it can be read in different ways. On one hand the policy was a cover-up which hid abuse, while on the other it suggests that this was a formal policy designed to properly investigate the matter and bring it to a satisfactory resolution to the benefit of all parties. Each diocese is independent of all others and it is the individual bishop as head, together with his advisors, to interpret Vatican policies in whichever way they see fit. Hence this discretion allows interpretation in differing ways. In some ways it appears to be more transparent while others are internally more forgiving. This is evidenced by Rossetti who argues that, when considering sexual abuse of a minor by a priest, however horrendous, it is not the unforgivable sin of the gospel (Rossetti, 1995). Some church authorities in the USA, like the Chicago Diocese, are more openly accountable and resort to the lay public and judicial structures, while others like New York tended to forgiveness and in-house resolution (Sipe, 1999).

The oath of secrecy and fear of excommunication were powerful reasons for victims not to disclose the matter to the proper judicial authorities or even to their friends. In this case the church's religious authority over its child victim is not only phenomenal but overwhelming. The weight of religious authority seems to have a more powerful influence than perhaps exists in normative organisational settings. It re-asserts the power relations of RIs over powerless child victims and further accentuates the dependent status of the religious adult. Children, like adults, try to protect themselves and discuss their inner feelings with their friends (MacLeod, 1999), and shutting off this avenue means that the victim opts out. Opting out means hopelessness, and survivors of child sexual abuse have considered a variety of strategies from running away to suicide (ibid.). While this situation continues, control rests in the hands of powerful adults and the abuse will continue, covered up, only to surface in years to come.

It would appear that 'On the Manner of Proceeding in Cases of Crime and Solicitation' not unusually, assumed primacy over state law at the time and it remained in force as a policy well into the 1990s. Bishops and senior clerics continued to act and decide on matters, independently making decisions which caused some observers to criticise the church over allegations of child abuse which just seemed to disappear. Any central consultation or intervention by Rome was shunned and more control seems to have been established at a local level, a factor which in many ways underscored the relative autonomy and independence of the bishop in such matters. Gallagher (1999) refers to institutional reluctance to develop appropriate policy as 'official inertia' but realisation of the grave situation in child protection in religious settings prompted action by the Roman Catholic faith. This policy minimised the effects of child abuse and reinforced denial which inhibits any investigation of the problem as a means of prevention (Sipe, 1999), so acceptance that a problem exists is the necessary starting point for any change.

The Nolan Inquiry

In 2000 Cardinal Cormac Murphy-O'Connor, responding to the conviction of twenty-one Catholic priests in England and Wales between 1995 and 1999 for child abuse, introduced a committee of inquiry in child protection matters. This inquiry was established after the cardinal had admitted responsibility on behalf of the Catholic faith for past errors in protecting children. This was not only a problem for the Catholic Church but also for all other religious organisations as well. The Nolan Inquiry was established and chaired by Lord Nolan (a former Law Lord) together with nine others to form a committee consisting of four Catholics and six non-Catholics. Members included two senior judges, senior officials from the Probation Service and psychiatric profession, and from a children's charity, and a senior Metropolitan Police officer. Their remit was to:

> Establish guide lines for church authorities dealing with cases of abuse, alleged or proven in the church, including the clergy, members of religious orders and lay people and to develop policy on dealing with child abuse so that there were clear goals that supported the creation of a safe environment for children. (Nolan, 2001)

In England and Wales the Roman Catholic institution decided to take child abuse by its clergy and laity seriously. This was a matter to be dealt with within the parishes if it was to become an example to others and give confidence to the general public and parishioners. They had accepted the limitations of previous policy guidelines as having a specific focus on child sexual abuse and the clergy and accepted a wider policy encapsulating all aspects of abuse. The Nolan Inquiry worked speedily and publicly issued its interim recommendations in April 2001. Best practice in child abuse cases suggested that a developed policy for action that provided guidance to church leaders should be produced at both national and diocesan levels. The committee decided among some of its recommendations that:

> There should be a national database of information on all candidates for the priesthood.

> There should be a designated child protection co-ordinator appointed at the level of each diocese who should ensure the effective implementation of child protection policies and practices based on Home Office procedures.

> Bishops and religious superiors do not overrule selection boards where reservations are expressed about a candidate's suitability for ordination on the grounds of a possible risk to children or young people.

> Allegations of abuse must be responded to swiftly, with police involvement.[7]

By September 2001 further recommendations were included in the final report. For example, confessionals between children and priests must be visible and Criminal Records checks on candidates for the priesthood mandatory in all cases.[8] The Nolan Inquiry stipulated that not only should there be a wider remit to include all types of abuse of children, but that new procedures should be introduced that allowed for a monitoring of the system to see if it was working correctly. Agreement was reached among the bishops, but not until after much discussion on maintaining an overriding principle in all matters concerning children called 'the paramount principle' taken from the Children Act 1989. This established principle was:

> The church believes unconditionally in the dignity of children and reasserts her unambiguous condemnation of child abuse. It is the pastoral duty of the church as a whole to protect and promote the spiritual and emotional needs of children.

So the Catholic Church introduced for the first time an overarching ethical principle into its religious setting for all members of its institution to aspire towards. The whole emphasis changed and where there were serious concerns regarding the safety of any child then the police were to be called using emergency procedures. Implementation and dissemination of the Nolan Inquiry recommendations called 'A Programme for Action' became the responsibility of Archbishop Vincent Nichols who set about creating a central child protection unit 'The Catholic Office for the Protection of Children and Vulnerable Adults' (COPCA). Keen to ensure that progress was being made Lord Nolan's final recommendation instructed that progress on implementation should be reviewed in five years. Accordingly in July 2006 Cardinal Cormac Murphy-O'Connor asked Baroness Cumberlege to chair a commission of experts for this very purpose. Their final analysis is awaited.

This committee of inquiry marked a change of ethos in RIs, in particular within the Catholic faith, from one founded on denial and deflection of child abuse to one based on recognising the unconditional dignity and need for the safety of children. Superseding the authoritarian-centred religious institution in this way in favour of a more egalitarian approach is in keeping with public expectation of RIs. RIs must strive to provide an environment for children that is safe, friendly and welcoming.

Witchcraft, exorcism and ritualistic faith-related child abuse

Another aspect of concern which is at present receiving media attention involves the harming of children who have apparently been possessed by evil spirits. Many newly arrived travellers from Africa originate from Nigeria, South Africa, Congo and Angola, the very nations where belief in witchcraft is rife (Reid, 2005). Many join breakaway fundamentalist churches with a potent mix of evangelical Christianity and traditional African religion. Even devout followers believe that exorcism only works if there is extreme physical pain carried out on the child (ibid.). As a result of recent trials there are deep concerns regarding child exorcism, witchcraft and ritual abuse following the jailing of three people in 2005. An Old Bailey jury heard evidence of a child who had been accused of being a witch, and who had been beaten, cut and had had chilli peppers rubbed in her eyes (Ward, 2005). She was cut forty-three times, beaten with a shoe and later placed in a laundry bag to rid her of the devil (Reid, 2005). The three convicted persons originated from Angola and attended the 'Combat Spiritual Church' in Dalston. There has also been the ritual (*muti*) killing or sacrifice of a Nigerian boy (Adam), aged between 4 and 7 years old, whose torso was found floating in the river Thames in 2001.

Concerned representatives of African churches in the UK met with ministers, the police and social services at a Government-sponsored forum to tackle the issue of ritualistic faith-related child abuse (Ward, 2005). Some religious groups involve themselves in dealing with children who have been possessed by devils and one most tragic case in 1999 involved 9-year-old Victoria Climbié who was taken by her aunt (*sic*) to a church to have her evil spirits cast out. So called 'Faith Healers' have been entering the country to perform exorcisms, break voodoo and black magic curses. Many people from African communities believe that deaf, blind or handicapped children are witches and that exorcisms are needed to rid evil demons from their minds and bodies. To be a child suspected of being possessed means being beaten with sticks, scalded with hot water and burnt with lighters, matches and hot irons (Reid, 2005). Among African parents the belief that their children are possessed is used to blame the causes of the parents' misfortune on the children and they are then subjected to the most cruel and brutal treatment. Project Violet was set up by the Metropolitan Police to engage with African communities to prevent abuse of this nature.

The London Child Protection Committee also introduced a separate strategy group comprising police, social services and health professionals to look into the matter. This not only raises the issue of the physical and emotional harming of children who, to some, appear possessed or who are behaving strangely, but also that of accountability on the part of self-appointed pastors. One senior police officer Detective Superintendent Chris Bourlet who was in charge of Operation Violet said:

> It is difficult to identify the scale of the abuse because it is a hidden crime that usually occurs in places of worship or in private homes. Few are prepared to speak out publicly. Others are frightened of revealing the truth for fear of reprisals from the powerful churches. Some questioned . . . said they would be dead meat if we tell you any more. (quoted in Reid, 2005)

There are a number of significant differences in this type of child abuse compared to those perpetrated by other RIs like the Roman Catholic faith and Church of England. Firstly this is child abuse, even though it claims to save the child from being possessed by evil spirits. Secondly driving spirits out requires a public show of extreme physical pain on the part of the victim. Thirdly self-appointed pastors practicing the occult are participating in ritualistic abuse of young children. Also witchcraft involves human sacrifice or ritual killing of young children. Lastly physical violence and even death is threatened to those who reveal the hidden secrets. This form of child abuse is an extreme and particularly brutal variant and attempting to understand its causes will require a greater degree of cultural knowledge and religious understanding in order to separate truth from fiction.

Conclusions

There is a natural assumption that all RIs offer an open, safe and principled environment for all visitors to their premises. Visitors will attend for a variety of reasons including worship, prayer, sanctuary, refuge, teaching, guidance, advice, learning and, in some cases, play. In the light of high-profile court cases of child abuse and child sexual abuse in RIs these assumptions cannot be taken for granted.

Reported figures for child abuse are small and low numbers as such will not command serious attention from the police. Even lower numbers can be found relating to harming children in the religious setting. Understanding child abuse in the religious context then needs evidence from investigation, although research in the USA has often been done in the psychological setting where deviant behaviour is being challenged in group work and not necessarily as a result of a referral from a criminal court. Examples of abuse can be found in most if not all RIs. The study of child abuse in the religious setting has suffered from a lack of access, openness and transparency on the part of RIs due in part to a fear of being found out and disclosing hidden dark secrets. Drawing attention to religious institutional child abuse has been left to media portrayals that contributed to increased public concern following criminal and civil court hearings. This form of disclosure is described by Gallagher (1999), as being 'scandal-centred' rather than child-centred. Not all children have been offered equal protection from all forms of abuse at the institutions they attend because of the diversity of RIs and the voluntary nature of the system to protect children. Being believed over an adult is more of a problem if that adult is a member of the clergy.

The reasons that child abuse was hidden had more to do with the relative powerlessness of children in relation to the dominant authority, and with the control of a powerful masculine-centred institution which has the ability to deny and deflect child abuse allegations. Historically, the rhetoric of denial has exacerbated the problem of child abuse, and especially when RIs act as magnets for supposedly rehabilitated sex offenders seeking spiritual guidance further compounds the threat to children (Harthill, 2000). The record on dealing with child abuse within the religious setting has been woeful, with naivety and bad leadership being responsible for the situation. Denial means the initiative stays with the religious institution and the lessons are never learnt from the mistakes made.

Statutory regulation dealing with religious institutional abuse may not be appropriate since it is one thing to create limiting legislation and quite another to enforce it. Preventing abuse through policy ensures a greater degree of accountability and must be a better way than reacting to scandal once abuse has taken place. This is why it is particularly important to get to the bottom of ritual abuse by break-away religious groups and to include them in the discussions to find answers. But not until recently has the principle of putting the child first been accepted in some, but not all, religious institutional settings, years after the Children Act 1989 first raised it as the 'Paramount principle'. Failure to acknowledge this principle and carrying on as before will be like a ticking time bomb, not only for unenlightened RIs but also for those religious groups practising the harming of children in the name of witchcraft. Child abuse committed in the past by clergy that went undetected may now surface, as victims who have grown up now feel confident enough to come forward to report these infractions to the police – as we are currently witnessing in Ireland and Jersey. Moreover, while child abuse has often been associated with richer religious settings, evidence is now emerging that poorer countries too are revealing that RIs are a safe haven for paedophiles and sex offenders.

RIs and the Roman Catholic faith particularly have changed their closed, secret and hidden environments into ones which are more open, honest and transparent by making their child protection strategies child-centred and egalitarian rather than authoritarian and oppressive.

Notes

1 www.cofe.anglican.org/about/the church of england today/ accessed on 13 June 2007.

2 There is a vast body of writing on theology and religion which is not reviewed in depth due to a lack of space.

3 For example in 1998, £13m was paid by the Catholic Church to eight altar boys in Dallas, Texas, and in 2001 £26m was paid to settle twenty-six cases of child abuse in Bridgeport, Connecticut. Payments to victims through the courts in the USA have led to the closure of forty parishes, the selling of fifteen church properties and 56 acres of land for £55m. In this case the Catholic Church in Boston was

ordered to pay a massive £67m compensation following some 550 law suits involving 815 children ranging over a fifty-year period in the USA, see also Petre (2005a).

4 http://newsvote.bbc.co.uk/mpaspps/pagetools/print/newss.bbc.co.uk.1/hi/uk/6594429.stm, accessed on 11 May 2007.

5 This was the case of Gilbert Gauthe, a compulsively disordered sex offender – disturbed and dangerous – who was able to wreak so much havoc among many prepubescent victims because the church neglected its duty of care to protect the young people in its charge. An institutional failure to respond attracts even higher civil court settlements against the defendant.

6 This policy was authorised by A. Cardinal Ottaviani who counter-signed the document on behalf of the Pope.

7 http://news.bbc.co.uk/1/hi/uk/1548098 accessed on 27 May 2007.

8 http://news.bbc.co.uk/1/hi/uk/1281367 accessed on 27 May 2007.

WEBSITES

Garden, M. (2004) 'Bad karma'. www.newhumanist.org.uk. Visited 5 August 2005.

Hopper, J. (1997) 'Child abuse statistics. Research and resources'. jim@jimhopper.com.

Chapter 7

Learning from mistakes

Understanding police failure in child protection

Peter Kennison

Introduction

Intense media coverage takes place when a child is abducted (Thomas, 2005), as evidenced in the search for 8-year-old Sarah Payne who went missing in the summer of 2000. Even greater coverage occurs when a child dies, or is found dead, in tragic circumstances which involve a carer, parent or guardian. Since the early 1970s there have been a number of high-profile child deaths that have included Maria Colwell aged 7 (1973), Jasmine Beckford aged 4 (1984), Heidi Koseda aged 5 (1985), Kimberley Carlile aged 4 (1986), Toni Dales aged 3 (1992), Tyra Henry aged 21 months (1984), Leanne White aged 3 (1992), Rikki Neave aged 6 (1994), Lauren Creed aged 5 (1997), Lauren Wright aged 6 (2000), Victoria Climbié aged 8 (2000), Ainlee Walker (Labonte) aged 3 (2002), and Natalie Mills aged 15 (2003). In the recent cases of Victoria Climbié and Ainlee Walker the media castigated the police, social services and other statutory agencies, for their lack of professional judgement in protecting the interests of a child, both having been tortured to death by their parents or carers. In the case of Ainlee Walker, the child's family were well known to various statutory agencies as violent abusers.

There is an assumption that during childhood, parents and carers provide the loving and caring environment necessary to properly bring up a child. Even if this is not happening the perception, as well as the expectation, is that defenceless members of our society, young or old, receive appropriate protection from the state, the police and other agencies, if the duty of care falls short. This protection involves joined-up care through partnership-working with other agencies which concentrates on ensuring the safety of the most vulnerable in society. In each of the cases of child death shown above there has been a gross human failure in some way.

This chapter discusses, and makes sense of, inter-agency partnership-working, especially where it goes wrong, predominantly using examples relating to the police. This is not to say that the faults only occur within the police: far from it, because similar failings can take place within all other agencies as well. When agencies fail to act in a manner that satisfies public and media expectation, they are rightly called to account. This chapter creates a case study that draws on the tragic events leading to the death of Victoria Climbié in 2000; a case which marked a watershed in child protection terms. Yet this was not the first case where communication and inter-professional working failed, in fact these failures were present in all the cases cited above. This chapter focuses on the failure of key agencies involved in child protection to work both individually and collectively to safeguard the welfare of this piteous child. It critically examines the central importance of the relationships between the agencies in the development of policies and the processes involved in child protection. For the purposes of this chapter external horizontal links refer to inter- or multi-agency working relating to the police, social services and the variety of health agencies involved in protecting children. Examples relating to critical failures of all agencies are chosen merely to show up the fault lines and to illustrate certain related and salient points.

Failures occur in a number of ways, and these can be mechanical, human or both. In this chapter it is human failure and not mechanical systems that is the subject of critical examination. Failure can be expressed as simply a 'shortfall between performance and standards' (Bignell and Fortune, 1984), however the issues of performance, together with the setting and maintenance of standards, are human activities often fixed by the law, agency or organisational policies, or work precedent and practice. The Laming Inquiry, which was set up in the aftermath of the Victoria Climbié tragedy, reported that:

> There were at least twelve key occasions when the relevant services had an opportunity to intervene. (Laming, 2003, p. 3)

These occasions were warning signs which occurred when Victoria had been taken or referred to hospital accident and emergency units, social services departments or to the police. This case underscores the relative powerlessness of children: had she been an adult, services would have been less likely to fail her.

Laming went on to conclude that those responsible never seriously reviewed the individual circumstances, leaving her to eventually die abandoned, unheard, in agony and alone. Laming suggests this was a gross failure and inexcusable (pp. 2–3).

The recent publication of 'Every Child Matters' and the introduction of the Children Act 2004 were inspired by the lessons learnt from the failure of agencies to protect Victoria Climbié.

Working with partners

In England and Wales the lead agencies with various responsibilities for children are the social services, the police, and the health service. All these agencies hold a duty of care under the Children Act 1989 to protect children. The roots of partnership working go back a long way, but in recent terms can be attributed to the Thatcherite New Right doctrine, promulgated through Home Office Circular 8/84, by suggesting that in policing terms the issue of crime prevention 'is a task for the whole community' (Home Office et al., 1984). For the first time it was being suggested that the police alone could not tackle crime and that it was a responsibility for everyone; the public and other agencies and partners. It meant also that the police lost their monopoly on policing. Since then the police have worked with other groups to help fight crime through partnership-working, which was not a new idea. Previous legislation was overhauled by the Children Act 1989 because, in terms of child protection, there was no simplified or coherent body of law and knowledge to aid practitioners. The legislation made no reference to partnership, but the concept did appear in DOH principles to underpin practice (DOH, 1989), which suggested that responsible authorities should work in partnership, not only with the parents of the child, but also with the child (ibid., p. 1). This is not to downplay the importance of the Act which created a legal mandate in terms of partnership-working between children and parents (Pinkerton, 2001, p. 250). The welfare of the child became the central theme of the legislation which was introduced in the wake of the child deaths of Kimberley Carlile and Heidi Koseda. Critics have argued that it is inappropriate to talk of partnerships in the context of relationships between powerful agencies and the children and families in whose lives they intervene and to whom they provide services (Ryan, 1999, p. 5). Therefore the unequal distribution of power relations within any child protection relationship must not only be purposeful in terms of shared goals, but also show recognition of the benefit of pooling resources, and have agreement on any collaborative working so that the goals can be met. On the surface though, partnerships between agencies make a good deal of sense because they have the potential to deliver coherent/ effective services and additional resources, and to pool ideas, knowledge and finance. This can generate new insights/solutions and synergy (Mackintosh, 1993) in an inter-professional and joined-up manner.

Within months of being elected to office in 1997 the New Labour Government introduced the Crime and Disorder Act 1998 (CDA) as the major thrust of its crime reduction programme (Home Office, 1998a). The culture of the police is an evolving process that increasingly recognises that they alone cannot prevent all crime (Home Office, 1991). They, like the conservative administrations before them, recognised that 'policing' was now a process that must embrace a multitude of agencies, organisations and individuals in order to succeed. In doing so, there must be a need for activity to be measured in ways that go beyond mere crime statistics because success often means different things to different groups. This was to be achieved through increased partnership co-operation that sought holistic solutions. This distinctive change became part of the modernising agenda where a discourse of partnership became widespread. Terms like 'joined-up government' and by association 'joined-up thinking' were essential in modernising public services (Parrott, 2005).

What are partnerships and how do they work?

Defining partnerships can be a difficult thing to do and depends very much on those who are responsible for making them work. Often contested in their definition, generally speaking they are considered to be:

> *The set of characteristics that differentiate provision agencies including legislative framework, powers and responsibilities, degrees of electoral accountability, codes and practices, career paths and so on.* (Balloch and Taylor, 2001, p. 36)

Crawford, on the other hand, considered partnerships within the field of crime control and criminal justice, suggesting that:

> *Partnerships . . . especially by their nature draw together diverse organisations with very*

> *different cultures, ideologies and traditions which pursue distinct aims through divergent structures, strategies and practices.* (1998, p. 171)

Parrott (2005) considered partnership-working from a social work perspective and suggested that, given the different array of professions involved in partnerships, it was clear that the business of partnership becomes a complex problem (p. 121). Simply put, partnerships are an agreement to work collectively between two or more independent bodies to achieve a common objective (www.improvementnetwork.gov.uk). Parrott suggests that this simple definition needs further clarification and hides other meanings which are also relevant when considering ethical issues (2005, p. 121). Bates (2005) suggests that partnership-working is often misunderstood because

> *Simply assuming that various partners share common aims and that conflict is a matter of failure to align aims misunderstands the issues.* (p. 52)

Partnership-working presupposes that participating agencies function well and will work effectively with one another, but partnerships are not without their difficulties. Firstly the partnership must be clarified at the start in terms of its relationships because it implies equality of status, role, responsibility, power, control, co-operation, funding and decision-making, etc. Furthermore, it also assumes that shared goals, shared responsibility and accountability existed amongst the partners. There can be conflict when these goals differ to those of the agency or vertical hierarchy in what is often referred to as silo thinking. There are also problems of culture and power relations where some agencies assume control and influence by imposing their own group norms, beliefs, socialisation, understandings and goals on others to the detriment of the partnership (Kennison and Fletcher, 2005, p. 125). The power relations and breakdowns between partners can be attributed to a lack of mutual respect for each other. Group dynamics are an important consideration because often the dynamics of cultural structures within the various agencies or vertical hierarchies reflect the differences of each cultural group (ibid., p. 128).

Partners delivering holistic solutions require different terms of reference otherwise conflict can be generated as each agency competes to deliver solutions that can promote the interests of their own organisation. Alternatively, agencies appease other more powerful participants and at times compromise and undermine their own position. Consequently partners are often involved in a fine balancing act between the various needs of their own organisations, their partners and those of the service user. The challenges and difficulties of exercising effective partnership-working are evident in all cases of child protection. In the case of Victoria Climbié, the failure of structures intended to facilitate such partnership was painfully evident and it is to the details of this case that the discussion now turns.

Ten months of tragedy

On 12 January 2001 Marie-Therese Kouao and Carl Manning were convicted and jailed for life for the murder of Victoria (Anna) Climbié, a small child aged 8 years from the Ivory Coast who had been entrusted into their care. The results of the post mortem showed that she had died from hypothermia which had arisen in the context of malnourishment, a damp environment and restricted movement (Laming, 2003). She had 128 separate injuries, showing that she had been beaten with a range of both sharp and blunt instruments. The last days of her short life were spent living in a cold unheated bathroom, bound hand and foot inside a bin bag and lying in her own urine and excrement (ibid.). For some who had contact with this matter, this had been the worst case of child abuse they had ever seen.

First contact

Victoria arrived in the UK from Paris on 24 April 1999 with Kouao, who appeared to be escaping the authorities for illegally claiming benefits to which she was not entitled. Victoria travelled on Kouao's French passport and entered the country as Anna – one of Kouao's daughters, although she probably wore a wig to make her look more like the child she had replaced (ibid.). Therefore, the first problem was the subversion of Victoria's identity to Anna, which meant that the status of the child within the family context had altered, with Victoria being treated by outsiders as the daughter of Kouao, rather than her niece.

On arrival, and travelling as EU citizens, they passed through immigration and went to a bed and breakfast in Twyford Crescent, Acton. Later Kouao visited Ealing's Homeless Persons Unit and obtained accommodation in a hostel in Harlesden. During later visits to Ealing Social Services the staff noticed a difference in dress between mother and daughter, with the latter being far scruffier (Laming, 2003, p. 27). By May 1999, a month after her arrival in the UK, there was evidence to suggest that Victoria was already suffering from neglect of development.

Failing our way to success

If systems work well, then there will be few problems; however, it is when they fail that the true nature of any organisation and its interconnections can be viewed. It is only from this point that lessons can be learnt. Reforming the process with checks and balances, where problems can be forecast in the light of previous experience and prevented, is the 'ex post facto' (retrospective) domain of management. Understanding failure within any organisation or hierarchy can be a painful process, none more painful than when it involves a small and vulnerable young child. All the agencies hold a duty of care to protect children: however in Victoria's case, this fell short in a situation where communication between agency partners was disparate, unco-ordinated, minimal or just non-existent. How did the systems in place, which were designed to protect young children, fail in such a spectacular way? In order for us to understand the failure we must first understand and deconstruct the decision- making elements of this case study.

Human factors are considered: especially those which relate to such things as human characteristics, expectations and behaviour. These not only concern the individual at the various levels within each agency, but also encompass the processes, procedures and the tools available to do the job. Within this paradigm it is necessary to also consider the allocation of function, group interaction, visual information and evidence, the physical environment, and training. The expectation of any human activity system concerned with child protection concentrates on the welfare and prevention of harm to children. These systems may operate at various physical and intangible levels.

The authority for protecting children is stated in section 1 of the Children Act 1989, under which the 'paramountcy principle' and common aim is the child's welfare. There are three sections which give powers to child protection agencies to take action. Section 17 empowers the local authority to 'safeguard and promote the welfare of children in their area who are in need'. Section 46 gives authority to a police officer who has reasonable cause to believe that a child would otherwise be likely to suffer significant harm, to remove the child to suitable accommodation or take reasonable steps to ensure that a child's removal from any hospital or other place is prevented. Section 47 places a duty on the local authority to conduct enquiries if they 'have reasonable cause to suspect that a child . . . in their area is suffering, or is likely to suffer, significant harm'. The only agents who have a power of entry to premises by force are the police, and other agencies summon police officers to addresses when they suspect child abuse. The main focus of this case study is the role of the police.

The police

In 1987 the Metropolitan Police Service (MPS) introduced dedicated teams of police officers, called Child Protection Teams (CPTs), who worked on joint investigations with social workers under a Detective Inspector. These dealt with child protection issues where prosecution and conviction was seen as less of a criterion of their success than establishing the truth and preserving the interests of child victims (Fido and Skinner, 1999, p. 38). These operated on a borough basis, usually from one location.

What the Laming Report showed was the serious failings of the police, not only at all levels within one force but also across police jurisdictions. The role of the police in this context makes them the lead investigative agency, responsible for making enquiries, collecting information and evaluating evidence for criminal prosecutions. The police submit evidence case files to the Crown Prosecution Service (CPS) who decide, amongst other factors, whether there is sufficient evidence to progress a prosecution or not.

Victoria's first visit to hospital occurred when she was taken to the Central Middlesex Hospital on 14 July 1999 where she was seen for injuries which were later described to be non-accidental (Laming, 2003, p. 65). Concern was such that she was referred to the Paediatric Registrar who recorded a large number of injuries on the whole of her body. Brent Social Services were informed that Victoria had been admitted for observation and further examination. The next day a doctor diagnosed scabies as the cause of her injuries and Victoria was later released into the custody of Kouao. No one sought to question or double check the diagnosis of the Paediatric Registrar in this case, perhaps because of the power wielded by doctors within the health service. The police also failed to visit and see the injuries after they were downgraded, for fear of catching scabies. A week later she was back in a hospital again, this time at the North Middlesex, where she was taken by Kouao who was concerned by the scald to her face, an apparent self-inflicted injury. She was detained for thirteen nights in the paediatric ward. On her third visit to hospital on 25 February 2000 Victoria was declared dead, aged 8 years and three months.

After the second visit to a hospital, the North Middlesex, Haringey, contact was made with Social Services who allocated a social worker, Lisa Arthurworrey, to the case. Contact was made with Social Services on a number of occasions after which the social worker visited

Kouao several times. Additionally, further contact was made when Kouao took Victoria to Haringey Social Services North Tottenham District Office to report that Manning had sexually assaulted Victoria – an allegation which she later retracted. Although she had been referred to Tottenham Child and Family Centre by the Social Services no one from the centre ever visited Victoria.

By the time of Victoria's death she had been to, or brought to the attention of, no less than five social service agencies (two of which were in the same borough) and two separate hospitals, which were visited on three occasions. The health professionals often see themselves as people who make others better by providing treatment for given ailments and injuries. Therefore it can be a common misconception that, certainly amongst them, the prevention and detection of crimes is outside their job description. This does not reflect a culture of partnership but that of an isolated group operating under difficult circumstances.

However, just to focus on one group of workers at the service delivery end of any business is to neglect the relationship with not only the rest of their vertical hierarchy, who must share some of the blame, but also those other agencies with whom they had an involvement. Furthermore, these connections seem to develop a cascade effect where, the further up or along one goes, the liability becomes shared or diffused.

The initial investigation

Laming showed that there was a lack of adequate initial investigation procedures during the early stages of these enquiries. What was obvious from an analysis of the investigation was the difference and quality of the investigation just because a child was involved. Had the victim been an adult and not a child, then there would have been a different response. For example normative arrangements in assault cases usually mean a visit to the hospital by a police response unit prior to the victim's release from treatment. It was the initial response by PC Dewar that was to give this case a low priority, even though the evidence showed that this was a very serious physical injury and was consistent with the definition of grievous bodily harm (GBH) under Section 18 of the Offences against the Person Act 1861. The officer created a Crime Report, classified it as GBH and identified her mother Kouao as the likely suspect (p. 297). The victim was in hospital and, in agreement with Ms Hines of Social Services, Victoria was placed under police protection, or a place of safety order, which effectively meant that a faxed Metropolitan Police Form 72 was sent to the hospital. PC Dewar never visited the hospital to see the child or visit the mother (Kouao) to give her the reasons for keeping the child under protection. PC Dewar simply went off duty at 7 p.m. and the next day attended a seminar instead of dealing with this matter further. Laming suggests that not to visit the child was a grave error of judgement because, had she done so, she would have found some twelve key pieces of information which would have given her grave cause for concern (2003).

Within two months of her arrival in the UK other people began to notice injuries on Victoria, especially the scars which Kouao explained away as resulting from a fall on an escalator. Kouao met Manning on 14 June 1999 when she boarded a bus he was driving. They exchanged details and this started their eight-month relationship. Three days after this a friend of Kouao, who had met the pair in the street, was sufficiently concerned at Victoria's appearance and behaviour that she telephoned Brent Social Services twice, anonymously. This was the first social services contact made; however by the end of this tragic affair further contacts were made with Haringey Social Services, Enfield Social Services and the Tottenham Child and Family Centre (Laming, 2003). The reason for so many social services agencies being involved was due to the increasing mobility of Kouao and Victoria as they moved between the different social service, health and police boundaries.

This meant that detection of child protection matters was further complicated by the subject's constant movement from one borough to another, a situation which not only showed a comprehensive lack of internal communication but also external horizontal contact as well. Within social services there was no unified internal system to track people or any robust system for inter-agency information exchange.

The physical setting: the workplace

Brent CPT was housed in 'rather scruffy accommodation' at Edgware Police Station. In the case of Haringey CPT they were based at Highgate Police Station in accommodation which Laming described as 'of poor quality'. He was told that the team were insufficiently equipped with staff, vehicles and IT equipment (p. 309), although Laming found that there was no suggestion that these problems hindered or affected the manner in which the investigation was carried out into Victoria's death. Whilst no real connection can be made between the quality of the overall investigation and the poor working conditions, this situation still reflects the grossly inadequate level of priority that CPTs were afforded within the Metropolitan Police Service. The quality of the work environment in at least two boroughs suggest problems of very senior management concerning under-resourcing and funding.

Computers, paperwork and the display of information

Another factor that can cause or contribute towards failure is how information is collected, recorded, presented and displayed. It is absolutely essential that any information can be quickly and easily recorded in a form that can be readily understood and evaluated by all those who are charged to view it. This is so that correct and appropriate decisions could be made on the basis of that information. Accordingly, that information must be accurate, reliable and sufficient. In this case the police had created a computerised crime report on their CRIS system (the Crime Reporting Information System). The police naturally have to handle masses of information on a daily basis and much of it is stored on a variety of databases.

In this case there were a number of failures relating to information-gathering and display. These occurred when considering, for example, the second referral by the Social Services in November 1999 when 'Sergeant Hodges carried out a routine check of CRIS some ten days after the original allegation and five days after the strategy meeting' (p. 327). Decision-making by supervisors, when questioning the CRIS database in respect of the investigation, appears to have been uneven, haphazard and nonchalant. Not only was this inadequate in terms of police supervision in the vertical hierarchy, but also in respect of horizontal connections with other agencies as well. In true partnerships, accurate information-sharing is the key to reliable problem-sharing and decision-making. If all the information had been pooled in what Laming describes as 'a Multi Agency assessment tool' then mistakes could have been avoided.

Training and work experience

Laming highlighted the lack of detective training and experience in both the relevant police CPTs. In the two boroughs' CPTs, Detective Inspector Anderson of Brent CPT was the only qualified detective with sufficient experience and training suitable to deal with child protection matters. Sergeant Cooper-Bland of Haringey CPT had undertaken a two-week Child Protection Course making him, as Laming suggests, 'somewhat of a rarity among the officers from whom I heard evidence' (p. 310). Other staff members had either never had a basic CID course or any other serious training related to child protection. For example, the Detective Inspector from Haringey CPT had had twenty years' police experience while serving in the uniform branch, but had not attended a basic Criminal Investigation Course and had had little practical CID experience. He admitted the fact that he 'did not have the practical skills to really supervise or take on child protection work' (p. 309).

How can an organisation charged with detecting and investigating serious crimes against children fail to properly select and train their staff without giving them the appropriate skills? This shows the organisation as one which often places or promotes people into a rank, rather than into a role. This situation also reflects an organisation which shows low priority and commitment to training (something also highlighted in 1999 by the Macpherson Inquiry) and to the under-valuing of police detective work. For some years prior to 1998 the Metropolitan Police Detective Training School at Hendon (seen in the UK, if not the world, as a centre of excellence in crime management) had been closed for some time and this only compounded this devaluation in the detective's role.

Supervision and the confusion of roles and responsibilities

The question of supervision was discussed in great depth in the report. What followed were examples of how not to supervise junior officers. The role of supervision at Haringey CPT, for example, was lax where PC Jones reported to the Detective Inspector directly, missing out sergeants in the direct chain of command, and consulting only with any sergeant who just happened to be about at the time (p. 324). Laming identified a lack of ownership in respect of supervision, 'where important issues can be missed and conflicting advice given' (p. 325), as a significant flaw.

There were blurred lines of accountability, not only between front-line staff and immediate managers, but also by more senior managers who presided over the supervision of child protection teams in the North West Crime Operational Command Unit. These included Detective Chief Inspector Wheeler, Detective Superintendent Akers and Detective Chief Superintendent David Cox. What confounded Laming in the case of DCI Wheeler, the most senior officer in the crime OCU, was that he felt his role to be purely administrative. Wheeler hardly visited the Brent and Haringey CPTs at all. Wheeler's immediate supervisors had the opposing view: that he had an inspection role with operational responsibility. There was overwhelming evidence to support the fact that Wheeler failed to supervise both Brent and Haringey CPTs, making the assumption, as did others above him, that all was well when it was not (pp. 342–3). The criticism of the blurred lines of accountability that existed both up and down the hierarchical ladder was that there was a fundamental weakness and that this was a direct cause of the failure to properly deal with deficiencies in the composition, resourcing and practices of the CP teams.

Laming also attempted to define the police roles and responsibilities in child protection at all levels of the police hierarchy. One of the failures he found underscores the disorganised nature of the police culture/organisation. For example, on 14 July 1999 social worker Michelle Hines contacted Brent Child Protection Team and told PC Dewar that Victoria had been admitted to hospital with non-accidental injuries. PC Dewar had just happened to answer the phone, effectively making her, by default, the officer in the case rather than having the matter allocated by supervisors. This underscores the immediacy of the police culture in the short term but failure to properly plan in the long term. This also demonstrates an organisation which is lax in its processes and supervision.

Individual and group behaviour: the problems of culture

Consideration must be given to the part individuals play in any system and, in particular, the extent to which human needs are met and the degree to which people provide what is required of them. The individual is seen in two parts, both as the resource (labour) to be used and also in the context of a 'thinking person'. These consider the needs, rights, goals, viewpoints and other attributes that distinguish the person from the robot (Bignell and Fortune, 1984, p. 192). Clearly one such viewpoint of the police in the case study concerned the fact that, in the eyes of a number of CPT Officers, the Social Services were the lead agency in child protection matters: a position which Laming severely criticised those police officers for taking. Thus far this case study illustrates graphically the problems regarding the individual failures; however, the group dynamics of this failure also need to be addressed.

A major influence in any situation relates to the behaviour of complete groups or organisations, namely, what control and influence is exerted in respect of group norms, beliefs, understandings and shared goals. These are often referred to as the organisational cultures, sub-cultures or the canteen culture. There can be conflicts, when, on occasion, group goals differ from those of the organisation. Organisational or group goals are set by those who are established at the top of those hierarchies. The group dynamics of cultural structures or vertical hierarchies reflect the differences of each cultural group. The cultural differences in Crime and Disorder partnerships were first highlighted in the Morgan Report (1991, p. 46) where five various models were identified that reflected the differences in co-ordination, structure and resourcing (Crawford, 1998, p. 170). Within these five models Morgan made particular mention of the local authority model, a police-centred model, and a police headquarters model. Crawford showed the variety in cultural structures which exist within the agency role, their processes and organisation. Individual agencies have vertical hierarchies with separate lines of communication, supervision and management functions.

In all vertical hierarchies these aspects provide difficulties, not only for the vertical organisational structure but also for other horizontal agencies involved, relating to joined-up thinking. If vertical links are not strong we cannot assume that horizontal partnership links are going to be any stronger. It is in any crisis that the true nature of any relationship can be viewed. Crawford illustrates this point:

> *Partnerships – especially within the field of crime control and criminal justice – by their nature draw together diverse organisations with very different cultures, ideologies and traditions which pursue distinct aims through divergent structures, strategies and practices.* (1998, p. 171)

In conflict situations where ideologies, traditions and interests head off in different directions, each group will possess different levels of authority and control. They will not only have variations in specialist knowledge and expertise but also in access to human and material resources (Crawford, 1998). Some have a superior legal authority over other partners, e.g. the police are the only group who have a legal authority to gain access to premises by force if access is denied. This dominance frequently attracts criticism and resistance which often isolates them. They were certainly isolated in their relationship with Haringey Social Services where, Laming added:

> *Tensions also existed between Haringey Social Services and the police. Ms Arthurworrey described the general feeling of hostility towards the police and other agencies which stemmed from [her bosses' view] that 'Social Services knew best . . . we worked the hardest and we knew our procedures. There was just very little consultation'.* (2003, p. 113)

The police have often been criticised for being in the dominant position in terms of crime control. They have a very distinct culture, or variety of sub-cultures, which have been seemingly resistant to change and this is particularly so the further down the hierarchical ladder one gets. These cultures are not unlike other agency cultures. There is insufficient space here to discuss and evaluate the police culture, however, suffice to say that they are a control profession who take charge and are well used to dealing with problems instantly. For example, if they have a specific crime problem or a murder to investigate, they often 'form a squad'. This reactive nature is perceived as a great short-term strength by those inside the police and one which is often tested in respect of street violence; however, long-term sustained effort is not a feature of the police culture. Bailey and Williams refer to this immediate response as 'rapid reaction which can cause friction with other agencies more accustomed to extensive consultation and reflection before major decisions are made' (2000, p. 73). The nature of control frequently pervades any inter- or multi- agency meetings with the police, who often take charge, organise and manage these gatherings. Bailey and Williams point out that the police activist approach often causes friction when they have arrived for meetings in good time, whilst social workers arrive late, seem unfocused and cause disruption by getting drinks (pp. 73–4). Police frustration frequently becomes apparent, and often good-humoured banter is used to defuse a tense situation that otherwise may deteriorate into argument and confrontation. This reaction, which is rooted in the police culture, is a by-product of the performance occupational culture (and therefore a blame culture) and also a reaction to coping with the competing demands placed on them, locally, nationally and organisationally.

The Laming Inquiry also attempted to look forward by staging a series of multi-agency seminars which focused on making recommendations as to safeguarding children by good practice. Firstly, there were discussions as to the discovery and inclusion of children within the system, keeping track of children, new arrivals in the UK, private fostering, and the hostility and exclusion that led to children being lost or frightened, and failure to access help and support from the various agencies. Secondly, the identification at the earliest possible stages of children at risk was also discussed. One of the main problems was in identifying a threshold which defined the nature of common intervention. Because of the differing priorities, demands and requirements of the varying agencies, this would be a difficult problem to surmount. Drawing on a clear line of accountability, being fully informed of service delivery and not accepting at face value what they are told were all improvements to the widespread organisational malaise (Laming, 2003, p. 5). The features of bad practice were common within all the agencies in this sad case.

Conclusion

In the foregoing, a general understanding and systemic account of partnership-working was shown predominantly focused on the police and between the police and other agencies, although the analysis was not exhaustive. The starting point of this analysis is premised on the fact that, if systems work well then there will be few problems; however, it is when they fail that the true nature of any organisation and its interconnections can be viewed. An error or failure is not mechanical but human and it is only from these failings that lessons can be learnt and measures put in place to ensure that these do not happen again. Understanding failure within any organisation or hierarchy can be a painful process none more painful than when it involves a small, vulnerable child.

Such was the nature of this failure that a public inquiry was summoned under Lord Laming to investigate how and why such a spectacular failure occurred. Not one of the agencies empowered by Parliament to carry out their responsibilities – in Victoria's case funded by the public purse – emerge from this inquiry with much credit (Laming, 2002). Lord Laming made 108 recommendations (specifically directing eighteen towards the police) for change and to ensure that lessons would be learnt for the future. Many of these recommendations had to be introduced within six months.

The role of the police, in terms of child protection, was woefully inadequate in this case, but what is also obvious is that not only is accountability complicated and diffuse but, in addition, the organisational nature of the police is fragmented and disorganised. Failing to get to grips with this complexity of internal functions also means that there is a lack of understanding in external matters. For example, the investigation and prosecution of adults in child protection matters rests with the police, yet in child protection matters the police perceived social services to be the lead agency.

The police had developed CPTs to help protect children, originally an impressive model of good practice but one which they doomed to failure by staffing them with people who had inadequate investigation skills, little practical work experience and poor training. It reflected a low priority situation which, in policing terms, afforded little in the way of status – in essence it was an un-sexy function of the police. It also showed the physical setting to be a sad and depressed one where police officers worked in poor surroundings, with a limited budget, shrinking resources and poor provisioning.

Blurred individual roles and disjointed lines of accountability, bad internal communication, supervision and management, further compounded the problem. Officers at ground level were incompetent and were effectively let down by their managers. Laming found the police response at all levels unacceptable.

He said:

> This is indicative, in my view, of the grand state of CPT in London in 1999, and it shows the priority they were accorded by the MPS as a whole. It would seem that the force was content to allow these teams to perform the vital work of protecting children with, in many cases, insufficient numbers of detectives and inadequately qualified managers. (2003, p. 335)

The MPS had given CPTs a low priority and as such, this was an organisation that was managerially flawed. Chains of command were breached in a number of places, which resulted in inefficient and ineffective management. Laming set police management a task to elevate the status of, and provide proper funding to, CPTs in his recommendations (Recommendation 105).

Snapshots of inter-agency work relationships were highlighted within the analysis and it showed a collection of individuals from all the agencies working separately with little respect for each other, little mutual consultation and hardly any exchange of information. It demonstrated an attitude of silo thinking across agencies, yet inside these organisations it was little better, resulting in communication up and down hierarchies as being grossly inadequate. What was also absent was any form of linked or joined-up learning or training between, and incorporating, all the agencies. Any communication or co-operation between agency partners was disparate, unco-ordinated, minimal or just plainly non-existent.

The social services came in for the lion's share of criticism with 47 recommendations, whilst 27 recommendations applied to the health service. All these were of varying importance and such was the urgency of the situation that most were to be implemented within six months. Primarily the bad practice within the health services was focused on the gathering and recording of information and not sharing such knowledge. No system of checks and balances ensured that these proper procedures were being carried out (Laming, 2003, p. 283).

Lastly, there was individual failure by a number of people from a variety of backgrounds which was further complicated by the group dynamic of organisational cultures, and especially by the fact that they had their own 'language'. A main Laming recommendation was aimed at providing a 'common language' framework across agencies which should be used by each agency in order that they are better placed to respond to concerns.

Chapter 8

Talking with children

Constructing victim-hood or agency?

Gwyn Daniel

(Editorial comments are displayed in italics.)

Introduction

Since the theme of this book is of children as victims, it quite naturally places great emphasis on the powerlessness and vulnerability of children. In this chapter I intend to discuss how we talk with individual children whose abusive or otherwise adverse experiences lead professionals to be concerned for their safety and well-being, and I argue that focusing on them only as powerless victims may not be the most helpful approach. There is inevitably a tension between the way that children's victimisation needs to be witnessed and documented at the macro level of policy and social action and the more complex, subtle and personal processes that infuse the micro level of our professional interactions with individual children.

I am a systemic family therapist, located within social work, who has specialised in work with families in three particular contexts. These are all situations where children are likely to be defined as 'at risk' or as victims: where there is past or ongoing domestic violence, where there is parental mental illness, or where separated parents are engaged in acrimonious legal conflicts over residence or contact. In each of these three areas there is a substantial body of research, clinical and policy literature (Gopfert et al., 2004; Osofsky, 1997; Rodgers and Pryor, 1998), which helps professionals identify risk, develop sensitivity to questions of immediate or long-term harm to children and intervene where appropriate. The statutory framework, including for example the Common Assessment Framework, is also important in structuring practice (DfES, 2006a). Equally importantly, highlighting children's victim-hood helps us argue for vital resources and services at the delivery end which are aimed primarily at protecting children and enhancing their physical and emotional well-being. What I argue here lies at the heart of social work practice and focuses on assessment and monitoring where evidence is interpreted and judgments made. The aim therefore is that resources are to be deployed in the best interests of the victim.

National Occupational Standards (NOS) have been set as a guide for social workers, and they clearly lay down values and ethics that are central to competence (Parrott, 2006).

Additionally, further assistance is provided by the General Social Care Council (GSCC) who have set codes of practice for social care workers and social care employees (ibid., p. xiii). Social work values set out to show respect for a person honour diverse and distinctive organisations and communities that make up contemporary society. Furthermore, they seek to advise on matters relating to combating processes that lead to discrimination, marginalisation and social exclusion (ibid., p. xii).

It requires the professional to reflect upon core practice issues and difficulties in maintaining the high standards in what Parrott (2006) suggests is a commitment to social justice through anti-oppressive practice on which social work values and ethics are grounded (p. xii). Here this may take the form of reflection in terms of 'negative assessment of such difference' especially where service user needs have been the focus of service delivery (ibid., p. 1).

Mental health and other professionals involved in offering services to individual children and their families need to be informed by professional and research-based knowledge of risk to help them make assessments of individual children. However they also need to find ways of working with children to promote their resilience and coping skills. Here a paradox may arise. Emphasising risk and victim-hood in work with children may create mind sets for professionals that can make it harder for them to engage creatively with children's agency (i.e. as active subjects) and with their unique coping skills and strategies. In trying to rescue and protect children, we may be less alert to what children themselves are actually trying to do with the resources available to them to protect themselves and often other family members too. In my experience, failing to engage with how children themselves think about their situations or to elicit from them all the ways they actively try to manage stressful or dangerous family processes can lead to silencing their voices and diminishing their agency. Children and adolescents, while often longing for and actively seeking protection, very rarely welcome being ascribed a victim identity, no matter how benign the intentions are of those who try to confer it. For children, in adverse family circumstances, there are generally complex issues of attachment, loyalty and protectiveness towards even the most abusive of parents.

In this chapter I will explore some of the ways that professionals who engage with children at risk can, whilst acknowledging adversity and potential harm, engage with their strengths and coping mechanisms and learn from the ways they think about their situation and from their ideas about what would be helpful to them. While my own work is located in therapeutic contexts both within the health service and in private practice, the ideas presented are intended to be useful to all professionals engaged in helping children.

I will explore three different discourses about children in adversity and discuss the ways in which they are likely to influence professionals in their work. I call these:

- Children as damaged

- Children as over-burdened

- Children as experts

I will argue that, while the first two carry a great deal of 'evidential loading'; the third is much more helpful at the level of our actual interaction with children. A fundamental tenet of the systemic approach (Bateson, 1973) is that the way we define phenomena, the patterns we choose to highlight and those we ignore, will have a profound effect on the 'reality' that we then 'discover'; this in turn has a major impact on the feedback we receive. To use more contemporary theory (Wetherell et al., 2001), positioning ourselves within each of these discourses will therefore influence the narratives we elicit from children. The possible consequences of operating from each of these discourses will be explored in relation to work with children where there is domestic violence, where parents are involved in legal disputes over residence or contact, or where parents have a mental illness.

While there are, of course, many other contexts in which children can be seen as victims, and child poverty is an overarching context which affects all of them, I have chosen these three partly because they are my specialities but also because they are situations where, whether or not children present symptoms, most professionals would consider that these children are the direct victims of their parents' difficulties.

Children as damaged – 'Harm-ism'

Much of the social legislation from the early nineteenth-century . . . has been, in part at least, concerned with protecting children from forms of neglect and abuse in the widest sense of these words. In nearly all of the legislation, the rhetoric has been that of the child as helpless, as acted upon, usually in some kind of damaging manner. (Hendrick, 1994, pp. 7–8)

Smart et al. (2001), in following the specific rhetoric applied to the effects of parental separation on children, use the term 'harm-ism' to denote the tendency in the media and among certain professionals and legislators to isolate divorce itself as harmful to children while glossing over those other factors more robustly identified in research such as poverty, impaired parenting, and parental conflict and violence. Children may then be assumed to require professional interventions to manage this transition. An example of 'harm-ism' can be found in a review of Trinder et al.'s (2002) research for the Joseph Rowntree foundation:

'out of the sample of 57 children, only 3 were referred for counseling, all of whom found it useful. The result of this lamentable state of affairs was that children were deprived of neutral support and *forced* [my italics] to turn to family members or friends for advice, comfort or support'.

This reviewer thus implicitly dismisses the natural support systems available to children as well as children's own capacity to help each other. Attitudes such as these can also be seen as profoundly culturally biased, ignoring the multiple ways that families cope through utilising the resources of the extended family.

When we are arguing for services to help children who do not have such natural support systems, it is, however, tempting to draw upon the discourse of 'harm-ism', to emphasise the worst outcomes and the most negative aspects of the experience. Even more significantly, Smart et al. also raise the question of how 'harm-ism' enters into structures of feeling within families. The fear of harming their children may lead a parent to stay in an abusive or violent relationship until the children are deemed old enough to cope. Notions of inevitable harm caused to children may also, paradoxically, prevent parents from acting in ways that *are* protective and resilience-building. These include giving children clear reasons for the decision to separate, giving them plenty of opportunity to ask questions, to return to issues about the decision that trouble them or involving them in decisions about the future. In interviews with children about divorce (Gorell Barnes et al., 1997; Smart et al., 2001), about parental mental illness (Gopfert et al., 2004; Gorin, 2004), and domestic violence (Gorin, 2004), their complaint about not being given information emerges as one of the most salient findings. The sequel of this after domestic violence, when parents may be too ashamed or fearful to accept that their children knew what was going on, may be that children are left as 'disempowered' rather than 'empowered' witnesses (Weingarten, 2003). This aspect is expanded on and developed later under the heading 'children as experts'.

In the case of parental mental illness, the fear that a parent has of causing harm to their children by talking about their illness may diminish the possibilities for closeness between parent and child as well as making children more likely to keep their own feelings of distress to themselves (Daniel and Wren, 2005; Focht-Birketts and Beardslee, 2000). When children are faced with adverse events and stresses within their own families the building of relational resilience crucially rests on adults' ability to appreciate their children's agency, their attempts to help and their desire to protect. Just as powerfully, there is a countervailing desire to protect their 'innocence'. The construction of children as innocent victims may also lead professionals to be more concerned with reassuring children that what has happened is not their fault than with finding out more about what children actually think and want under the circumstances.

Pathologising children

In the past few years there has been increasing anxiety about the state of children's mental health, with children in Britain being described in the press as 'the unhappiest in Europe' (e.g. The Times, February 2007). Attention has been drawn to the number of children presenting with depression, with self-harming behaviours and with ADHD (Attention Deficit Hyperactivity Disorder). Various hypotheses have been advanced for this, including pressure on children to perform academically, bullying and violence within schools and communities, pressures on children as consumers, family conflict and breakdown, and the long working hours of parents. To explore the relationship of these factors to unhappiness and symptomatology in children is well beyond the scope of this chapter: however, what I am concerned with is more specific. Here I will explore the possible effects of medicalising distress and pathologising children through diagnosing and treating them rather than through tackling the structural issues mentioned above. In a recent research project on childhood depression (Campbell et al., 2003) one of the more striking findings was that, although all the children taking part had been diagnosed as depressed through self-report and a psychiatric interview using the Diagnostic and Statistical Manual of Mental Disorders (DSM, vol. 4) criteria, when interviewed with their families they showed a range of behaviours and preoccupations. Among the findings was the extent to which children showed feelings of anxiety, responsibility and protectiveness towards a parent. The significance of this for therapy is that these feelings provide opportunities in conversations with children to address feelings, thoughts and actions in an interpersonal context rather than focusing only on the child's inner state.

A particularly good example of the risks of pathologising children lies in the enormous rise in diagnoses of ADHD over the past decade and the treatment of it through medicating children. (See Newnes and Radcliffe, 2005 for a trenchant analysis of this trend.) Research into the effect of this on children themselves (Brady, 2005) highlights the way that children come to view themselves as impaired or damaged and also with many feeling that their medicalised self suppresses other aspects of selfhood. Yet, while medication has been the most common intervention, locating the problem firmly 'within' children, other social and environmental factors have featured less strongly in professional discourse. One factor of particular interest here is the relationship between the kind of restless and unsettled behaviour which gives rise to diagnoses of ADHD and children's experience of domestic violence. Cooper and Vetere (2005) have alluded to emergent research evidence on this connection which certainly accords with my own clinical experience. Children who grow up in volatile households, who need to constantly be 'on the alert' to signs that a parent is becoming angry and to take action to protect themselves, may find safety in keeping on the move and may indeed find concentration difficult. These symptoms, rather than being taken only as pointers to a medical condition of as yet unidentified neurological origin, could, in these circumstances, also be seen as a logical response to a highly stressful context. Since domestic violence is under-reported, professionals need to be persistent in inquiring about these factors. However, a recent report to the Family Justice Council (2007) into the impact of domestic violence on contact arrangements found that there was a serious lack of awareness among mediators and Child and Family Court Advisors on the incidence and effect of domestic violence.

Accessing services

In order that social workers can intervene in a situation they must morally justify their conduct, since the aim of social work often lies between two points – the best outcome or the least harmful effect (Parrott, 2006, p. 12). Yet there are no right or wrong answers to many of these problems and social workers can be pulled in a number of competing directions in their search for innovative solutions in resolving difficult cases. Professionals in social work stand at the centre and they owe their responsibilities not only to the victim but also to society, the social work profession and the employing agency as well.

In this situation there is a diversity of services available to troubled children, but in the UK much of it is fragmented and often patchy. However, one universal service is available and that is the Child and Adolescent Mental Health Service (CAMHS). The three family contexts mentioned above are ones which, as most highly trained and experienced professionals working within CAMHS will say, are among the most complex and difficult that they engage with, and where therapeutic intervention may be extremely beneficial in protecting children's emotional well-being. However, even if children are significantly troubled, this will not in itself gain them access to CAMHS unless they meet a certain threshold of symptomatology. Being primarily in need of help because of distress about the contexts in which they live, or the levels of stress, unpredictability and danger they face, is unlikely to gain children access to CAMHS unless they themselves can be defined as having mental health problems. Asking about a referral to CAMHS for a child caught in the middle of a particularly vicious legal dispute between her parents, I was once told that 'she'd pretty well have to be cutting herself to get onto the waiting list'. Even if children *are* displaying symptoms, the fact that a parent has a serious mental health problem or their parents are engaged in litigation may well exclude them from these services. In the case of domestic violence they are more likely to be accepted if it can be argued that they are suffering from post traumatic stress disorder. These services are, of course, hugely underfunded – given the need in these demanding situations – so fund holders have to find ways of managing their resources and in this case that relates to strict referral criteria, but there are two results of this policy which contribute towards my argument here. One is that, when services are offered to children on the basis of their symptoms rather than on the situations they have to manage, the contexts in which they have come to be so distressed, and the 'logic' of their attempts to manage this, may fade into the background. The other is that parents or referring professionals may have to 'talk up' children's symptoms in order to get help for them and this can find its way into how children's behaviour is subsequently constructed by family and professionals alike.

To secure the agreement of others in decision-making, social workers owe a duty in terms of professional accountability, by persuading their managers that their actions are reasonable, given all the evidence, and that the decision to favour one course of action over another is a good one (Parrott, 2006). Often though, professional loyalties or working practices lead to rigidity in deciding on what is the best context within which to help children. For example, when providing services for families with parental mental illness, there is a strong case, as many child carers themselves have argued (Gopfert et al., 2004), for involving children much more in adult services. This means that children's concerns about their parent can be directly addressed, information and support can be given, and children themselves do not have to be pathologised. However, this requires a significant leap of faith and change in both thinking and culture in which more skills in talking with children are needed than is currently the case within adult mental health services.

Social workers need an attitude that values difference, which literally means that it requires them to inhabit the world of the other, so that they may be able to value empathy in order that they are able to understand the victims' world and its values (Parrott, 2006, p. 29). Reflecting on their own values is also an important function for the social worker, since in recognising and understanding difference they must be able to value their own position in society and recognise ways in which power can be shared (Parrott, 2006). Highlighting situations like these only underscores the relative powerlessness of children in an adult world, which often results in their voices being lost, and may lead to more appropriate solutions being ignored. Social workers and health professionals alike who operate in a social work environment will need to engage in an internal political struggle within the confines of their social work role and profession to achieve change. This will then recognise the contribution made by children in mental health cases but also maximise the effective outcomes not only for their parents but also for them as service users.

Children as burdened – *'Parentification'*

Children who grow up in families where parents are either vulnerable, volatile, dangerous, or all three may end up taking a great deal of responsibility and often become defined by professionals as 'parentified' (Byng Hall, 2002; Earley and Cushway, 2002; Minuchin, 1974). This means that children, even at young ages, take up roles in their families which are more commonly ascribed to adults. At the practical level, they may carry out 'grown up' tasks such as physically looking after a parent, carrying responsibility for younger siblings, intervening in violent interactions or calling emergency services. At the emotional level, they may feel anxious and responsible for parents who are struggling to cope; they may suppress their own needs and desires in order to pacify angry parents or to avoid being drawn into the acrimony between their separated parents.

While much of this can, of course, have long-term detrimental effects on children's emotional development, labelling such children as 'parentified' is not always helpful. It can have the unwitting effect of pathologising a position which children have needed to adopt in order to manage otherwise overwhelmingly stressful experiences. It can also ignore cultural and contextual diversity, and differences about the 'proper' role of children in families. For some fragile families it is the very fact that children take on these more 'adult' roles that keeps the family viable. It also ignores the flexibility achieved by many families in which parents try to resume their parenting roles as soon as they are well.

Children with violent or vulnerable parents constantly have to appraise situations in order to assess risk to themselves, to one or both parents and to other children in the family. Having the skills and competence to do this can be a source of pride and self-esteem to children, however much the doing of it may conflict with developmental theories of children's capabilities, with social norms about adults' and children's roles, or indeed with their own long-term emotional well-being. Young Carers' Groups are an example of services which do explicitly recognise the roles children take on and which provide contexts where children can be less isolated, can access help and can have opportunities for other kinds of experiences.

Child development

Inevitably discussion of 'parentification' takes us into the realm of child development and theories about what can be expected of children of different ages in cognitive and emotional terms. The role of social, economic and familial context is, however, insufficiently taken into account in our theories about what children are capable of and at what age. For example, a young child who lives alone with a parent who overdoses may have skills in calling emergency services that another older child in a different context would never need to learn. Children living in violent families may develop skills in reading minute changes in body language that children in calmer households do not need. Having rigid ideas about child development may constrain us because, if we assume that children of certain ages cannot understand certain things, we may never ask them the questions that would enable them to demonstrate that they indeed do. Thus, even while legislation from the Children Act 1989 onwards includes the requirement that children be consulted about matters affecting them, this often does not happen because of professional perceptions about children's age and understanding.

When we think of children mainly as victims or over-burdened, we may never ask them about how they have developed skills or find out how they achieve a sense of agency, which helps them avoid feelings of overwhelming impotence and fear. Parents and professionals alike are organised by beliefs and canons of 'good parenting', and these in general tell us that parents should look after children and not vice versa. Therefore the very active way in which children may in fact perform these tasks carries the risk of becoming another hidden story and children may be left in a position of having responsibility without power or recognition.

In the case study that follows I show how in conversations with Josefa a change in approach alters the focus of any likely intervention.

CASE STUDY 1

*Six year old Josefa, who was referred to a CAMHS service for bed-wetting, sleep disturbance and school difficulties, moved between the households of her mother and father who had separated acrimoniously two years previously. Since then, there had been several violent incidents between the parents witnessed by Josefa who also had countless experiences of hearing each parent criticise and 'bad-mouth' the other, behaviour she described as 'naughty'. A therapist met with Josefa alone and, on hearing about this, kept saying to Josefa how hard this was for her and it must be too much because she is only six years old. Josefa was having none of this and kept insisting 'I can manage'. The therapist, understandably, didn't believe her and persisted in the line that it was too hard for her, receiving more of the same response. Then the therapist changed tack and asked Josefa to describe the ways in which she **did** manage, Josefa talked about how she told each of her parents off when they were 'naughty'. She thought that this sometimes worked. What did she do if they didn't listen? If they didn't listen, she went off to her room. In the middle of this discussion about her heroic attempts to have an effect on her parents, she turned to the therapist and said spontaneously, 'but sometimes I can't manage'.*

Comment

This example demonstrates that, while the level of stress a child experiences is usually not in question, respecting and engaging with children's knowledge and skills in managing these adverse situations can lead to a more realistic mutual appraisal of what is possible and what is not. Once recognised, it was possible to talk with her about how the therapist could help her and to locate responsibility where it properly belonged – with her parents.

Children as experts

It will be clear by now that this author, in her therapeutic practice, has a strong preference for the children as 'experts' discourse! As a psychotherapist, I am well aware of the tendency of our profession to look more closely at deficits and vulnerabilities than at strengths and resources and to be overly keen to interpret communications rather than follow the logic of the narrative. This is a particular risk when working with children who are indeed vulnerable, may lack verbal fluency and whom we will be anxious to understand. They are also likely to invite us through silence or through playful or disruptive activity to articulate our own meanings on their behalf. All of this, however well-intentioned, can lead us into 'doing to' rather than 'working with'.

Identifying strengths and resources

Much recent thinking about children now emphasises their position as actors in their social worlds rather than as passive recipients of welfare or protection (Smart et al., 2001). Without in any way challenging the idea that the welfare and protection of children is central to the social work task, this does create a different framework for engaging with children and with their understanding of their familial and social worlds.

In recent years, there has been an upsurge in research into children's worlds, within a broadly social constructionist framework, and this challenges many traditional, universalising and essentialising assumptions about childhood. This involves conceptualising children as active citizens (Brannen and O'Brien, 1996; Cockburn, 1998; Smart et al., 2001), as active participants in decision-making (Butler et al., 2006), and deconstructing the psychology of children's cognitive development (Burman, 1994; James et al., 1998). In the therapeutic field, privileging children's competence in their social worlds and their ability to access skills in adversity (Burck, 2003; Daniel, 2003; Daniel and Wren, 2005), has involved questioning assumptions about the inevitable harm done to children if they take up roles and responsibilities more 'properly' ascribed to adults.

Smart et al., in their research with children after divorces, have described approaches which engage with the ideas children themselves have about their social worlds rather than those adults think they should have. They point out that the notion of the 'child as project' tends to assume that childhood is a unitary category where age or developmental stage is privileged over social, economic or cultural context. 'Child as person' on the other hand, involves thinking about the pluralities of childhood experience and considers children as 'active and interactive practitioners of social life.' Children are seen to have certain skills and knowledge, often different but not considered to be inferior to those of adults. This recognition also brings childhood research into the domain of power, politics and hierarchy where explorations of children's positioning within generational hierarchies are explored, and indeed the whole tenor of and assumptions about adult–child relationships are called into question.

Systemic therapists try to understand the different contexts influencing their clients and relate this to behaviour. They are fully cognisant of all the profoundly harmful effects of neglect or abuse, yet they choose, in conversations, to highlight the positive or logical ways in which people have come to think or act in the way they have. In work with children, this involves tracking, carefully and respectfully, how they have come to make sense of their relational world and acknowledging the thinking that has gone into its construction, however bizarre, troubling or misguided, this may appear to adults. (See Cooklin (2001) for an excellent discussion of conversations with children which highlight their own constructions rather than the therapist's interpretations.)

Engaging with children's expertise in the context of domestic violence involves understanding not just the impact of the violence on them but also the actions they have made or tried to make in response to it. The ideas of Kaethe Weingarten about disempowered and empowered witnessing (Weingarten, 2003) are helpful here. Adapting Weingarten's ideas to children who witness violence (Burck, 2003) enables us to engage with the common experience of children who are exposed to violence, but have no opportunity to construct a narrative for themselves around this experience. *Schon (1987) suggests that professional workers learn from the people they serve in their practice and Parrott (2006) asserts that professional workers reflect back on practice using theory both in action with service users and later when evaluating practice (p. 79).* This experience may then remain unarticulated, fragmented and accessible only in relation to physical stimuli such as perceived threat or other types of arousal.

Lack of comfort by a trusted adult who may either themselves be too traumatised, unwilling to acknowledge that the child has witnessed the violence or may themselves be objects of fear, may leave children uncontained and prey to overwhelming anxiety and impotence. Parents may convince themselves that children could not possibly have seen or heard the violence and do not want to hear a child's assertion to the contrary. This lack of acknowledgement constitutes, for children, disempowered witnessing.

Empowerment by contrast involves, in effect, observing a child's witnessing through giving credence to their experience and through hearing the account of all the things the child did or thought about doing, which generally includes their attempts to keep themselves or others safe. This is, of course, not an alternative to ensuring safety in the household, which is the adults' responsibility, but keeps children's own agency at the foreground and helps them to locate their own experience within a shared narrative. The fact that believing children and acknowledging their experience has a beneficial effect, even when violence or abuse **does** continue, can be confirmed by the feedback of children to the provision of confidential telephone services such as Childline.

'The plan'

In the following case study I consider the often unbearable stresses on children managing conflict and associated relationship difficulties. I met with six-year-old Curtis after he was referred for acute anxiety and sleep problems.

CASE STUDY 2

Curtis's parents were separated and he and his two younger siblings lived with his mother who had a physical illness and had suffered from mental health difficulties. Curtis's father had been violent to her and the relationship between the parents was very hostile, with continuing allegations of violence from each parent. I met with Curtis two years after a particularly violent episode, which had occurred after he and his siblings had been to their father for the weekend and were being returned to his mother's house. Neither parent thought he could remember this incident as he was only four years old at the time, but Curtis had a clear recollection of his father hitting his mother. When I asked him for more details about this, he said that they were outside the house and he tried to get himself and his younger siblings into the house but the door was locked. 'So what happened then?' I asked. Curtis said 'I tried to get them to stop, but I didn't have a plan' What sort of plan? 'A plan to get them to stop fighting' I asked Curtis if he thought that, at four years old, he was too young to have a plan? He agreed but said that now, at six years old he could have a plan. We continued this conversation for a while and, with each question, Curtis advanced his age a bit further until he was certain that, at age sixteen, he would definitely have a plan. I asked him if he would like it if there was a time machine so that he could go forward to being sixteen and get the plan. He said he would. I said that that might be a good idea but could be a pity because he would miss out on all those years between six and sixteen which, in my recollection, could be pretty interesting years. 'Oh no', he said 'I wouldn't miss out, because I'd get the plan, get back in the time machine and go back to being six!' After admiring his ingenuity, I asked Curtis if he thought it would be easier if his parents had a plan to stop fighting. He thought it would. I asked him if he would like me to help them get a plan and he said he would. The rest of the work with this family revolved around my work with the parents to reduce risk to the children. Curtis was involved from time to time in sessions as my 'consultant' when I would ask him how well he thought the plan was working.

Comment

This is an example of work in which the intolerable nature of the stress experienced by the child and his siblings was not in question. However, engaging with Curtis's own expertise and agency was helpful in the service of reducing the violence between his parents and in challenging the adults to take responsibility for their behaviour. While this in no sense burdened Curtis with responsibility, he was able to be involved in monitoring the work with his parents in a way that reflected both his realistic level of anxiety for himself and his younger siblings and his sense of pride about how much he had tried to help.

When there is parental mental illness, a parent can sometimes be extremely moved to learn how much their child has worried about them and has tried to be helpful. For other parents this may conflict far too much with their ideas about how things between parents and children *should* be. In this case, as well as trying to help, children may experience a denial from their parent that it ever was so.

Consulting children

Services for children are often developed with only a passing reference to what children actually say they want. Audrey Mullender (2002) and her colleagues, who interviewed 1,400 ethnically diverse children about their experience of domestic violence, highlighted two findings which are relevant to service development – that they want to be listened to and have their views taken seriously and that they play an active part in making decisions and helping to find solutions. These findings have been mirrored in the advice given to mental health professionals by children from a Young Carers Group:

- Introduce yourself, tell us who you are and what your job is.
- Tell us what is going to happen next.
- Give us as much information as you can.
- Remember to talk to us; we have first hand experience of what is going on.
- Keep on talking to us and keep us informed. Tell us it's not our fault.

- Tell us if there is anyone we can contact.

  Please don't ignore us. Remember we are part of the family and we live there too. (in Gopfert et al., 2004)

Carol Smart, Bren Neale and Amanda Wade's research into children's views on contact and residence post-separation also confirms that children want to play an active role in deciding how these arrangements are made.

Conclusion

Constructing children *only* as innocent victims of failed parenting or abusive systems, however firmly based in reality this is, can constrain professionals from exploring how children themselves make sense of their reality. While children are obviously not responsible for their parents' inability to parent them, or for their violence or volatility, a focus on victim-hood creates many limitations in interactions with children. It may lead a professional to be overly protective and anxious to interpret the child's experience in particular ways, for example, to reassure children that none of this is their fault, that they have done nothing wrong. It may make us less alert to all the skills that children have learnt in order to manage such experiences, or to learn from them how they have come to evaluate and monitor adults' behaviour. In constructing children as experts, I find that I can engage more readily with their pride and self-esteem, address dilemmas of loyalty to vulnerable parents and access their own ideas about what help they need. It is not easy for parents whose greatest fear is often that they have damaged their children by their actions to listen to them talking about how much they know and how hard they may have tried to be helpful.

Social workers and other professionals involved with domestic violence and as mediators helping parents in conflict post-separation, or in adult mental health, may find themselves leaving children's perspectives out of their thinking. We need to be able to challenge previous understandings, and sharing good practice is essential in informing future policy as to what works. Challenging previous working practices and questioning pre-conceived ideas, which in this case is about the powerlessness of children, may bring better outcomes for victims. In achieving this, professionals may find the increased policy emphasis on integrated working together with a focus on outcomes for children (DfES, 2004a) helpful. In all of these fields, we need to accept that children are generally scrutinising the adult world with great attention, a world which may be failing them, and are taking, or trying to take, actions for self-protection. Consulting children who are at the receiving end of the adults' difficulties and conflicts means learning from their expertise. This can be done in the form of focus groups of children, involving them in the design of research projects as is increasingly the practice in the Joseph Rowntree Foundation. Increasingly, organisations charged with disseminating good practice to professionals have demonstrated a commitment to ensuring that the voices of children, and other service users, is clearly heard (see, for example, Aubrey and Dahl, 2006; Wright et al., 2006). At the very least, it means making sure that in work with individual families, the children's views and opinions, in all their detail, are always in the foreground.

Chapter 9

Child protection from a diverse inner-city primary school perspective

Sue Goodman and Anthony Goodman

Introduction

What can be expected from the teaching profession, and their colleagues, in terms of their ability to raise and share concerns about child protection (CP) within a primary school setting? If worries about a child do arise, how is this recorded and shared with other professionals? How is it handled? Who has responsibility? This chapter will describe the process whereby these concerns within the school are transmitted internally and externally. Schools have their set procedures and designated staff, from the head teacher downwards, to do this. The chapter will also draw on case studies to highlight the process with all of its complexities. Contrary to what might be expected, young people rarely openly disclose when they have been abused, whether this is physical, sexual, neglect or emotional in its nature. Rather, it is the familiarity with and knowledge about the young person that may alert school staff. A child may appear withdrawn or aggressive, he or she may in some way demonstrate that they are distressed. There are times when young children innocently talk about a family event in a news-sharing forum, which alerts adults. However, distress does not indicate that there is necessarily a major problem and the skill of the school team is to try to discover what is upsetting the young person, without causing even more stress to them.

This chapter will be looking at the role of the designated CP professional or team in a mainstream primary school, in terms of role and responsibility. It will examine the reality of CP in this setting, and the part it has to play within the wider educational remit. It also looks at the theory and the legal responsibility behind the role.

In 2006 the Government published an inter-disciplinary guide entitled *Working Together to Safeguard Children. A Guide to Inter-agency Working to Safeguard and Promote the Welfare of Children* (Department for Education and Skills, 2006b). This was under the 'Every Child Matters: Change for Children' agenda. The document highlighted the shared responsibility for 'safeguarding and promoting the welfare of children – and in particular protecting them from significant harm' (p. 33). The role of the school is covered very concisely (pp. 66–8), and the document includes an earlier Department for Education and Skills (DfES, 2004b) document on child protection in its bibliography. This document, *Safeguarding Children in Education*, is still relevant to the school environment. Schools have a responsibility under the Education Act 2002 to safeguard and promote the welfare of their pupils. *Safeguarding Children in Education* states that the school 'will have important information about the child's level of understanding and the most effective means of communicating with the child' (p. 67). It adds that the school should not investigate possible abuse or neglect but has a key role in referring these issues on and that it can contribute to assessments.

CP is not an exact science and sadly the years have been punctuated by highly publicised tragic cases, from Maria Colwell onwards, where professionals have got it wrong. In 2003, after the tragic death of Victoria Climbié, the Government produced *Every Child Matters* (ECM), which described the formation of Children's Trusts where local authority education and children's social services as well as some children's health services, Sure Start and Connexions would be brought together to integrate these key services under the Director of Children's Services as part of Children's Trusts. ECM coined the five outcomes that were seen to matter most to children and young people and the role of the school is self-evident:

> *Being healthy: enjoying good physical and mental health and living a healthy lifestyle.*
> *Staying safe: being protected from harm and neglect.*
> *Enjoying and achieving: getting the most out of life and developing skills for adulthood.*
> *Making a positive contribution: being involved with the community and society and not engaging in anti-social or offending behaviour.*
> *Economic well-being: not being prevented by economic disadvantage from achieving their full potential in life.*
>
> (DfES, 2004a, pp. 6–7)

How child protection responsibilities and practice have evolved in primary schools

Teaching in schools over a forty-year period has given one of the authors (SG) a long-term perspective on CP. At the start of her career it was still permissible for teachers to smack children. Knowledge of CP was very rudimentary and not part of training. In the early 1970s CP came to the fore in the aftermath of the Maria Colwell tragedy, when professionals failed to protect her and she was killed by her parents. She was kicked to death by her step-father. Her class teacher is reported as saying:

> *One day Maria burst into tears during a disturbance in the class. She sat on my knee and held her arms round me. I shuddered when I felt how thin she was. She was like a bird, and I was frightened of crushing her.* (Dickson, 2003)

This highlighted the need for CP to be taken more seriously, which was recognised and then influenced the 1975 Children Act. When the other author (AG) worked as a probation officer many years ago, the idea of inter-disciplinary training was only beginning as trust between the professions, especially social services and the police, was not developed (Garrett, 2004). Jean Moore (1985) noted the class divide between the professions, e.g. medicine and the police. She also commented that an abused child was a small part of the teacher's work. Parents would prefer the teacher to spend time educating their child and not be 'side tracked'. The teacher works with groups, whereas the social worker works on a one-to-one basis. The definition of what is a problem is likely to depend on the professional background of the discipline. Writing fifteen years later, Hawtin et al. (2000) discussed the unique position of teachers in relation to child abuse, in terms of recognition, referral, support and prevention. To achieve this, 'teachers need to be able to examine their own feelings and attitudes to the subject.' (ibid., p. 126). Teachers would need to be taught about possible indicators of abuse and what to do if their suspicions were aroused. The authors comment that 'the teacher might be the only adult in a child's life that the child feels he or she can trust with a disclosure . . .' (ibid., p. 126). Finally, they point out that the school has a role to play in empowering children through the communication of information and strategies for self-protection. Children have become much more au fait with the knowledge of sexual abuse in recent times (Renvoize, 1993).

The main role of the primary school is to introduce young children to learning in a formal setting, and to provide them with a wide range of educational opportunities of a high standard. Children in inner cities can start their nursery education at 3 or 4, often leaving their parents or carers for the first time. They attend school for part of 195 days a year, so members of school staff have contact with the children second only to their parents/carers. School staff may spot the withdrawn child, who will rarely say anything, a child cowering when an adult raises a hand; sexualised behaviour which is inappropriate for young children; children whose clothes are always dirty and whose shoes are worn out and far too small; children with unexplained injuries, cuts or bruises. Children are often coerced by family members into hiding what goes on at home. They may not have an understanding about what is acceptable in the interaction between an adult and a child, they may collude, consciously or otherwise, with what is occurring behind closed doors. Thus, for a variety of reasons, professionals are not necessarily aware of these behaviours and incidents. The child's experiences may go unnoticed.

Increasingly, schools are establishing CP teams, as the time commitment required may be great. There needs to be at least one member of the team who does not have a full teaching commitment, as not only do relationships with pupils and their parents need to be established, but the staff member needs time to gather information, prepare reports, check attendance records, attend meetings, and liaise with outside professionals. Meetings can include: formal discussions of concerns with parents or carers; initial meetings with social workers and police; attendance at case conferences; family group conferences and core group meetings looked after reviews; liaison with education welfare officers, nurses, etc.; and the preparation of a Pastoral Education Plan (PEP). It may be that pupils are also on the school's educational special needs register.

Process

When the school is alerted to a concern about a child, there is an agreed school CP policy, but there may not be hard and fast processes, as each concern is handled in an appropriately individualised manner. Each school has developed its own practice. The Common Assessment Framework (CAF) will ensure that the outcomes of the process become more streamlined and consistent.

A typical chain of events when concern is triggered is outlined below:

The CP co-ordinator gathers concerns from person who raised the alert.

One or two members of staff talk to the child, without coercing or asking leading questions. They try to gather some information about the events that triggered the alert. Notes are kept, recording the child's words. If there are siblings in the school, they may also be spoken to.

A decision is made within the CP team about the next step to be taken. The head will be kept informed throughout, and may wish to take a lead. If it is decided that parents/carers should be called in, to discuss the concerns further, the children are informed. The children's responses are noted.

If parents/carers are called to come to the school, they are asked to come as soon as possible. They are informed that something has come to light about which the school has concerns and that school staff would like to discuss it with them.

On parents'/carers' arrival at school, they are spoken to by a senior member of staff, in the presence of another member of staff whenever possible. The concerns are highlighted in the face-to-face meeting, but it is made clear that should there be serious concerns that this will passed to social services as the school does not undertake child protection investigations.

As mentioned above, social services are often contacted during this process, as the school may check whether the family are already known to them, or to talk through the concerns gathered by the school. These may be deemed of such a level that progressing the process to a referral should be made. By making this contact, the school are able to talk to a front-line social worker.

At other times, especially if the family are already known to the authorities, following the phone discussion, a direct referral may be made.

The front-line social services CP team work in conjunction with the police CP team. There are times when the joint CP team decide that it should be the police who come to the school to interview the child. (If the alert comes towards the end of the school day, then the interviewing process may take place within the family home.) The police remit and their methods of interviewing children are different to those of social services and schools. These are discussed in appropriate chapters of this book.

There then may follow a joint assessment involving both police and social services. A decision is made about whether to take the case to conference or not.

An initial case conference may be held shortly after the investigation. Professionals from a variety of agencies are invited.

Even in the most extreme case, when the alert leads to the removal of the child from the family home, the school remain involved, and often form the only point of familiarity, continuity and routine for the child. It is seen by professionals that children should be able to continue to attend the same school, if this is at all possible.

Communications between the groups of professionals are not as straightforward as they could be, and it is anticipated that once the CAF is established, this will clarify and improve the process, as well as cut down the amount of preliminary work which has to be done by individual agencies.

The impact of 'Every Child Matters'

Although not directly focused on schools Lord Laming's report has become a blueprint for the development of joined-up practice in the ensuing publications under the heading of 'Every Child Matters'. Lord Laming in the first Victoria Climbié Memorial Lecture highlighted five deficiencies in how she was treated by professionals. Firstly, he noted that disputes between services as to whether the case was a Section 17 'Child in need' or a Section 47 'Child protection' affected how she was seen. There was no response to the needs of the child until the situation was viewed as a crisis situation. Schools would hope to pick up issues of need before they turn into a crisis and it is essential that other services respond to these and not wait until the situation deteriorates.

Secondly,

> *services focused on the needs of the adults in the life of Victoria . . . she did not feature in the focus of their responses . . . The key message here is that once work gets off on the wrong footing bad practice gets compounded and the situation becomes almost impossible to recover.* (Laming, 2007, p. 4)

Schools, almost by definition, are child-focused and unless the child is very new to the school, they will have some knowledge of how the child copes with everyday life. This experience should be utilised by other professionals.

Thirdly, there was poor recording and use of data across all agencies. Important facts in Victoria's details were missing, such as who authorised her discharge on the second occasion from hospital. In the school there is not necessarily a record of contact with outside agencies like hospitals and generally medical information is still not shared with the school. Thus the danger of lack of communication is still present.

Fourthly, the different staff that dealt with Victoria 'did not follow the basics of good practice and, even more worrying, this was never picked up by their managers.' (ibid.). In the school scenario it is essential that all staff are trained to understand the basics of child protection but this is still not always the case. Newly trained teachers, especially on intensive one-year conversion courses, are not necessarily being given even the most rudimentary insights into child abuse and how schools should react to concerns or be pre-emptive to less dramatic circumstances. All relevant staff with child protection responsibilities should undergo regular refresher training, but the demands of the national curriculum, OFSTED, league tables and SATS outweigh other issues in order to meet Government targets.

The final point is worth quoting in full:

> *Fifthly, the level of communication between the key agencies was seriously deficient. In my view this was due to both to the absence of a shared understanding of each other's respective responsibilities and a destructive lack of trust.* (ibid.)

The school is often not seen as being so important in child protection conferences but, as Laming clearly states, there should be no hierarchy between the different organisations and no organisation is more important than any other. It is worth repeating that children spend more time in school than in any other place outside of the family.

Laming is critical of the roles played by senior managers in all the different services that had contact with Victoria. A head teacher, although not necessarily the person who will deal with child protection issues directly, is the focal point for what goes on within the school, so it should be easier for concerns to be centralised through this person. It is essential therefore that head teachers are trained and regularly updated on child abuse and that this is cascaded down to all staff within the school, to include non-teaching members.

In September 2004 the DfES publication *Safeguarding Children in Education* laid down good practice procedures for schools and further education colleges. Governing bodies have to ensure that schools have 'a child protection policy and procedures in place that are in accordance with locally agreed inter-agency procedures, and that the policy is made available to parents on request' (DfES, 2004b, p. 16). As schools give the opportunity for staff to work with young people it is essential that safe recruitment and vetting procedures are in place. In the event of accusations against members of staff, procedures have to be in place for dealing with allegations.

It is not necessary that the head teacher has to take lead responsibility for dealing with child protection issues but it has to be a senior member of the school's management structure who is not necessarily a teacher. Where there are separate senior and junior parts on different sites or with a separate management line then each part or site requires a designated person. This person must be trained in 'basic child protection training' and have refresher training at two yearly intervals.

> *The head teacher and* all other staff who work with children [our emphasis] *should undertake training that equips them with the knowledge and skills necessary to carry out their responsibilities for child protection that is kept up to date by refresher training at 3 yearly intervals, and temporary staff and volunteers who work with children are made aware of the school's arrangements for child protection and their responsibilities.* (DfES, 2004b, pp. 16–17)

An important role for the school, within the personal, social and health education (PHSE) curriculum, is to make children and young people aware of what is acceptable and unacceptable behaviour (both physical and mental) towards them and how they can keep themselves safe.

The later document restates the need for trained strategic staff in child protection. It is by no means clear that these targets have been achieved either for new staff entering the profession during their training or for employed staff within schools.

CASE STUDY: SEXUAL ABUSE CONCERNS

Claudine was a girl of ten, with complex learning difficulties. All of the siblings in the family had learning difficulties to some extent, and several older ones had already been removed from their mother's care. There were always questions about who her father was, and it was believed that her father may have been her uncle, her mother's brother.

As a result of her learning difficulties, her unkempt presentation and the fact that she did not live in the school's catchment area, Claudine had difficulties making friendships. Questions of neglect arose, and she was closely monitored by school staff. When Claudine was nine years old, she was befriended by another family, about whom members of staff had a sense that sexual abuse might be taking place between the father and his daughters. He was very secretive, and allowed no professionals, especially the school nurse, near his daughters. There was no clear evidence to suggest that he was involved in child sexual abuse, but the children were very subdued and the father, who was very sharp, had formed a relationship with a woman who was withdrawn. She was the mother of three daughters. He was a school governor, and showed an interest in helping out in classes. When the staff's concerns were shared with the head teacher, although there was no evidence, it was decided that he should asked to stop all activities directly involving pupils within the school. No evidence was ever found within the school to raise concerns formally, although he was open about previous allegations made about sexual activities with children relating to his former partner.

Claudine visited this family after school, and came back to school telling her support teacher that she did not want to go there again, as they were asking her to do things she did not want to do. When this was mentioned to her mother and to the father of the friends, they both said that she had lied. The school reported their concerns about Claudine to social services and immediately the second family moved from the area. Claudine and her siblings were removed from their family shortly after, following concerns raised about activities within their own family.

On the very night that Claudine was placed with a foster carer, she started to reveal the extent of the sexual abuse she had encountered, within her own family setting and within the home of the ex-school governor. It was then discovered that her younger brother and baby sister had also been abused by family members. It was never clear who the fathers of any of the children were, and for each of them there were always questions about the male relations within the family. Nothing was ever clarified to confirm the school's concerns.

The school later heard how well Claudine had settled with her new carers, and how she had been able to apply herself far better within her new school, despite her learning difficulties. She was able to take more pride in her appearance once she felt safer in her home environment.

Discussion

This case raises a number of interesting issues. The neglect and sexual abuse that Claudine suffered, combined with her learning difficulties, made her especially vulnerable. Perhaps the father from the other family saw that she was isolated and that she was therefore willing to be befriended. Furthermore he may then have realised that she was sexually experienced and he 'homed in' on her. The school was the vehicle that he used to target children, from a respectable position.

This case stemmed back to the time before all adults, including governors, involved in school matters had to have a Criminal Records Bureau (CRB) check as recommended in the Bichard Inquiry (Home Office, 2004). This is now a minimum safety measure.

Claudine was brought into school, and taken home each day by school coach, as she did not live within the catchment area. Her mother came only for parents' evenings, so there was very little opportunity for members of school staff to establish a relationship with her. Claudine was always very happy to be in school. She talked openly about family members including a sibling who was so profoundly disabled that he never came home from hospital and died before reaching a year. She said very little about what went on within her home, or her extended family.

The school were aware of her mother's inability to parent well. She too had learning difficulties, as had her other children to a varying degree. There were annual review meetings to discuss Claudine's special educational needs, and the progress she was making with her support teacher, but apart from this, there was very little information-sharing. There were concerns about neglect, and communications which resulted in the involvement of social services.

Mainstream school responsibilities

Schools have a number of essential educational tasks and expectations placed on them by the DfES that they must to complete. They monitor attendance and punctuality, highlighting pupils who are frequently late, those not picked up after school, or who rarely complete a whole week without medical evidence. This is the clearest monitored and accountable method of spotting possible or potential abuse, as concerns about attendance often go hand in hand with parents' difficulties with coping. Difficulties experienced include financial, housing, mental health, abuse, domestic violence, drug, alcohol, learning or medical.

Primary school staff have daily contact with most parents and carers of the younger children. They try to build up a rapport with them, which they develop throughout the time that the children remain in the school. Within each school there is a head teacher, who has overall responsibility of running the entire school. This includes pupils, curriculum, staffing, Government guidelines, OFSTED, budget, premises, policies, routines and parents. Staff include teachers, teaching assistants, office staff, lunchtime staff, cleaners and a site supervisor. Increasingly, primary schools have learning mentors who have a pastoral role outside the curriculum and they have opportunities to work with individuals and groups of young people, as well as with significant adults in pupils' lives. Within inner-city settings such as this, there is often a high turn-over of both staff and pupils, many of whom migrate for one reason or another. The annual pupil turn over may exceed 20 per cent. For many pupils and their families, English is an additional language.

Increasingly, primary schools have teaching assistants in classrooms. They often spend break and lunchtimes out in the playground with the children, playing and chatting with them in less formal settings than the classroom. At such times, children are more likely to talk about what is going on outside school or about something that is worrying them. Walking to the library, the park, the swimming pool, standing in the lunch queue, sitting on the bus on a school trip day, are often times when young people share their worries with familiar, and even more importantly, safe adults who have undivided attention for them. Residential trips, which as health and safety measurements increase, are sadly too few and far between, offer staff opportunities to notice habits and fears in the children in their care.

Physical abuse

The case of Maria Colwell highlighted the danger of ignoring serious concerns with the welfare of the child. Cases are not always so clear cut. Within a school children will arrive with cuts and bruises and with a parental explanation about how they were caused. The class teacher may be the first person to take note of this and if they are uneasy they would report the injury to a more senior member of staff or the child protection co-ordinator. There is no statutory requirement to record every bump or bruise. If there is a concern the parent may be asked to explain what had happened and a record may be kept. Each school is left to develop its own recording system, although guidance is given with reference to what specific facts get recorded, as there is an agreed method. There is an understanding that all records kept within the school are subject to the Data Protection Act 1998, and parents have right of access to them. Schools therefore have to be extremely clear about what they record.

CASE STUDY: PHYSICAL ABUSE CONCERNS

Raymond had professional parents. His behaviour was very challenging from the day he, and his brother, arrived at the school. They were both fighting in the playground, independently, from day one. This behaviour continued. When challenged about his violent interaction with others who were strangers to him, Raymond was much more anxious about the school reporting his behaviour to his parents than about getting into trouble with school staff. He was clearly willing to accept the consequences of his unacceptable behaviour from the school. He gradually began to describe punishments that were meted out at home which included being forced to hold a kitchen chair up, over his head, by its legs. When his arms ached, and he began to lower the chair, he was beaten. It was as if he had never been encouraged to develop his own boundaries of acceptable behaviour, but physically punished for what was perceived to be wrong-doing. The parents were immediately called in to discuss what had been reported to the staff by the boy. They were told that this was a child protection concern, and that social services would be informed. A social worker arrived to talk to the parents. The father was honest and acknowledged that he chastised his children in a way in which he felt acceptable. His wife, who appeared to be the more forceful parent, was not so forthcoming. She was very defensive, and verbally confrontational with the visiting social worker. Their legal position was explained to them, and alternative behaviour management within the home was discussed. With the social worker, they also discussed the impact on personal behaviour management of children who are used to being chastised outside school, and therefore never given the opportunity to take responsibility for managing their own behaviour. An agreement was reached that the parents would reconsider their relationship with their children within their home, and that not only would Raymond's behaviour in the playground be monitored, but that the school would be alert to any comments he made at school. Social services retained an overall monitoring role.

Discussion

This is frequently a very difficult cross-cultural issue, in that within some families, physical punishment is perfectly acceptable, but the law in this country forbids it. Such meetings with parents are often the first realisation that the fact they have been physically chastising their children is against the law, and is being noted by professionals. For school staff, conversations like this are extremely challenging but essential, as parents may feel that their parenting skills are being questioned, and they are being humiliated and angry, as their private circumstances have entered a public arena.

However, all staff and parents need to be aware that we operate within the context of legal obligations and constraints of English law and these must be adhered to. (Thus practices like female genital mutilation may be acceptable overseas but are illegal in this country.) Hitting children with belts and other implements will not be acceptable forms of corporal punishment.

The parents were supported by both school staff and a social worker to reflect on their behaviour management techniques. They were given the option of attending a course in which parents were able to discuss the behavioural challenges they experienced with their children within the home and encouraged to share alternative methods of managing such behaviour. The courses were available at the school led by the learning mentor and were also offered by a local voluntary agency. The boy's behaviour gradually became less challenging but he continued to benefit from firm boundaries, which were set for him.

Procedures – theory and practice

Systems of communications within any organisation are vital. Within a school, staff observe and hear a lot. Professionals working in schools are sensitive to the needs and the feelings of the young people in their care, but at the same time, the pressures on schools, as in all public sector settings, are increasing. Being prepared for looming OFSTED is ever present. Curriculum, planning, observation and assessment are demanding on teachers, but as this has increased, so have the number of support staff. They are often the people to whom children will go if they are unhappy or worried. It is these adults who, as part of their role, can be an observer and chat with parents informally. Communications systems have to be excellent. Schools have child protection policies, which alongside all other school policies, should be reviewed annually.

When there are concerns about children, good rapport with parents and carers is vital, as it is a school's duty to inform them of their concerns, and invite them in to discuss them. Such conversations can be tense, and require an empathic manner at the same time as direct information-sharing. These meetings can be extremely traumatic. Parents can feel vulnerable by being forced into opening up an area that they would rather have kept private, or they could hear about observations or conversations about which they know, or claim to know, nothing. On the other hand, this may provide parents with a welcome opportunity to discuss experiences in their lives and events over which they feel they have no control, or about matters they would like help, but have been unable or unwilling to ask.

Each local authority or county council has their own procedure and training package, but the core of the identification and referral process is the same. The CAF will be a national process of information-gathering and sharing, and therefore should ensure that information gaps do not occur. Entries can be made by a number of professional agencies, and each case will have a key worker. As in all public sector areas, different authorities have different needs, be they related to community, staffing, funding or facilities. Responses therefore are not uniform. In a poorer/more stretched local authority, such as Newham, there is always a need for more services for the diverse and ever changing community where English is not the family's first language and the children may have experienced severe trauma which resulted in them fleeing to this country.

The implementation of the CAF as a shared assessment tool in England is now being initiated; it involves many other agencies including educational psychology, social services, education welfare, medical services (nurses, occupational, speech and language therapists and physiotherapists, health visitors, midwives), parents' advocates, Children and Family Court Advisory and Support Service (CAFCAS), child and family consultation service (C&FCS), police, schools for other family members, foster carers and staff from assessment centres, amongst others. Its aim is to enable practitioners to 'develop a shared understanding of a child's needs, so that they can be met more effectively. It will avoid families having to tell and re-tell their story.' (DfES, 2006a) The decision whether to do the assessment within the CAF is a decision that must be made jointly with the child and/or their parent. Furthermore: 'Apart from a pre-natal assessment, it is not possible to do a common assessment without seeing or involving the child.' (DfES, 2006a, p. 15).

Funding issues within, and financial responsibility on the school

The designated school CP co-ordinator must be able and in a position to prioritise work, as initial CP issues do not happen steadily over the year. When they do, other responsibilities have to be put in second place. Staff members need to use the process effectively. Ideally there is a common language between the professionals, although there must also be recognition that each person is viewing the case from a different perspective. The CAF is a confidential online system of recording. Local authorities are increasingly responsible for correct documentation. Such documentation needs to be kept in an agreed way, as the CP team need to have access to it at all times. Time commitment on the part of a school is a large point to be considered when designating a senior member of staff, as their other commitments may need to be covered at short notice, or for meetings. Such meetings are very time-consuming and, with travelling, preparation and debriefing time can take up to four hours.

Conclusion

What may be considered as a CP referral in one area may not reach the same level of concern in another. This could be for a variety of reasons, including workload, regularity of low -level risk, movement of families, and family and cultural expectations. However there should be local area agreements about procedures and it is essential that all staff in schools that have contact and knowledge about children should be trained and familiar with policy and procedures. The CAF is a tool for early intervention to enable a multi-disciplinary approach to working with families. In situations where there is concern of harm or risk of harm then procedures must be followed as set out by the local safeguarding children board (LSCB). Thus there should still be an overall consistency in approach.

Furthermore, all staff should have a regular programme of refresher training as it is all too easy to fall into the trap of assuming that knowledge and skills in this area is a static phenomenon and not a dynamic one. By this we mean that child protection should be on a visible agenda to ensure that staff are aware and alert to the possibility of abuse.

ECM (DfES, 2004a) was full of constructive possibilities for ensuring that inter-disciplinary co-operation became the norm, and it highlighted a number of good practices that could be developed nationally. More specifically for this chapter it commented on the need to look at opportunities for families, especially for the father to become more involved in school life. It talked about working more closely with parents to strengthen their understanding of how to help their child's development. It also stressed the need for a joint approach. All these are fine points in theory. As in all issues dealing with human behaviour, parents can use their child to fight their relationship battles, children sometimes need to be protected from their parents and carers, and from paedophile-inclined professionals. That is why knowledge about child protection in the age of the Internet is vital. This is a potentially traumatising and dangerous area for young people: consequently it calls for vigilance and a suitably trained workforce. Regularly updated knowledge and skills have to be the order of the day.

Chapter 10

Minimising the risk to children and young people

The police response

Chris Bourlet

Introduction

Victoria Climbié died on 25 February 2000. On 12 January 2001 Victoria's great-aunt, Marie-Therese Kouao, and Carl John Manning were convicted of her murder. Victoria's death was tragic enough but it wasn't just the 128 separate injuries recorded on her young body that sent shockwaves through the child protection community. It was the identification of a catalogue of systematic errors that resulted in all the key agencies failing to protect Victoria. Lord Laming chaired a public inquiry into Victoria's case which discovered that on twelve key occasions an intervention could have been made to save Victoria. Laming made 108 recommendations and this chapter considers how the Metropolitan Police Service (MPS) responded to the challenge set out by the public inquiry and made sweeping changes to better protect children from harm.

Policies, practices and systems in child protection are changing in a variety of ways. In fact, over the years they have been in a state of flux, due often to the impact of another preventable tragedy occurring. In 1973 Maria Colwell died at the hands of her stepfather despite over thirty calls from neighbours to social services. Even though practices were refined, lessons highlighted and learnt, and with communication improving between child protection agencies, there have been further victims who have died at the hands of their carers since this tragic event. In fact, nearly every year there have been cases highlighted which reveal child victims to whom closer attention should have been paid by the appropriate authorities and which then could have prevented harm coming to them.

Victoria's legacy was the government review of child protection resulting in the 'Every Child Matters' agenda. This new policy aims to raise awareness, improve multi-agency working, and protect children better in the future than they have been in the past. The central aim of this strategy is to ensure that every child, no matter what their background or circumstances may be, should have the support they need to be healthy, stay safe, enjoy and achieve, make a positive contribution, and achieve economic well-being.

In this chapter I show the level of police response, the policy changes, the reorganisation, and how the investigation of child deaths has become highly committed and professionalised. These changes have caused the Metropolitan Police Service to develop new methods and procedures which have become more proactive rather than reactive, and have moved from solving a crime after it has been committed to intervention and prevention. The changes were not straightforward, and along the way a number of problems and challenges for policing practice have surfaced.

Investigating child abuse

The investigation of child abuse is one of the most challenging within the police service, for although the three basic elements of policing – intelligence, prevention and enforcement – are present they apply more in child abuse cases than in any other crime. The challenge lies in the combination of volume, complexity and risk not faced in any other type of police work. The MPS deals with at least 100,000 reports of children coming to its notice every year. Most of those reports will be of limited concern to any of the child protection agencies and only a small proportion will be crimes to be investigated by the police. However, the very nature of child abuse by their carers is that the crime is hidden away and often committed in the privacy of the home. A misplaced accusation of abuse can have a dramatic impact on a family; as of course can be missing the signs of abuse. Child abuse investigators always try to place the best interests of the child first, and deciding on what course of action to take in a child protection case is rarely clear or straightforward, but it is none the less crucial. Additionally, these decisions cannot be made in isolation. Child abuse investigators need to work with a wide range of partners from social services, health, education and others, all circumstances which add to the complexity and challenge of communicating effectively. Although there are, thankfully, only a handful of child homicides each year, there have been several high-profile cases over the past thirty-five years which were potentially preventable, thus demonstrating the extreme risk when the agencies get it wrong. These notable and highly publicised child deaths have included Maria Colwell in 1974, Jasmine Beckford in 1984, Heidi Koseda in 1985, Kimberley Carlile in 1986 and Victoria Climbié in 2000. It is fair to say that the case of Victoria Climbié became the watershed for change. Lord Laming in his report concluded that the legal framework was effective; it was the implementation of the system that was flawed and acerbated by poor management and leadership in the child protection field.

The death of Stephen Lawrence and the ensuing public inquiry led to the MPS fundamentally reviewing the professionalism of its murder investigation systems which led to a cultural change in how race and diversity were addressed by the police. In addition, the death of Victoria and Laming's report achieved similar major changes.

Development of police teams

The first child abuse teams in London were formed in the late 1980s and became known as Child Protection Teams (CPTs) in the early 1990s. Policing in London was organised into geographical 'Areas' like spokes of a wheel. Each Area consisted of a number of police divisions, known as Operational Command Units (OCUs), plus a headquarters consisting of support functions. It was here that the CPT was housed under the Crime OCU, which also consisted of murder teams and proactive crime squads. The weakness of this organisational structure was highlighted in the public inquiry, as the CPT were often perceived as being of low importance and under-resourced, and responsibility for the teams at senior level was, to say the least, confused. These units were often staffed by uniform officers with limited detective training and investigative experience. Systems to manage referrals from other agencies, and expertise, also varied from team to team. The opportunity for error to turn to tragedy was present because the conditions for 'organisational malaise' as Lord Laming described it, were clearly evident, albeit only with the gift of hindsight.

In 2000, Sir John Stevens became the Commissioner and moved the MPS towards a borough-based policing model in order to align the police with the new Crime and Disorder Partner-ships across the capital. Consequently Areas were abolished, thus creating a requirement for a new model to deliver the specialist policing functions. In the very week that Victoria died, it was decided to break up the old Crime OCUs into their constituent parts and re-form them into specialised OCUs within a new centralised Serious Crime Group. Within that group, the first specialist OCU of child abuse investigators was formed and given the title of Specialist Operations 5, or SO5 for short.

The main advantage of a centralised command was the MPS's ability to push through the change of programme required to meet the demands of Laming's recommendations and take the protection of children to a higher level. The formation of SO5 allowed the MPS not only to bring together a variety of child-related departments under one group but also to think about and develop co-ordinated strategies designed to put the care of children at the forefront of policy. The new department covered a variety of aspects relating to child-related offences and was designed not only to be reactive to events but also proactive in attempting to predict offending behaviour, which will be referred to later. Also brought within the remit of SO5 were the Paedophile Unit and Major Investigation Teams – originally tasked to investi-gate complex historic children's home abuse investigations – later to take responsibility for child homicides. Although too late for Victoria, the advantage of such a model provided the MPS with the ability to find solutions to the criticisms Laming was to identify later. This was referred to as the Change Programme.

One main problem originating from the Laming Inquiry was the issue of accountability and this meant that any new command structure had to have clear lines of responsibility and line management. The OCU had a Detective Chief Superintendent in overall command with a Chief Officer supervising strategic issues from a central perspective, thus satisfying Laming's demands for accountability. The staffing and the availability of resources for CPT were documented for the first time, allowing for greater transparency and accountability rather than being hidden away as part of a multi-faceted Crime OCU where the voice of children could be lost. Consistency of approach is a long-standing problem in policing, but the new structure offered a solution for each CPT in the new OCU to work to the same standard operating procedures. This was further supported by the launch of the London Child Protection Committee (LCPC) pan-London protocols in 2002.

The MPS, because it is the largest of the forty-three police forces in England and Wales, often has the ability to produce policies and procedures for change ahead of others. Because the UK has a locally based policing structure rather than a national force, one size does not fit all.

Other forces around the country find the MPS model difficult and challenging for reasons of organisational structure, resourcing and resilience. Generally, smaller forces tend to prefer a variant to the MPS model, using a devolved structure, with only child protection policy centralised. One criticism of this set-up is that the focus on children can be diluted by the demands of other investigative priorities, but it has the advantage of integrating the various operational family protection elements, such as domestic violence, into a more holistic overview.

The Change Programme

The first Commissioners of the Metropolis, Rowan and Mayne, stated in 1829 that the primary objectives of policing were the prevention and detection of crime. Although Laming praised the murder investigation which followed the death of Victoria, when a public inquiry concludes that the MPS failed in its primary objectives and failed a vulnerable child, a substantial and concerted response is required to promote positive change. The MPS does have a good record in responding to such challenges – the Lawrence Inquiry has led to fundamental cultural change in procedures and attitudes in policing. Therefore the introduction of a change programme to address the weaknesses of the Laming criticisms should perhaps not have been surprising. The amount of change required to achieve the desired results in a large organisation needed substantial commitment and leadership from managers at all levels in the MPS. Not only is there organisational 'inertia' to be overcome in order to implement change, but child protection did not feature in national policing plans; there were no police targets to achieve. Reducing burglary and robbery can be easily measured and therefore often attract managerial focus and resources – what gets measured, gets done. In spite of the dice being loaded against child protection, senior managers recognised the need for a major change programme. Set up within Specialist Operations under the command of Assistant Commissioner David Veness, who oversaw the changes and much of the reorganisation, the programme was driven by the enthusiasm of certain Chief Officers such as DAC Bill Griffiths and Commanders Carole Howlett and Dave Armond. Established under the newly formed Serious Crime Group, child protection was restructured in London and child protection gradually fought its way into the National Policing Plan priorities. These measures raised the awareness and importance of child protection in policing terms.

The first major step was to actually set up the Operational Command Unit – the basic organisational structures to bring together the disparate units from the old Area model. Administration staff were required to manage finance and human resources for about 600 police officers and staff. This required accommodation, budgets, vehicles, stores, trainers, policy writers and so on. Under the leadership of a Detective Chief Superintendent the largest group of child abuse investigators in the world slowly came together. The basic building blocks were now in place, but to address the concerns of Laming and move the police service forward in professionalising child protection a co-ordinated change programme was required.

A small team of experts and professionals were gathered together in order to set up and manage the process. What was to follow not only mapped out a programme of change but also took the MPS beyond the requirements and expectations originally set out by Lord Laming.

Changing structure

The importance of a structure for the new organisation of child protection post-Laming was more than merely logistical. The new structure had to be able to demonstrate the accountability demanded by Laming to enable quality service delivery at the front line. Secondly, to drive through the changes required effective leadership was needed, which, in a hierarchical police rank structure, needed clear lines of communication to allow the change programme to roll out. Communication across over twenty geographical locations where the teams were actually based across London would present challenges to the management of the programme. Workshops were held to forge the new structures, consulting staff, partners, HMIC and even Lord Laming himself.

From these discussions and consultations, London was divided into four administrative regions, each headed by a Detective Chief Inspector, clustering the CPT (each led by a Detective Inspector) into manageable groups. A borough alignment for the CPTs was maintained, but with some boroughs brigaded for economies of scale and practicality. A formula was devised to provide some objective assessment of workload per officer, which then determined the size of the teams. As time progressed, the command moved towards more brigading to provide greater resilience.

From the ad hoc inquiry teams set up to address complex child abuse investigations, two Major Investigation Teams (MITs) were created with responsibility for East and West London. These teams provided the basis for investigation of suspicious child death, Sudden Infant Death Syndrome (SIDS or cot deaths), and complex and serious child abuse cases. The two MITs provided additional capacity both for proactive work, mainly against paedophile networks, and also providing support for work by the CPTs when additional resources were required. The MIT also provided the capacity and opportunity to increase the professionalisation of dealing with child death.

Under the Headquarters operations were clustered other specialist functions. Training and policy work was co-ordinated from here and a partnership and prevention unit was set up to promote a range of innovative projects tackling child protection issues. Operation Paladin Child scoped the emergence of trafficked children through Heathrow Airport, resulting in the formation of a multi-agency Ports Safeguarding team.

Following requests from operational detectives investigating child deaths from London and beyond, it was recognised that available information fell short of requirements and that the command needed an intelligence management capacity with the ability to respond 24/7. The intelligence unit was formed in accordance with the National Intelligence Model, which provides a structured intelligence system to support both reactive and proactive work against child abuse. The unit provided intelligence support to the Paedophile Unit, and a Source Unit which managed informants who were connected loosely to paedophilia and child abuse. A child abuse detective was posted to New Scotland Yard in the Specialist Crime operations room to provide out-of-hours expert advice and co-ordination capability. An on-call set-up was also arranged to ensure that any critical incident would receive expert child abuse input.

Intelligence functions grew to cover the emerging use of technology to abuse children with the formation of the High Tech Crime Unit, which was able to tackle child abuse on the internet and which soon achieved an international reputation for its capabilities. The Intel Unit produced information on patterns of child abuse, enabling more efficient targeting of resources, and could respond to emerging threats such as concerns regarding paedophiles targeting children affected by the Tsunami of 2004.

Whilst structure is important, Laming identified that the quality of leadership as being crucial to improving the service delivery at the front end of policing.

Improving leadership

With the internal structure of the OCU completed, the work to change the capabilities of the organisation could begin. Lines of accountability ran from Chief Officer level through to the OCU Commander, and down through the Senior Management Team to the individual CPT on the front line. The MPS also decided to professionalise the leadership within its review function. As a result, a team of dedicated review officers, experienced in child protection issues, were formed to provide the police input to Chapter 8 reviews – so-called because the guidance is found in chapter 8 of *Working Together to Safeguard Children* (DfES, 2006b). They conduct reviews of cases, examining practice and procedure, and enabling the organisation to continue to learn and improve. Dissemination of the learning is achieved through training, workshops and the modification of policy, all of which is recommended through an OCU policy board.

The culture associated with child protection in the MPS had come under intense scrutiny during the public inquiry. The 'Cardigan Squad' was one of the terms used to describe the old CPT when they were attached to an Area and this label reflected the perception of a lack of commitment and prioritisation given to child protection. The aim of the change programme was to professionalise child abuse investigation. Its first task was to change the name and so the Child Protection Command became the Child Abuse Investigation Command, CPT became Child Abuse Investigation Teams or CAIT – where the emphasis on the term 'Investigation' highlighted the 'what it says on the tin' message. It was important to raise the status and capability of child protection staff, so all investigating officers were elevated to substantive Detectives. This meant that they received the full training given to other detective departments in the MPS rather than just to 'branch' detectives, a title given to uniform officers on attachment. The national accreditation scheme for Detectives, which professionalised the Investigative Process, was piloted on the OCU and ensured that minimum standards of investigation were implemented across the whole command.

In his evidence to Lord Laming, DAC Bill Griffiths, Head of the Serious Crime Group, had stated that in the A to Z of investigation Victoria's case had not got past B. Not only was increasing the capability of the investigators crucial, but also the supervision of investigations. A supervision model was introduced, building on MPS corporate policy to ensure high-risk investigations were suitably supported. Complex situations such as 'Fabricated' or 'Induced Illness' and historic child abuse allegations were addressed through a range of workshops in order to improve training, influence policy and re-define guidance. Leadership days were also held to support managers and share experiences.

Applying sufficient resources

Sufficient resources are essential for any change programme to be effective and the CPT had been criticised for not being sufficiently resourced and funded under the old Area model. Secondly, the quality and quantity of resources are often seen by staff as a benchmark of the value placed by the organisation upon them. CPT accommodation was often described as 'Dickensian' and totally inadequate for the provision of quality service to young child victims of crime. This led to an accommodation strategy to upgrade the building stock to support child protection across the capital. Of course, property development time-scales are more costly and long-term than operational ones, but the OCU gained substantially improved accommodation across London in the years following the publication of the Laming report. This strategic move saw a shift towards more brigading of units into purpose-built sites with family-friendly interview suites and modern standards of office accommodation for staff. HQ functions were brought together in a modern office block, which improved lines of communication in the senior management team.

Sharing of information is crucial in the effective protection of children. Substantial challenges lay ahead in sharing information between agencies, as pre-Laming CPT had stand-alone computer systems, and passing of information between front-line uniform officers and CPTs relied on paper forms sent through unreliable internal despatch. The change programme introduced a networked IT system called Merlin which enables officers to record information electronically and in a form which is searchable throughout the whole MPS. Whilst these are still early days, work continues to improve the functionality as more and more improvements are demanded from the system so as to make information flow more accessible and efficient. Eventually the aim is to tie the Merlin system into a database with a national information-sharing capability.

Supporting systems

Structure and leadership will count for little if the systems employed are not fit for purpose. It became evident during the public inquiry that the systems employed to protect children in London were too ad hoc and varied across the city. Receipt and control of referrals into a CPT seemed to rely upon whoever answered the phone, regardless of their capability or capacity to do so. In response to these criticisms, a 'Referral Desk' was introduced in every CPT, which was staffed by a supervisor responsible for the decision-making process, and new processes were designed to systematically handle incoming information. Instead of relying on subjective professional judgement and experience, more objective criteria were applied, backed up by a documented risk assessment. On the downside, Referral Desks increased the bureaucracy of the system but improved the accountability of the decision-making and provided protection for the decision maker through improved documentation.

Since the introduction of Referral Desks, efforts have been made to improve the efficiency of the systems employed. This could be achieved through single key searches of police information (an important priority in many other areas of policing), better use of IT through secure use of email, and increased brigading of administrative functions to achieve efficiencies of scale with regionally based Referral Desks.

To provide a more accountable management of crime investigations, the command introduced its own Crime Management Unit – each front line Borough OCU has a CMU to manage the administration of the MPS Crime Recording Information System (CRIS). The unit acts as a quality assurance system to manage the complexity of crime investigation administration. Through the CMU the command was able to introduce minimum investigative standards and drive up the overall quality of crime investigation. The MPS standard operating procedures for child abuse investigation were largely adopted in the national standards introduced by the National Police Improvement Agency (NPIA) in 2004.

In an effort to drive increased efficiency and harmonise working with partners at case conference level, the MPS introduced Police Conference Liaison Officers (PCLOs), who were members of police staff (i.e. not police officers). These dedicated staff members were tasked with partnership liaison with social services so as to manage the progress of ongoing child care case conferences. Not only did this allow police officers to be released back to crime investigation but PCLO also were able to improve the quality of files and paperwork within the CAIT.

Aiding partnership working

The whole theory of safeguarding children is based on the ability of the different agencies involved to be able to work together. The change programme did not challenge this fundamental assumption, but there was a period of reclarification as to how the CPT worked with other agencies, in particular social services. The focus placed on professionalising the investigative process in child abuse made the police rethink the whole system. Police no longer did 'joint investigations' but worked in partnership with social workers. It was felt that the boundary of responsibilities had become blurred between the different professions and that the police had to clarify the role officers were expected to undertake. The method of joint investigations have changed. Joint investigations were previously viewed as the two branches of a police criminal investigation and social services child care assessment coming together in the shape of a letter 'Y'. However, since Laming was critical of this approach the police have adopted an 'H' method of police investigation where parallel inquiries with the social services are linked together as in the letter 'H' – a subtle but important distinction. This approach has increased the value of communication and information sharing and recognises the need for a clearly defined frame of reference for each part of the investigation. Sometimes however, it has been perceived by partners that the police pulled back from truly working together through this approach.

To overcome such views, work was undertaken to build on partnership training such as the high tech Multi-Agency Critical Incident Exercise, which brought partner agencies together in a high tech, immersive training environment (named Hydra). Joint training was undertaken both through the MPS central training unit and locally through Area Child Protection Committees (latterly Local Safeguarding Children Boards). The police played a key role in the development of the London Child Protection Committee (now the London Safeguarding Board) promoting a pan-London approach to strategic issues across the capital. Regional Partners' meetings were facilitated by the police to engage local child protection managers from a range of agencies on emerging issues.

Another advantage of the change programme was that the MPS now had a central point of contact for agencies to come to. This was particularly important to the voluntary sector and non-governmental organisations such as the NSPCC and Barnardo's, amongst many others. Ministers and mayors visited the command and relations with other key organisations in combating child abuse were also formalised and strengthened. For example, regular meetings were held with Great Ormond Street Hospital and projects addressing the sexual exploitation of young people were initiated with Barnardo's. Such relationships helped drive forward joint child protection agendas.

One of the challenges of working in the MPS is the scale of the operation. The MPS covers thirty-two London boroughs, each an independent organisation. Overlay Government departments, primary care trusts and voluntary organisations – each with their own regional structures – and strategic partnership working becomes even more challenging. Area Child Protection Committees (now Local Safeguarding Children Boards) fulfilled a co-ordinating role at the local level and the formation of the London Child Protection Committee (now the London Safeguarding Children Board) did the same on a pan-London level. Supported by the London councils – an umbrella organisation for local government in London – the committee consisted of representatives from all the relevant agencies to address strategic partnership issues for London. The MPS, as one of the few pan-London organisations, was helped by the LCPC to drive through elements of the change programme for mutual benefit. The first success was to gain acceptance of the need for child protection procedures that could be adopted across the capital so that practice and procedures would be the same in every London borough. This work went hand in hand with standardisation of operating procedures in the CPT within the MPS. Further ground-breaking work has been undertaken with London leading the debate on child protection issues nationally. Recognising the change in accountability with the Children Act 2004 and the move towards Safeguarding Boards, LSCB chairs were given more representation on the London Board and supported the work of the Board through a London Chairs sub-committee.

Information-sharing

Originating from the 2004 Bichard Inquiry, the handling of information for police purposes and use by others was the subject of intense scrutiny in the wake of the double child murders of Holly Wells and Jessica Chapman in August 2002. During the murder inquiry it was discovered that the murderer Ian Huntley had managed to obtain employment as a school caretaker in Soham, Cambridgeshire, even though there was information available in Humberside, a neighbouring police force, which tended to indicate he was a real threat to children. Information on Huntley was either mishandled mislaid, destroyed or neglected when certain checks relating to his character were carried out. Nothing of substance was found or communicated that alerted the authorities inquiring into his background and suitability for the position of school caretaker.

As a result of the Bichard Inquiry the handing of information held and managed by police was reviewed, leading to the development of the IMPACT programme (Information Management, Prioritisation, Analysis, Co-ordination and Tasking). This led to significant changes in working practices, and also technology, to greatly reduce the risk of the kind of failings in information-sharing which formed part of the background to the Soham murders. Part of the programme was the production and development of a comprehensive code of practice on police information management that came into effect in November 2005. The programme and codes of practice were supported by extensive training and operational guidance. The introduction of new technology also enables information-sharing between forces for Child Abuse Investigation Units was brought into use at the end of 2005. This new capacity for sharing information, together with a development capability, is an ongoing process and will be progressively extended as systems develop through to 2009 and beyond.

Diversity

Although Laming said little in his final report regarding diversity and racism, the change programme developed a greater understanding of community issues in relation to child abuse than the MPS could have grasped without the development of a specialist child abuse command. In the first instance Mr and Mrs Climbié visited the command at New Scotland Yard to unveil a memorial to their daughter. Their challenge to the new command was: 'The community were the only ones who tried to help Victoria, what are you doing to help the community?'

The first response was to sponsor a Community Partnership Project working in two London boroughs with two consultants tasked with engaging with communities regarding child abuse issues. The project built bridges of trust with communities and highlighted an assortment of concerns ranging from physical chastisement to spirit possession. A leaked copy of the report led to sensationalistic out-of-context reporting by the press but it also led to the successful Project Violet that sought to support communities. (See Chapter 6 for further information on this police-led initiative.) Amongst some of the matters dealt with by this initiative were spirit possession and female genital mutilation (FGM), projects that gained the MPS national recognition for their positive work. The Community Partnership Project developed further, receiving funding from the Government and London Safeguarding Board to enable it to expand the work into a further eight London boroughs, engaging with London's diverse communities to help reduce child abuse.

To support the development of the change programme to realise Laming's aim of improving front-line service delivery, a key element of the progress of the programme was the involvement of a new Safeguarding Children Independent Advisory Group (IAG). IAGs had originally come about in the MPS following the Lawrence report, but have grown to advise the police on a wide range of operational and policy issues from a community perspective. The Safeguarding IAG provided advice and support to the change programme and beyond, providing relevant advice and reassurance that the programme was still heading in the right direction.

Internal diversity was also playing a key part in developing success from the change programme. The command consists of over 50 per cent female police officers, a higher proportion than other similar-sized commands, and significantly more than other specialist detective commands. Work was done to support and promote opportunities for women in the organisation, such as flexible working opportunities, workshops and additional training. The nature of the work is not always easy and so all members of staff were supported by regular counselling and welfare assistance.

Beyond Laming

The change programme not only began to address the main concerns of the Laming report but, by creating such a momentum of change, other benefits not envisaged at the beginning have started to emerge. The death of any child, even in accidental or natural circumstances, is a tragic and heart-rending situation for parents, carers and police to cope with. Cot death is one of the most challenging situations for the police since most cases are simple tragedies or accidents, but each needs careful and sensitive investigation to ensure no foul play. The 'Back to Sleep' campaign in the 1990s dramatically reduced the overall numbers of cot deaths or SIDS. However, the police response was fragmented and patchy in London, and because of the number of murder investigation teams spread across the capital, there was no centre of excellence in the investigation of unexplained child death. Project Indigo sought to improve the quality of the investigation into the deaths and the service given to grieving parents. The decision was made that intra-familial homicides would be investigated by the Child Abuse Major Investigation Teams, and the initial investigation of SIDS would be undertaken by the CAIT Detective Inspector rather than front-line borough-based police officers as had previously been the case. Although the number of suspicious deaths is small in number, the two MITs soon developed a great deal of expertise and experience as they dealt with about a dozen or so homicides a year. Child Abuse Senior Investigating Officers (SIOs) have become expert in areas such as 'Shaken Baby Syndrome' and 'Which One of You Did It' cases. Training and support was given to the CAIT on the complexity and challenges that dealing with a SIDS case can create, including input from parents who had lost children. The change programme has led to a dramatic improvement to the quality of service that a child can expect in London from the police

In many areas of policy development, the MPS has been able to drive safeguarding forward. The command had strong links with the national co-ordination of child protection and, in partnership with the London Safeguarding Board, was able to influence policy and practice on a range of issues, such as forced marriage, FGM and the development of child death screening teams.

The broadening of the 'Every Child Matters' agenda into Safeguarding has resulted in a similar broadening of responsibility for the protection of children in the MPS that takes us beyond Laming. The change programme, initiated by a dedicated team of passionate investigators of child abuse, has now been taken on by other parts of the MPS in order to address the demands of Government legislation introduced under Sections 10 and 11 of the Children Act 2004 to ensure the well-being of children. Of course the safeguarding of children does not rest with one small part of the policing organisation, and the Every Child Matters Programme Board for the MPS is now led by Territorial Policing, which has responsibility for policing the 32 boroughs. The migration of responsibility for managing the change from a specialist policing command to the more generalist Territorial Policing acknowledges the role that the whole of policing has to play in safeguarding children. It has a new programme of work being undertaken to meet the requirements of the new Act and safeguard the futures of the millions of children living in London.

Conclusions

One of the aims of this chapter was to highlight the problems, dilemmas and challenges facing the police in protecting children given the criticisms brought to light from the Laming Inquiry. Its most important objective though, was to show how the MPS reacted to the mistakes made and the challenges it faced in learning from them.

This took the form of the change programme which was implemented by the MPS to deal with the faults in the system and, in doing so, set out to professionalise the police response by ensuring the effective investigation and prevention of child abuse in London. Significant benefits have come about as a result of the change programme. The investigation of child abuse or child death is now recognised as being more of a challenge for police investigators than is the case if the victim is an adult. This makes it all the more important to raise the status and standards of investigation in child protection matters especially given its complexity. Raising standards to increase the level of professionalism in this difficult area was one of the over-riding principles. Casework is now allocated according to a given formula rather than being taken on by whoever happened to be in the office at the time or answered the telephone. In this way there is a fairer distribution of casework and also the monitoring of standards is made easier.

Against the backdrop of increased professional standards has been the introduction of new methods and procedures that have galvanised and regenerated child protection staff to be more proactive rather than reactive, thus ensuring that prevention is the key. Changes have required root and branch treatment from the top and down to the very bottom. Improving structures, reorganising and amalgamating staff who jointly work in child-related areas under one command has not only helped the flow of information up and down the chain of command but also broadened responsibility, improved leadership and accountability. Outside the organisation information-sharing is being developed amongst partners. Although the nature of policing in England and Wales presents its own problem with its forty-three autonomous force areas, change beyond the MPS will progress at a different pace and with varying amounts of success since not all chief officers will be in a position to allocate appropriate resources to the same degree.

Here I have shown many of the challenges which were faced in order to ensure change. It is often said that the police culture is resistant to change, but this has not been the experience of child protection in the MPS. If anything staff have seen an improvement in status, have been rewarded with new systems and better technology, and benefited from cleaner and more professional working conditions. The new methods have also created a momentum of their own producing benefits previously un-envisaged during the planning stages. Economies of scale have also been shown to have a positive benefit since the pooling of resources, amalgamating staff, sharing in expertise and good practice offers a better chance of success. Chapter 8 reviews also ensure that casework is monitored in such a way that it will be more proactive when it comes to intervention in problematic cases.

The programme continues as the MPS moves towards addressing the broadening challenge of the 'Every Child Matters' agenda. Even with all the systems implemented and prevention strategies in place, it is an unfortunate fact that some children will still be abused and killed by those expected to care for them. Victoria's legacy is that there is a team of dedicated, skilled and passionate professionals who will stand up for the rights of those children whose voices cannot be heard.

WEBSITES

Home Office (2006) *Every Child Matters – Working Together To Safeguard Children 2006 – A guide to interagency working to safeguard and promote the welfare of children*. www.cambslscb.org.uk/leaflets/Working%20Together%20to%20Safeguard%20Children.pdf.

LCPC (2006) *Community Partnership Project Final Report*. www.londoncpc.gov.uk.

Morris Inquiry (2004) *Report by Sir Bill Morris into the Way the Metropolitan Police Service (MPS) is Managed*. www.morrisinquiry.gov.uk/default.htm.

National Police Improvement Agency (2004) *Guidance on Investigation of Child Abuse*. www.mpa.gov.uk/committees/ppr/2007/070116/07.htm.

Victoria Climbié Inquiry: Report of an Inquiry by Lord Laming. www.victoria-climbie-inquiry.org.uk/finreport/finreport.htm.

Chapter 11

Statutory social work processes involving children

Prostitution and other areas of vulnerability

Nic Hinrichsen and Anthony Goodman

Background

This chapter outlines the stages of the statutory social work agency processes in the investigation and subsequent response-planning in relation to concerns that there may be reasonable cause to suspect that a child is suffering or is likely to suffer significant harm. This information is essential, for it is based on the process stages identified in the Quality Protects Children's Social Services Core Information Requirements with reference to the Integrated Children's System (ICS) framework for working with children in need and their families and on *Every Child Matters – Working Together to Safeguard Children*.

It is a process overview designed to give the reader an understanding of the sequence of events and stages of social work involvement. It is not intended as a comprehensive guide to each of the specific stages. The particular example of children involved in prostitution will be drawn on as an exemplar of vulnerable young people. This client group is not always easy to help and indeed they may reject assistance, not least because 'help' may be synonymous with exploitation. The chapter concludes on the interrelationship between protection and punishment and the implications for children involved in prostitution, whereby punishment is conflated with protection so that a punitive response is seen as being in the best interests of the child (Phoenix, 2004).

The Government's view of professional responsibilities was spelt out in *Safeguarding Children Involved in Prostitution: Supplementary Guidance to Working Together to Safeguard Children* (SCIP) (May 2000). The sections of the Children Act that it refers to are detailed later in the chapter:

All professionals must be able to recognise situations where children might be involved in, or are at risk of becoming involved in, prostitution. They should treat such children as children in need [section 17 of the Children Act 1989], who may be suffering, or may be likely to suffer, significant harm [section 47 of the Children Act 1989]. Services that come into contact with these children have a responsibility to safeguard and promote their welfare and to co-operate effectively to prevent children becoming involved in, and to divert children out of, prostitution. (p. 9)

David Barrett (1997) commented that social policies towards children both contributed to them entering prostitution and made it difficult for them to leave. Yet, those under 18 were then supposed to be protected by the Children Act 1989 as they include those who are 'children in need', 'at risk' of 'significant harm', which should invoke procedures as laid down in statute. Swann and Balding (2001) were commissioned by the Department of Health to provide basic quantitative data on how well SCIP was working. The Government published its *National Plan for Safeguarding Children from Commercial Sexual Exploitation* in September 2001. Swann in her introduction to the report highlighted that children were being bought and sold for sex in the UK and this was not an overseas issue or problem.

Her three diagrams, reproduced below from the report, demonstrated that language defined perceptions and attitudes:

Figure 1. Prostitution/Sex Industry Triangle

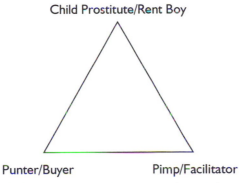

The first triangle implied that young people were making informed choices about their lifestyle.

The second triangle re-labels the participants from being part of the sex industry to being part of an abusing relationship.

Figure 2. Abuse Triangle

By inverting this in the third triangle the focus is put firmly on to the 'abusers and coercers' and not on the pathology of the young person or victim.

Figure 3. Prosecution/Protection Triangle

(Diagrams from Swann and Balding (2001))

In the SCIP supplementary guidance, a model developed by Barnado's on how young girls may be abused is described. It is essentially an entrapment model where the young girl is identified by an older man and is then groomed into becoming emotionally dependent on him and detached from other influences, both family and friends. Then emotional and physical violence is used to progress her into selling sex for money. For boys and young men it draws on the experience of an organisation providing support to victims, Streetwise Youth. In this model many of the boys and young men experience homophobic reactions to their sexuality and are left unsupported and vulnerable. They may have suffered a multiplicity of neglect, sexual, physical and emotional abuse, as well as separation from one or both of their parents (DOH, 2000, pp. 15–16).

The story of 'Louise' given in Barrett (1997) is a harrowing tale of abuse, official indifference and rejection by her mother. It is the systemic failure of and by authority to a child in need who ended up working as a child prostitute feeling trapped, without escape. The SCIP document is explicit that the identification of a child being actually involved or at risk of becoming involved in prostitution should always trigger the intervention of the local Area Child Protection Committee (ACPC) both for the sake of the child and to gather evidence about the 'abusers and coercers'. (SCIP, May 2000, p. 9)

Swann and Balding (2001) found mixed reactions to child prostitution by the 146 ACPCs, with 111 ACPCs saying that this was an area that they needed to address:

> 76 per cent of ACPCs said that there were children involved in prostitution in their area,
> 5.5 per cent did not know,
> 90.9 per cent of the 111 ACPCs who said that children were involved in prostitution in their area indicated that girls were involved,
> 62.2 per cent of the 111 ACPCs who said that children were involved in prostitution in their area indicated that boys were involved,
> 49.65 per cent of the 111 ACPCs who said that children were involved in prostitution in their area indicated that girls and boys were involved,

8.1 per cent of the 111 ACPCs who said that children were involved in prostitution in their area could not give a gender breakdown of children involved.

The degree of proactive activity varied greatly, with some areas demonstrating good pro-activity through outreach work, whilst others did not perceive there to be a problem, indeed two areas 'seemed horrified and outraged that it may have been suggested that they had any young people involved in their area' (ibid., p. 4). They reported one respondent's classic understatement: 'We have 3 or 4 girls involved here, I call them the "good time girls".' (ibid., p. 5).

This can be contrasted with the findings of Pearce et al. (2003) that focused on case studies of fifty-five young women at risk of, or experiencing, sexual exploitation and/or prostitution. They were aged between 13 and 18 years and had histories of physical or sexual abuse, heroin use, running away from home, truanting, getting into unknown men's cars. This would not appear to be consistent with 'good time girls' and underlines the ignorance and naiveté of that comment. Most had been abused and/or been the victim of violence from older men, including abduction and rape. The researchers produced a typology whereby the women fell into three categories of risk: firstly those who were at risk of exploitation; secondly those who swapped sex for favours, including accommodation etc.; thirdly those who were self-defined as prostitutes (see diagram 3, Swann and Balding).

Cusick et al. (2003) interviewed 125 young people with experience of sex work and drug use and found that there were three significant 'trapping factors' namely:

Involvement in prostitution and/or hard drug use before the age of 18,
Outdoor sex work or as an 'independent drifter',
experience of at least one additional vulnerability indicator such as being 'looked after' in local authority care or being homeless. (ibid., 2003, p. v)

In regard to the last factor 78 per cent of the group had been 'looked after' by their local authority and of these 71 per cent had been living in or had run from local authority care when they had first prostituted. That many of these children were already in contact with services led to a recommendation that opportunities to identify children at risk of involvement in prostitution needed to be maximised. To end the selling of sex, the report highlighted two factors, separating private and commercial sex and ending the link between problematic drug-taking, funded by selling sex. In January 2006 the Home Office published *A Coordinated Prostitution Strategy* that was five-fold:

prevention, tackling demand, developing routes out, ensuring justice and tackling off-street prostitution. In particular, with regard to children and young people it commented on the need to raise awareness, for prevention and early intervention; and to adopt a holistic approach with continuity of services.

The current context of child protection: processes and procedures

The context of social services involvement in child protection is now based on Section 11 of the Children Act 2004, which places a statutory duty on key people and bodies to make arrangements to safeguard and promote the welfare of children. The current guidance and associated circulars are based on the Every Child Matters document – *Working Together to Safeguard Children – A Guide to Interagency Working to Safeguard and Promote the Welfare of Children* (2006).[1] It lays out the expectations of how individuals and organisations work together in carrying out their duty. The current guidance updates and replaces the 1999 version, to reflect developments in legislation, policy and practice. In *Working Together to Safeguard Children* 2006 the government announced that the separate Child Protection Register would be phased out by 1 April 2008. The functionality of the register is to be replaced by the Integrated Children's System (ICS) through the existence of a Child Protection Plan. The ICS systems will be required to record and report the periods during which the child is the subject of a Child Protection Plan. The term 'Child being the Subject of a Child Protection Plan' replaces 'Child on the Child Protection Register' from 2008 and the term is used in this context in this chapter.

The First Safeguarding Report and the Victoria Climbié Inquiry Report (2003)[2] have both resulted in major developments in policy for children's services. These were realised in the Every Child Matters programme, underpinned by the Children Act 2004,[3] which aims to improve outcomes for children in five key areas: being healthy, staying safe, enjoying and achieving, making a positive contribution and achieving economic well-being. The 2002 Department of Health review found that whilst all agencies had accepted their responsibility to ensure that children were safeguarded, it was not always reflected in practice. It found that agencies were not always sufficiently committed to, or willing to fund, the work of Area Child Protection Committees (ACPCs). There were also severe difficulties in recruiting and retaining professionals working in child protection and child welfare, which were reducing the effectiveness of measures to safeguard children. This would accord with the low priority in some areas of safeguarding children and young people involved in prostitution.[4]

The second Joint Chief Inspectors' Review of Children's Safeguards 2005 led by CSCI[5] was **published on 14 July 2005, and included the following** summary of key findings:

> *At a local level, the priority given to safeguarding children across local government, health services and the justice system has increased in the three years since the last review and the status of work in child protection and child welfare has improved. There are many examples of good practice and agencies are working together better to safeguard children.*
>
> *Nonetheless, some recurring themes over the past three years across sectors and agencies cause significant concern:*
>
> > *Some agencies still give insufficient priority to safeguarding and children's interests and there are some groups of children, including those with disabilities and those living away from home, whose needs are not always given sufficient recognition or priority;*

There are still considerable concerns about the differing thresholds applied by social services in their child protection and family support work and about the lack of understanding of the role of social workers by other agencies; and

Continuing difficulties in recruitment and retention in some services affect their ability to safeguard children effectively and may restrict their capacity to deliver the new Every Child Matters arrangements.

(www.safeguardingchildren.org.uk/)

In relation to safeguarding and staying safe, revised Statutory Guidance on the safeguarding duty was issued in April 2007. This established Local Safeguarding Children Boards (LSCBs) in each council with social services responsibility. The work of LSCBs is part of the wider context of children's trust responsibilities that aim to improve the overall well-being in the five Every Child Matters outcome areas, listed above, for all children in the local area. Whilst the work of LSCBs contributes to the wider goals of improving the well-being of all children, it has a particular focus on aspects of the 'staying safe' outcome (*Working Together to Safeguard Children*). The LSCB has responsibility for co-ordinating local work and ensuring its effectiveness. This responsibility includes: the development of policy and procedures for safeguarding and promoting the welfare of children; participating in planning activity; communicating the need to safeguard; procedures to ensure a co-ordinated response to unexpected child deaths; monitoring effectiveness; undertaking serious case reviews; and collecting and analysing information about child deaths. The responsibility covers: activity to identify and prevent maltreatment or impairment of health or development; proactive work aimed to target particular groups; and responsive work to protect children who are suffering, or at risk of suffering, harm.

The LSCB has lead responsibility for developing policies and procedures in the area of the authority, including

policies and procedures in relation to the action to be taken where there are concerns about a child's safety or welfare,

setting thresholds for intervention including concerns under Section 17 and Section 47 of the Children Act 1989.

The safeguarding requirements and thresholds for specialist services should also be addressed in the local Children and Young People's Plan. This would be consistent with addressing the concerns of children and young people involved in prostitution. The scope of the new safeguarding measures also includes:

Private fostering. New private fostering guidance and the national minimum standards for private fostering which came into force on 1 July 2005.

Missing children notifications. The Department for Children, Schools and Families holds a list of all the designated managers in local authorities in England who are responsible for ensuring that missing children notifications are dealt with properly.

Vetting and barring scheme. Following the Bichard Inquiry Report (2004), the Safeguarding Vulnerable Groups Act 2006 lays the foundation for a new scheme which aims to help avoid harm, or risk of harm, to children and vulnerable adults. It establishes an Independent Safeguarding Authority which will be phased in. Under the terms of the Act, an Independent

Safeguarding Authority scheme will be implemented which will protect both children and vulnerable adults by preventing those who are known to pose a risk of harm accessing these groups through their work. The ISA scheme is intended to provide a most stringent vetting and barring service.

The Integrated Children's System (ICS)[6] was developed with the intention of improving outcomes for children defined as being in need, under the Children Act 1989. It provides a standard approach to the key processes of assessment, planning, intervention and review, with exemplar documentation for each process stage. It is based on the Assessment Framework developmental needs: child's developmental needs; parenting capacity; family and environmental factors. These records form the basis of the e-social care record for children and are supported by IT software systems. Local authorities are expected to have fully compliant systems by 2008.

In relation to social services involvement in safeguarding cases the key principles are set out in the guidance under Section 11 of the Children Act 2004; these seek to ensure that the work should be:

Child-centred

Rooted in child development

Focused on outcomes for children

Holistic in approach

Ensuring equality of opportunity

Involving children and families

Building on strengths as well as identifying difficulties

Multi- and inter-agency in approach

A continuing process, not an event

Providing and reviewing services

Informed by evidence

The processes by which these principles are applied are assessment, planning, intervention and reviewing, informed by the Core Information Requirements (DfES) – process model v3.1.[7] and in the Integrated Children's System (Department of Health, 2002).[8] These identify key stages of process from the point when concerns raised about a child are referred to a statutory organisation empowered to take action to safeguard and promote the welfare of children (Children's Trust, Children's Department, Social Services Department (SSD)).

LSCB partners should have locally agreed criteria as to when and how it is appropriate to make a referral to the local authority children's social care service in respect of a child in need. There should be an agreed format for making a referral and sharing the information recorded. (The Common Assessment Framework offers a basis for early referral and information-sharing between organisations.)

The key stages of the social work safeguarding involvement are:

Contact

Referral

Initial Assessment

Strategy Discussion(s)

Section 47 Enquiries (and Best Evidence interviews – if required)

Strategy meeting/decision

Initial Child Protection Conference – Decision whether to register/ not register(until April 2008) – Record of the Child being the Subject of a Child Protection Plan. (from April 2008)

Completion of the Core Assessment

Formation of the Core Group/ Core Group meetings

Development and implementation of Child or Young Persons Plan – Child Protection Plan / Child or Young Persons Plan – Child in Need

Safeguarding Visits

Review Conference/Deregistration/ Record end of Child being subject of a Child Protection Plan

The process commences with the *Contact* to the agency, which may be from: another local authority, other agency or professional; friend, neighbour, parent, relative, the child or young person themselves; anonymous source or other source. The children's social care service must clarify with the referrer (including self-referrals from children and families):

the nature of concerns;

how and why they have arisen; and

what appear to be the needs of the child and family.

This process should always identify clearly whether there are concerns about maltreatment, what is their foundation, and whether it may be necessary to consider taking urgent action to ensure the child(ren) are safe from harm. Where the referral is from an agency/other professional, the agency/professional should confirm the referral in writing within 48 hours.

The local authority social worker in consultation with the manager and other identified professionals, should decide and record the next steps of action within one working day. This should be recorded using an ICS compliant *Referral and Information Record.* If it is decided that there is a need to investigate further whether there are concerns about the child's health, development, actual and/or potential harm and to establish whether this child is possibly a child in need, an *initial assessment* should be commenced (other action may include referral to other agencies, the provision of advice or information, or no further action.) Sometimes immediate emergency action may need to be taken to safeguard and promote the welfare of the child. Where such action is being considered it should be preceded by an immediate *strategy discussion* with the police and other agencies as appropriate, in parallel with the commencement of the Initial Assessment. The referrer should be informed of the initial outcome of the referral within 48 hours.

If the child or family is known to social services and there is active ongoing involvement, a new initial assessment may not be required. The record-keeping should relate to the individual child, not a sibling group file. The purpose of the *Initial Assessment* is to determine whether:

the child is in need,

the nature of any services required, and

whether a further more detailed assessment should be undertaken (Core Assessment).

The ICS compliant *Initial Assessment* should be completed within a maximum of seven working days of the date of referral, using the *Framework for the Assessment of Children in Need and their Families* (Department of Health et al., 2000), (often referred to as the assessment triangle).[9] Where the criteria for initiating Section 47 Enquiries (see below) are met, the initial assessment period may be very brief. If a Common Assessment Framework assessment has been undertaken, information from this should be used to inform the Initial Assessment.

Strategy Discussion

Where there is reasonable cause to suspect that a child is suffering or is likely to suffer significant harm, a *Strategy Discussion* must be held immediately. Where risk of significant harm is suspected but is not an urgent factor the Strategy Discussion should be held as soon as possible. The Strategy Discussion will involve the CSSR, police (normally the Police Child Protection Team) and other agencies as appropriate. It can be undertaken as a face-to-face meeting or can even be by telephone. The purpose of the Strategy Discussion is to:

Share information;

Decide what action, if any, is needed immediately to safeguard the child;

Decide whether Section 47 Enquiries should be commenced (or continued if already begun) and if not commencing Section 47 Enquiries, deciding whether or not the child is a 'Child in Need' and if so whether interim services and support are required;

Plan how the Section 47 Enquiries will be undertaken, and who will undertake it;

Decide whether a medical examination is necessary and, if it is, who will undertake it;

Determine what information will be shared with the child and his/her family members, unless such information-sharing may place a child at risk of significant harm, or jeopardise police investigations into any alleged offence(s);

Determine whether disciplinary action is necessary against staff;

Determine whether criminal investigations should commence or continue.
(Core Information Requirements process model)

The Strategy Discussion should be chaired/convened by a manager and recorded using the ICS Record of Strategy Discussion format. The Strategy Discussion may consider all children living in a household where appropriate, but a separate record should be completed for each child.

The key decisions of the Strategy Discussion will determine how the case is taken forward. They are as follows:

Is immediate protective action required? If so commence the immediate protective action. This may be that police take action to protect the child or that social services take action to protect the child, in which case the following need to be considered:

A decision about whether an Emergency Protection Order (EPO) is appropriate;

A decision about whether to apply for an exclusion requirement when applying for an Emergency Protection Order under Section 44 of the Children Act 1989;

A decision about an immediate placement for the child.

Is a *Section 47 Enquiry* appropriate? – see below – Section 47 Enquiry

Is this still a Child in Need? – if so complete the initial assessment, consider a Core Assessment; commence any immediate services agreed.

Is disciplinary action necessary against CSSR staff to be initiated? If so the department's disciplinary process must be initiated.

Will criminal investigations commence/continue? If criminal investigations need to commence or continue, then it will need to be further determined whether or not an '*Achieving Best Evidence Interview*' will be required – see below.

Will an *Achieving Best Evidence Interview* be required? When criminal investigations are involved a further decision must be made about whether the social services and police should interview the child in order to gain evidence to be used as part of any criminal proceedings. This information can also be used in any Family Court Proceedings and in the Core Assessment. The interview is to be conducted in accordance with the guidance for 'Achieving Best Evidence' (Home Office et al., 2002).[10]

(based on Core Information Requirements process model)

If the Strategy Discussion has identified the need for a Section 47 Enquiry, the Strategy Discussion should also consider whether to gain parental permission or to override potential parental objections to contacting other agencies. If these arise subsequently, they should be decided by a team manager. It may be that more than one Strategy Discussion will take place during the investigation, in which case a further Strategy Discussion Record must be completed for each discussion and each child.

Undertaking a Core Assessment under Section 47 of the Children Act 1989

It is likely that the Section 47 Enquiries are taking place in tandem with other investigations and activities, particularly where criminal or disciplinary enquiries are involved, and those undertaking the Section 47 Enquiries should be mindful of 'Achieving Best Evidence' issues. The Section 47 Enquiry forms part of the Core Assessment and should be used to determine whether concerns are substantiated and whether the child is judged to be at continuing risk of significant harm.

Key issues to consider in undertaking a Section 47 Enquiry are that it must always involve seeing and interviewing the child, so specific arrangements may be needed to interview the child such as a joint visit with a co-worker, interpreter, signer and a suitable venue. Is the parent/carer aware of the enquiry? Are other children involved? Does the child require a medical examination under child protection procedures? Many authorities have produced publicly available guidance and checklists specifically on undertaking a Section 47 Enquiry.[11]

Section 47 Enquiries are part of the *Core Assessment Process* and should always be undertaken in a way that minimises distress to the child, so that throughout the enquiry the child's views, wishes and feelings should be ascertained and recorded. The scope and range of people to be interviewed needs to be addressed, considering all those who are personally or professionally connected with the child, and/or their parents/carers, siblings and extended family members. The Framework for the Assessment of Children in Need and Their Families age-specific Core Assessment domains should form the basis for collecting, analysing and recording information as this informs the completion of the Core Assessment process.[12]

In tandem with the commencement of the Section 47 Enquiry, an ICS Chronology Record should be commenced/updated. When a Section 47 Enquiry is concluded, it will need to be determined whether:

Concerns are not substantiated: Where concerns about the child being at risk of or suffering significant harm are not substantiated, the Core Assessment should be completed (within 35 working days of the completion of the Initial Assessment/commencement of the Section 47 Enquiry) and Child in Need planning undertaken in order to consider with the family what support and/or services maybe helpful. In exceptional circumstances child protection concerns are not substantiated and no further action is required.

Concerns substantiated, but child is not judged to be at continuing risk of significant harm: There should be sound reasons, based on analysis of evidence obtained through Section 47 Enquiries, for judging that a child is not at continuing risk of significant harm. These may include a change in family circumstances, where the event was an isolated incident, where the most involved agencies judge that the family will work co-operatively to ensure the child's safety and welfare. In these circumstances a child protection conference/ safeguarding plan is not required, and the Core Assessment should be completed as above, with Child in Need planning in order to consider with the family what support and/or services maybe helpful.

Concerns substantiated and the child is judged to be at continuing risk of significant harm. See below.

The decision may be made by a reconvened Strategy Meeting, or in a single-agency enquiry by the team manager. A record of the outcomes must be completed by the social worker. It is the responsibility of the team manager to ensure the record is completed. It should be completed as an Integrated Children System record. The parents, the child (if appropriate) and the professionals involved should be informed of the outcome in writing.

There may be circumstances in which discontinuing Section 47 Enquiries is an option because it is clear that the criteria for Section 47 Enquiry are no longer satisfied. Such decisions should be taken by a manager following consultation with the police and other agencies involved, in particular the referring agency.

Where the concerns have been substantiated and the child is judged to be at continuing risk of significant harm, an *Initial Child Protection Conference* should be convened (within 15 working days of the Strategy Discussion which initiated the Section 47 Enquiry). The social worker and manager should identify those to be invited to the conference. The social worker should complete the Initial Child Protection Conference Report (pt. 1) based on the information gained to date in the Core Assessment. The social worker should provide parents and children, where relevant, with a copy of the report in advance of the conference. It should be explained and discussed in advance of the conference itself, in the preferred language(s) of the family members, and the social worker should also outline the purpose of the conference, explain who will attend and their roles, and the possible outcomes and what they might mean.

The *Initial Child Protection Conference* will be chaired by a professional who is independent of operational or line management for the case. There is detailed guidance on the conducting of child protection conferences produced by many of the area Safeguarding Boards. The chair will determine whether anyone should be excluded from attending, and how the conference will be conducted, and arrange for the minutes and completion of the ICS Initial Child Protection Conference Report.

Shropshire Safeguarding Board has produced a useful guidance on the Initial Child Protection Conference, which is on their website.[13]

The key decision for the Initial Child Protection Conference is whether the child is at continuing risk of significant harm. If the Initial Child Protection Conference decides that there IS NOT a continuing risk of significant harm, then this must be recorded in the minutes and the child protection process ends. The conference may consider the child's needs and what further help would assist the family in responding to them. The Core Assessment should be completed (within the 35 working days of the completion of the Initial Assessment/commencement of the Section 47 Enquiry) and a Child in Need meeting held in order to consider with the family what support and/or services maybe helpful; where appropriate, an ICS Child/Young Person's Plan (Child in Need Plan) should be drawn up and reviewed at regular intervals.

If the Initial Child Protection Conference decides that there IS a continuing risk of significant harm, this must be recorded in the minutes and the child made subject of a *Child Protection Plan* according to a decision by the chair of the Child Protection Conference, recording the applicable categories of abuse or neglect. These are:

neglect

physical injury

sexual abuse

emotional abuse, or

combinations of the above

The conference should:

agree the outline *Child Protection Plan*;

appoint a key worker who should be a qualified, experienced social worker;

identify the membership of the Core Group to develop and implement the Child Protection Plan;

agree the date for the first *Child Protection Review Conference* and specify the changes in circumstances that would warrant holding the review conference earlier than planned;

recommend whether Family Proceedings are appropriate.

The decision to make the child subject of a *Child Protection Plan*, and the category should be recorded in the *Child's Chronology*.

The key worker and Core Group will develop the plan to protect the child based on the Outline Plan that was agreed by the Initial Child Protection Conference. The development of the plan will be based on the information available from the Core Assessment that was begun under Section 47 of the Children Act 1989. It can be seen from the above that a child under the age of 16 who cannot legally consent to sex would be seen as being abused. This does not preclude older young people also being viewed as abused.

The *Child Protection Plan* should:

Set out what work needs to be done, why, when and by whom;

Describe the identified needs of the child, and what therapeutic services are required;

Include specific, achievable, child-focused objectives intended to safeguard the child and promote his or her welfare;

Include realistic strategies and specific actions to achieve the objectives;

Clearly identify roles and responsibilities of professionals and family members, including the nature and frequency of contact by professionals with children and family members;

Lay down points at which progress will be reviewed, and the means by which progress will be judged; and

Set out clearly the roles and responsibilities of those professionals with routine contact with the child, e.g. health visitors, GPs and teachers, as well as any specialist or targeted support to the child and family. (Core Information Requirements v3.1)

The *Integrated Children's System Child's Plan* should be used for the *Child Protection Plan*. The key worker/allocated social worker is responsible for convening the *Core Group* and for undertaking regular Statutory visits to the child.

The *Core Group* is responsible for monitoring and implementing the child protection plan and for reporting on progress on the Plan to *Child Protection Review Conferences*. The social worker is required to produce a report in advance of the *Review Conference*. This should be prepared using the *ICS Child or Young Person's Protection Review form – Part 1 social worker's report*. It should include the details of the Statutory Visits, Core Group meetings, other meetings and updating on progress on the plan and factors from the Core Assessment.

The *Child Protection Review Conference* will also be chaired by someone independent of operational or service management and the responsibilities of the Conference Chairperson, social worker and other agencies are as for an Initial Child Protection Conference. Its function is to review the progress made against objectives set out in the Child Protection Plan and to determine whether the child is still at continuing risk of significant harm. At each conference, the child protection plan should be reviewed.

Where the child IS still at continuing risk of significant harm the Child Protection Plan will be revised, the key worker and Core Group will continue to implement the plan, undertake Core Group meetings and Statutory Visits. If the child is no longer at continuing risk of significant harm, the conference may consider the child's needs and discuss with the family what support and/or services maybe helpful; An ICS Child/Young Person's Plan (Child in Need Plan) should then be drawn up and reviewed at regular intervals. The reasons for discontinuing a Child Protection Plan are because:

EITHER It is judged that the child is no longer at continuing risk of Significant Harm requiring safeguarding by means of a Child Protection Plan. Only a Child Protection Review Conference can decide that the Child Protection Plan is no longer necessary.

OR the child has moved permanently to another local authority area. There are specific arrangements for children moving across local authority boundaries.

OR the child has reached the age of 18 years.

OR the child has died.

OR the child has permanently left the UK. In that case all reasonable efforts will be made to liaise with relevant agencies in the receiving country.

Once the Child Protection Review Conference has been held, the Conference Chair should complete *part two (the Chair's Report) of the Child Protection Review Record* recording the decisions of the child protection review conference – this should be completed at the Child Protection Review Conference by the Conference Chair. The *Chronology Record* should be updated. The process of review, revise plan, implement plan, Core Group meetings, Statutory Visits, updating the Chronology continues until a Child Protection Review Conference decides that the Child Protection Plan is no longer necessary as outlined above.

Child protection and the unborn child

Where there is concern relating to the welfare of an unborn child and where a Section 47 Enquiry Core Assessment gives rise to concerns that the unborn child may be at future risk of significant harm, a *Pre-birth Conference* should be convened. A Pre-birth Conference has the same status, and should proceed in the same way, as other initial child protection conferences, including decisions about a child protection plan. The involvement of midwifery services is vital in such cases. Where it is decided that the unborn child is likely to be at risk of significant harm and will require a Child Protection Plan, the Core Group should be established and the Child Protection Plan prepared prior to the expected date of delivery. The key worker must inform a designated manager responsible for child protection of the date of birth of the child, and its name. The process thereafter is as above.

This mechanism and new practices enable consultation to take place in cases where harm to a child is suspected or real and allow partners to pool ideas, gather information and make informed choices regarding intervention. It makes for better partnership working and a high degree of professionalisation.

Linking good practice to children and young people involved in prostitution

Joanna Phoenix (2002), in critically examining the impact of the Department of Health/Home Office guidance SCIP, argued that this document made 'child and youth prostitution an explicit issue of social policy' (p. 353), with an emphasis on victimisation. There were two implications that she commented on in linking youth prostitution to the Children Act; the first was that children's need's can be 'identified, recognised and accommodated' and second was that 'it . . . provides a set of resources that young people involved in prostitution can access and through which their criminalisation can be challenged' (ibid., pp. 357–8).

However she contended that SCIP also distinguished between the deserving young, who were victims of grooming (etc.), and the undeserving, who actively engaged in prostitution despite the best endeavours of formal organisations.

The danger is that 'older' young people could be seen as not deserving of scarce local authority funding, yet it is the 16–17 year olds that typically progress on to adult prostitution. Many of the young people (often in care), as Sutherland's differential association theory would predict, learnt to become prostitutes as a form of economic survival from their peers. It is the 1517 year age group that is most likely to be known to the statutory agencies and the question is: will the response be a child protection plan or criminal prosecution, i.e. will it be to punish the young person in order to protect them? Why might this latter possibility be the outcome rather than the former? Phoenix (2004) outlined a sequence of events in which police fear of community demands to 'clean up the streets' required a reaction in order to demonstrate that they were responding. Arrest and charging, what Phoenix described as 'creeping welfarisation of punishment' (ibid., p. 166) provided a rationale and avoided the need for child protection actions. In her research she found this approach was also described as an 'exit strategy', whereby police action made further prostitution difficult for the young person. She was sympathetic towards the police as they had few resources beyond arrest or referral.

The problem of effective interventions with children and young people involved in prostitution is complicated by the expectation of exchanging information between the statutory and voluntary agencies that are required to adhere to the procedures described in this chapter. Phoenix (2004) highlighted the issue that voluntary organisations were obliged to share information on young people, and the police and social services could invoke Section 47 of the Children Act 1989 to force them to do so. Furthermore this information-sharing was described as being 'one way', with little information given back. An example was given of a 15-year-old girl working in a parlour: when the outreach worker informed the police and social services they lost their ability to get into many other similar establishments. Clearly there had to be sensitivity in how this type of information was used by statutory agencies.

The solution appears to be to draw on the concept of 'immediate danger' so that cases are reported when there is a risk of death or serious injury.

More recently, Natalie Valios in an article in *Community Care* (2007) reported on two projects run by the NSPCC in East London. Street Matters works with 10 to 18-year-old girls in the Whitechapel area of East London who are at risk or who have been sexually exploited. BFree is a national consultation service for trafficked and sexually exploited young women. Staff are qualified social workers and youth workers. It must be recognised by those working to safeguard and protect children and young people that solutions will not always be simple and quick. The young person may not alter their behaviour quickly and they are likely to need long-term support to be able to lead a near normal lifestyle. Valios's (2007) article included a case study of a 16-year-old girl that had been sexually exploited by a number of older men, had had sixteen police missing person reports, had been gang raped, and had a sexually transmitted disease. Nevertheless, with sensitive outreach work and support from Street Matters she had become reconciled with her mother and step-father and was slowly turning her life around.

The projects underline the need for a service that also recognises the need for an anti-discriminatory approach to this work: many young women have been trafficked from Africa, while but 31 per cent of the young women worked with by Street Matters between April 2004 and March 2005 were of Bangladeshi background and 22 per cent were white. It would be very easy to miss ethnic minority children and young people who are vulnerable to forced marriages and where sexual matters are not easily discussed within the family. Outreach work in schools is an important component of the work.

Conclusion

This chapter has highlighted a number of important factors relating to safeguarding children. Using key documentation it has deliberately plotted at length the new social work procedures and processes which need to be applied when safeguarding vulnerable children. This is important to do as often outsiders and some insiders fail to understand not only what is in now place, but also how the system has changed and how it works. This change in policy replaces older methods often associated with the casework model but builds on good practice taken from years of successful working in child protection. Altered and different priorities, improved standards and ensuring better service delivery to clients have all brought about these changes. At another level it has allowed for greater practice professionalisation.

This chapter has revealed the complexity of addressing the needs of vulnerable children and young people. It has also guided the reader through the lengthy, complex and highly specialised social work processes which have been put in place as part of the risk assessment now applied to each case. It has also help to raise the issue of prostitution as an exemplar in which the problem may be ignored or may invoke a punitive response, not least to protect the services themselves from criticism. What this means is that priorities have changed by empowering children and parents who must be included and consulted as a matter of course. This is a bureaucratic and complex system which still faces the criticism that some lazy professionals may be protected from any responsibility because it allows them to do just enough to cover their own back rather than developing a child-centred focus. Under this new system this becomes less likely, since greater partnership working may reveal this lack of professionalism. Furthermore, shared goals and joined-up working with others will help to develop successful interventions and show good practice as described by Valios.

It will not only provide for more improved methods at the service delivery end in providing holistic solutions but also ensure greater responsibility and accountability on the part of those whose who have a duty of care to protect children at risk. Used sensitively, these processes will protect vulnerable children and young people as they were designed to do. Another dynamic of this chapter has been that the emphasis has been placed firmly on the 'abusers and coercers' and not on the pathology of the child, young person or victim. In agreeing with Phoenix this chapter emphasises the importance of treating children and young people involved in prostitution as victims rather than offenders.

It is essential therefore that professionals should know, understand and work with the procedures as laid down, but professional judgement also requires knowledge, values and skills. The new Home Office (2006) strategy on prostitution is more concerned with safer communities than with the welfare needs of the women (Melrose, 2007). Whilst this relates more to adults than children, nevertheless the message was that resources are needed if support rather than punishment is to be offered, particularly in individuals with multiple issues, such as drug abuse. This is certainly pertinent to many young people involved in prostitution. The investigatory procedures detailed should ensure that the young person is treated as a child in need, rather than an offender to be punished. The label should not define what support is going to be offered.

Notes

1 Every Child Matters, *Working Together To Safeguard Children 2006 – A guide to interagency working to safeguard and promote the welfare of children*. www.cambslscb.org.uk/leaflets/Working%20Together%20to%20Safeguard%20Children.pdf.

2 The Victoria Climbié Inquiry: Report of an Inquiry by Lord Laming, inquiry.org.uk/finreport/finreport.htm.

3 Children Act 2004, – Chapter 31, www.opsi.gov.uk/acts/acts2004/ukpga_20040031_en_1.

4 These comments accord with similar views raised by authors in Chapters 7 and 10 relating to policing (Editor's note).

5 Second Joint Chief Inspectors' Review of Children's Safeguards, 2005 – CSCI, www.safeguardingchildren.org.uk/default.htm.

6 The Integrated Children's System (ICS) – Every Child Matters, www.everychildmatters.gov.uk/socialcare/integratedchildrenssystem/about/.

7 Core information Requirements (DfES) – process model v3.1 2003 – DfES, www.everychildmatters.gov.uk/resources-and-practice/IG00009/.

8 Integrated Children's System: The Exemplar Records for Assessment, Planning, Intervention and Review (Department of Health, 2002), www.everychildmatters.gov.uk/socialcare/integratedchildrenssystem/.

9   Department of Health (2000) *Framework for the Assessment of Children in Need and their Families*, www.dh.gov.uk/en/Publicationsandstatistics/Publications/PublicationsPolicyAndGuidance/DH_4003256.

10 Achieving Best Evidence in Criminal Proceedings: Published by Home Office Communication Directorate Jan, www.homeoffice.gov.uk/documents/achieving-best-evidence/guidance-witnesses.pdf?view=Binary.

11 Bristol Children & Young People's Services, Issues to consider when making s. 47 Enquiries (E) www.bristol-cyps.org.uk/socialcare/procedures/childprotection/pdf/s47-enquiries.pdf.

12 Cambridgeshire Local Safeguarding Children Board, Action To Be Taken Where A Child Is At Risk Of Significant Harm – Practice Guidance, www.cambslscb.org.uk/professionals/procedures/proc_ch4.shtm#ema.

13 Shropshire Safeguarding Board, Initial Child Protection Conferences Manual Version: 1 (11/10/2007) Chapter Revision: 1 (03/07/2007), www.herefordshire.gov.uk/hscb_SafeguardingChildrenProcedures/chapters/p_initial_cpc.html.

Chapter 12
Concluding themes

Peter Kennison and Anthony Goodman

Her Majesty's Inspector of Constabulary (HMIC) undertook a thematic inspection entitled 'Keeping Safe, Staying Safe' (2003) of police child protection procedures following the recommendations made by the Laming Inquiry into the death of Victoria Climbié. Other agencies as well as the police were also looking at their procedures to see if improvements could be made. The HMIC published its recommendations in October 2003 and later the Home Office issued Memo 44/2003 to provide greater clarity in child protection matters to agencies. Additionally in 2003 a Green Paper entitled *Every Child Matters* was issued that built on preventive plans to safeguard all children by proposing changes in policy and legislation.

The introduction of this new Government approach in 2006, which took the same name 'Every Child Matters', was designed with a number of key themes in mind. The aim of this strategy is to ensure that every child, no matter from what background or in what circumstances, should have the support they need to be healthy, stay safe, enjoy and achieve, make a positive contribution and achieve economic well-being. Stemming from this initiative was the introduction of legislation, the Children Act 2004, which introduced a Children's Commissioner with sweeping new powers. The launch of Children's Trusts as part of this initiative brings together all services for children and young people, which will aid multi-disciplinary working with the aim of ensuring improved inter-agency co-operation, integrated strategies and governance. The new agenda has been designed to empower children and young people and to give them a voice in an adult-centric world. Empowering and listening to children and young people is essential in our understanding of crime and victimisation. Children and young people are frequently stigmatised, labelled and demonised as offenders when in fact explanations regarding crime drawn from research suggest that children are more often than not the victims of crime, rather than perpetrators. Thus one of the main themes of this book has been to explain why and under what circumstances the labelling of children in a variety of contexts and settings takes place. Other emerging themes have been explained as they were raised within each chapter. Here we address some general themes that are common to a number of chapters.

Chapter 1 focused on the social construction of these common labels which were applied to non-adults as a way of explaining their context. The social construction of child, childhood, child abuse and child sexual offending is contingent upon many components. What is evident is that it shows a lack of public and professional agreement, certainly in respect of defining these key concepts. It is also important and necessary to take into account the motivations of those constructing these concepts, especially those relating to child sexual abusers. From what standpoint are their motivations derived, and are these doctrines moral, political or something else? Moreover, child protection guidance has been dependent on how policy makers interpret the risk and actual threat. Also, heightened fears of child maltreatment by child sexual offenders, when added to media exposure, emphasise and exacerbate the problem, and the moral panic that reinforces itself creates even more pre-dicaments. Thus, it is necessary to move away from the extreme end of social constructivism and adopt a realist perspective. The evidence suggests that media portrayals of sex offenders are often unhelpful and fuel the moral panic to a point where the fear of crime outweighs the actual threat.

The same message was developed in Chapter 2, where children and young people appear to be demonised as offenders rather than seen as victims. As Martin et al. (2007), Newburn et al. (2007) and Pain (2003) suggest, when children and young people inhabit public spaces they feel over-policed, under-protected and viewed with suspicion rather than care. The evidence from official police statistics and from victimisation surveys suggests that children and young people are as, if not slightly more, likely than adults to be a victim of a street crime, broadly defined so as to include inter-personal violence and thefts occurring in public spaces (outside of the home and not in school/college). Amongst the under-18 population, street crime victimisation is not evenly distributed. Children and young people living in inner city neighbourhoods, characterised by relative social and economic disadvantage, are exposed to higher levels of street crime in general, but in all neighbourhoods, not least city centres, older boys, particularly ones who have themselves offended, are most at risk.

Qualitative research also highlights the need to distinguish between forms of victimisation, between, for example, the 12-year-old robbed at knifepoint by a group of young men, the 15-year-old wounded in a street-level conflict between rival groups and the 17-year-old assaulted outside a city centre night club by her ex-boyfriend. At the same time, victims in each context seem to share a sense of the inevitability of crime, a sort of casual fatalism – 'shit will happen' – from which follows the notion that whether one becomes a victim or not is as much a matter of luck as of anything – the risk is built into the environment rather than the individual.

Whilst at a general level, therefore, there is certainly a need to take young people's victimisa-tion seriously and to focus efforts on the prevention of crime *against* as well as by young people, too great a focus on victims as such risks distracting attention from the all-important contexts in which youthful forms of street crime occur.

In the area of substance misuse highlighted in Chapter 3, one of the greatest difficulties facing those seeking to implement policy is the initial reluctance of problem-substance users with children to come forward and identify themselves as such. The main parental fear surrounds the issue of having their children removed from their care if they are judged to be unfit parents. Social stigma and negative stereotypes fuel this reluctance to come forward, not only on the part of heavy substance-using parents, but also their children as well. A paradox exists where at one end there is a strong desire for treatment, whilst at the other they suffer in silence without resorting to support, and in an often insurmountable way. Treating both parents and children as victims rather than offenders is the key theme, and support not punishment may be a better policy solution. As Caroline Chatwin suggests there is often a gap between child and adult services that allows some children to slip through the net, so perhaps a more holistic approach is necessary, involving parents, children and wider kin, that would better resolve the dilemma. Furthermore, intervention points were highlighted; support during pregnancy and also when treatment programmes were implemented provided positive change in both parents and children. The message to service providers is clear: the key is inclusion in treatment programmes and other support networks, rather than alienation and exclusion.

Developing and building on notions expressed in the first chapter, Caroline Metcalf placed more emphasis on the welfare and safety of children and the understanding of the dynamics of sexuality, together with the importance given to gender roles in the maintenance of a child's well-being. Fear of paedophile crime is fuelled by negative media portrayals, particularly with the apparent risk of Internet sex offending. As primary definers, the media as a powerful institution presents child sex offending as a continued and significant threat to children, with only incarceration as the answer to the problem. These sensational portrayals that normalise serious sex crime as typical not only lead to a deviance amplification spiral, which fuels fear of further offending, but also seek to attach labels like 'beast', 'monster' or 'depraved' to the term 'paedophile'. This has the effect of excluding these groups and, given the shift in emphasis as to how social, political and ideological influences impact on public attitudes towards sex offenders, this results in ever more punitive policies that reflect enforcement, tightening procedures, increased surveillance and monitoring as the answer to the threat.

Reintegrating the offender back into the community is not an easy task: long-standing research supports the view that decreasing socio-affective deficits, such as emotional loneliness, reduces the risk of re-offending. New methods and ideas like 'name and shame' campaigns are designed to reassure the public, but these not only run the risk of driving individuals underground and out of sight but will also *increase* their emotional loneliness and isolation whilst at the same time also affecting them emotionally with a further lowering of self-esteem. We are unaware of the risk to the public of Internet sex offenders at one end but must avoid an over-exaggeration and stigmatisation at the other end. Sex offenders are not a heterogeneous group and misconceptions of them may lead to a gross over-estimation of risk amongst the lay public without offering any real or suitable alternative to protecting children from becoming victims.

Sally Angus dealt with children as victims from a different perspective by discussing the issue of restorative justice and Youth Offending Teams who have a duty to involve victims when dealing with offending behaviour on the part of young people. What is evident from research is the fact that the process tends to deter young victims from participating. This may be due to a number of factors, not least cultural-professional attitudes that implicitly minimise offender responsibility through the attribution of some responsibility for the event to peer victims. Restorative processes can actually exacerbate feelings of exclusion from the processes of justice and leave victims with unchallenged perceptions that offenders are systemically excused. More effort and commitment is needed on the part of YOT staff to ensure victim participation in the process. We saw in Chapter 2 how it is more likely that children are victims rather than offenders and that there is, for a variety of reasons, serious under-reporting of crimes, which makes it all the more important to encourage and ensure victim participation.

Very few sociological publications have appeared in the UK that highlight the plight of children or young people who have been the subject of child abuse in the religious setting. However, some individual biographies have emerged in recent years that often reflect a harrowing and tragic tale of institutional abuse of children involved with religious groups. What emerges from Chapter 6 is that religious institutions have dealt with child abuse by denial in a variety of ways and at a number of levels. Greater awareness that child abuse was taking place in the religious setting is a recent phenomenon. When child abuse has been discovered in a religious setting, RIs have tended to deal with the matter no differently from any other institution that had a duty to protect children in their care. RIs are similar to other institutions and, in some cases, mirror them, since they will share common characteristics that allow child abuse and, more particularly, child sexual abuse to take place. Child abuse is an under-publicised crime; investigation is hampered by the lack of reporting and by the secrecy surrounding it. The settings and conditions are ripe for the further exploitation of children. These characteristics are about power, authority and control over the child by an adult, usually by a dominant male. Such power within a closed, secret or hidden institution means that those in charge are able to deny malpractice. Detection in the institutional setting requires the abuse to be followed up and confronted, factors which create a daunting challenge to child protection (Gallagher, 1999). Examples of abuse can be found in most if not all RIs. The study of child abuse in the religious setting has suffered from a lack of access, openness and transparency on the part of RIs, so reported incidents are rare. More RIs are awakening to the fact that they must be aware of child protection and put procedures in place that ensure their safety. The Roman Catholic Church have taken the initiative and made their child protection policies child- rather than adult-centric.

Chapter 7 drew on the case study relating to the tragic events leading to the death of 9-year-old Victoria Climbié in 2000, a case which marked a watershed in child protection. Yet this was not the first case where communication and inter-professional working failed: in fact these failures were present in all the notable child death cases since Maria Colwell died in 1973. It would be untrue to say that nothing had been learnt in the intervening period and much good work in child protection has taken place in that time. Yet with the complexity of organisation, management, policy considerations and working practices in mind, this chapter showed up the failure of key child protection agencies to work, both individually and collectively, to safeguard Victoria. It critically examined the central importance of the relationships between the agencies and of partnership-working, finding that while either systems or agencies or both can be inadequate, in the end it was simple human failure that let this child down. It highlighted how partnership-working presupposes that participating agencies function well and will work effectively with one another, but the reality of it was that the system was failing and it was only with the benefit of hindsight that this was realised. Partnership-working assumes that shared goals, shared responsibility, and accountability exist between the partners. Yet there can often be conflict as agencies may compete to deliver solutions that promote the interests of their own organisation, but at the cost of real partnership-working. The Laming Report showed there were serious failings on the part of the police, not only at all levels but also across police jurisdictions. The initial investigation was flawed, and Laming suggests that for the investigating officer not to visit the child was a grave error of judgement, because, had she done so, she would have found some twelve key pieces of information which would have given her grave cause for concern (2003). Blurred individual roles and disjointed lines of accountability, and bad internal communication, supervision and management further compounded the problem. Whilst officers at ground level were incompetent, they were effectively also let down by their managers. Snapshots of inter-agency work relationships were highlighted within the analysis and this showed a collection of individuals from all the agencies working separately with little respect for each other, little mutual consultation and hardly any exchange of information. Communication up, down and across hierarchies was grossly inadequate and any form of linked or joined-up learning or training between, and incorporating, all the agencies was also missing. Any communication or co-operation between agency partners was disparate, uncoordinated, minimal or just plainly non-existent.

Chapter 8 showed how constructing children *only* as innocent victims of failed parenting or abusive systems, however firmly based in reality this view may be, can constrain profes-sionals from exploring how children themselves make sense of their reality. Whilst children are obviously not responsible for their parents' inability to parent them, nor for their violence or volatility, a focus on victimhood creates many limitations in interactions with children. It may lead a professional to be overly protective and anxious to interpret the child's experience in particular ways. Using the concepts of children as damaged, as over-burdened, and as expert, Gwyn Daniel has argued from each of these discourses. She has shown that consult-ing with children as experts often means that they engage more readily and give profes-sionals a better idea about their needs. Consulting children who are at the receiving end of the adults' difficulties and conflicts means learning from their experience. Good practice has demonstrated a commitment to ensuring that children are listened to and kept in the foreground of any problem-solving.

Sue and Anthony Goodman showed in the primary school context how, for a variety of reasons, child protection referral in one area may not reach the same level of concern in another. These reasons can include workload, regularity of low-level risk, movement of families, family and cultural expectations. This chapter raised the issue of local area agree-ments about procedures on CP and how these must be brought to the attention of all staff in schools that have contact and knowledge about children. They must be trained and familiar with policy and procedures, including having refresher training at intervals later. The Com-mon Assessment Framework tool for early intervention enables a multi-disciplinary approach to working with families to enhance CP work. In situations where there is concern of harm or risk of harm then procedures must be followed as set out by the Local Safeguarding Children Board (LSCB). Thus there should still be an overall consistency in approach so that staff are aware and alert to the possibility of abuse. ECM (2003) was full of constructive possibilities for ensuring that inter-disciplinary co-operation occurred, and it highlighted a number of good practices that could be developed nationally. Specifically it stressed the need to engage with parents and especially for the father to become more involved in school life. It talked about working more closely with parents to strengthen their understanding of how to help their child's development. It also stressed the need for a joint approach. It developed the idea that parents can use their child to fight their relationship battles, and so children sometimes need to be protected from their parents and carers, as well as from paedophile-inclined professionals. Moreover, knowledge about child protection in the age of the Internet is vital.

This is a potentially traumatising and dangerous area for young people, and consequently it calls for vigilance and a suitably trained workforce.

In Chapter 10 Chris Bourlet showed how, in the aftermath of the Laming Inquiry, the Metropolitan Police Service (MPS) engaged with the problems, dilemmas and challenges facing the police in protecting children. Its most important objective though, was to show how the MPS reacted to the mistakes made and the challenges it faced in learning from them. This took the form of the Change Programme which was implemented by the MPS to deal with the faults in the system and, in doing so, set out to professionalise the police response by ensuring the effective investigation and prevention of child abuse in London. Significant benefits have come about as a result of the Change Programme. The investigation of child abuse or child death is now recognised as being more of a challenge for police investigators than if the victim were adult. This makes it all the more important to raise the status and standards of investigation in child protection matters generally, especially given its complexity. Raising standards to increase the level of professionalism in this difficult area must be one of the over-riding principles. Casework is now allocated in a systematic way, according to the nature of the case, rather than on the basis of who happened to be in the office at the time or who answered the telephone. In this way there is a fairer distribution of casework and also the monitoring of standards is made easier.

Against the backdrop of increased professional standards policing has seen the introduction of new methods and procedures that have galvanised and regenerated child protection staff to be more proactive rather than reactive, thus ensuring that prevention takes precedence. Changes have required root and branch treatment from the top down to the very bottom. Improving structures, reorganising and amalgamating staff who jointly work in child-related areas under one command has not only helped the flow of information up and down the chain of command but also broadened responsibility, improved leadership and accountability. Outside the organisation information-sharing is being developed between partners. Although the nature of policing in England and Wales presents its own problem with its forty-three autonomous force areas, change beyond the boundaries of the MPS will progress at a different pace and with varying amounts of success since not all chief officers will be in a position to allocate appropriate resources to the same degree. Here the challenges that were faced would ensure change and given that the police culture is resistant to change (this has not been the experience of child protection in the MPS). If anything staff have seen an improvement in status, have been rewarded with new systems and better technology, and benefited from cleaner and more professional working conditions. The new methods have also created a momentum of their own, producing benefits previously un-envisaged during the planning stages. Economies of scale have also been shown to have a positive benefit, since pooling resources, amalgamating staff, sharing in expertise and good practice offer a better chance of success. Periodic and structured checking of live casework files has been introduced in such a way that the system will be more proactive when it comes to intervention in problematic cases. The programme continues as the MPS moves towards addressing the broadening challenge of the 'Every Child Matters' agenda. The chapter argues that even with all the systems implemented and prevention strategies in place, it is an unfortunate fact that some children will still be abused and killed by those expected to care for them. Victoria's legacy is that now there are dedicated, skilled and passionate teams of professionals who will stand up for the rights of those children whose voices cannot be heard.

Chapter 11 saw a number of important factors relating to safeguarding children. Using key documentation it has deliberately plotted at length the new social work procedures and processes which need to be applied when safeguarding vulnerable children. Often outsiders and some insiders fail to understand not only what is in place, but also how the system has changed and how it works. This change in policy replaces older methods often associated with the casework model and builds on good practice taken from years of successful working in child protection. Altered and different priorities, improved standards and ensuring better service delivery to clients have all brought about these changes. At another level it has allowed for greater practice professionalisation. The chapter guided the reader through the lengthy, complex and highly specialised social work processes which have been put in place as part of the risk assessment now applied to each case. The issue of prostitution was used as an exemplar, showing that the problems faced by the young person may be ignored or may invoke a punitive response, not least to protect the service providers themselves from criticism. What this means is that priorities have been changed by empowering children and parents, who must now be included and consulted as a matter of course. This is a bureaucratic and complex system which still faces the criticism that some lazy professionals may still be protected from any responsibility because the system allows them to do just enough to cover their own back, rather than acting with a child-centred focus. However, under this new system this becomes less likely since greater partnership-working may reveal any lack of professionalism. Furthermore shared goals and joined-up working with others will help to develop successful interventions and show good practice as described by Valios (2007).

The new procedures will not only provide for more improved methods at the service delivery end in providing holistic solutions, but will also ensure greater responsibility and accountability on the part of those who have a duty of care to protect children at risk. Used sensitively, these processes will protect vulnerable children and young people as they were designed to do. Another dynamic of this chapter has been that the emphasis has been placed firmly on the 'abusers and coercers' and not on the pathology of the child, young person or victim. In agreeing with Phoenix this chapter emphasises the importance of treating children and young people involved in prostitution as victims rather than offenders.

Professionals should know, understand and work with the procedures as laid down, but professional judgement also requires knowledge, values and skills. The new Home Office (2006) strategy on prostitution is more concerned with safer communities than with the welfare needs of the women (Melrose, 2007). Whilst this relates more to adults than children, nevertheless the message was that resources are needed if support rather than punishment is to be offered, particularly in the case of individuals with multiple issues such as drug abuse. The investigatory procedures detailed should ensure that the young person is treated as a child in need, rather than an offender to be punished. The label should not define what support is going to be offered.

General themes

Consistent themes emerge from the chapters. Several of the authors have suggested that in many instances in the past professionals within organisations have indicated that there has been a general and historical lack of interest in child abuse, even denial that child abuse exists or is taking place. Such was the lack of commitment that often a low or insufficient level of priority was given to some areas of working to safeguard children (see Chapters 7, 10, and 11). Also, there has been a consistent under-valuing of work and staff in this area, together with insufficient recognition or support for the needs of children who either have disabilities, or live away from home, or are carers for parents with drug/alcohol problems. To improve matters the Government agenda has been to ensure improved and consistent quality of service, service delivery and better standards across the agencies in child protection work.

In terms of partnership-working there has often been a blurring of roles and responsibilities, with poor or non-existent communication not only within jurisdictions but also more particularly across agencies. The redefining of lines of communication, roles and power relations has also been a significant challenge for agencies. Maintaining shared goals, understandings, objectives and a common communications framework are all positive features of successful partnership-working. The Every Child Matters agenda has introduced guidance to allow the agencies to build better and more resilient partnerships so that they do not fail. Differing intervention thresholds not only in social work and family support but also across agencies has also been a stumbling block for practitioners who often failed to consult and also to agree on solutions. Child protection work is very challenging and difficult, so there have been difficulties in retaining and motivating staff. Yet given the variety of agencies who have a duty of care towards children, and granted the complexity of systems, processes and procedures, there is little wonder anyone has a strategic handle on what goes on. Over the last twenty years not one of the agencies has stayed the same: all of them have experienced dramatic change. Because of the constant changes and reorganisation of the police, the health service, education and social work, both insiders and outsiders often have little idea about what may be available. New initiatives, better decision-making and innovative solutions to child protection issues have meant that the old regime of managing casework has moved on to that of managing risk. This is where the political agenda, in what is known in Government circles as 'arms length but hands on', attempts to provide more in the way of choice, innovation and better funding support for child protection. As a result these procedures have not been straightforward, becoming long, detailed and difficult to comprehend. Constant change not only means agencies and their staff are constantly retraining or up-dating their knowledge but it has also introduced a high degree of complexity and fragmentation when often what is required is a system which practitioners not only understand but which is also integrated, co-ordinated and simple to use. Also with complexity comes fragmentation, and when systems fail then they are even harder to put right. We have seen the positive benefits of change where new working practices, better working conditions and improved technology have been introduced. Furthermore, enhanced partnership-working has exposed the police to other partners, and this has begun to induce positive change, shared responsibility and a greater sense of ownership. The professionalisation of child protection has also been an emerging subject in social work, policing, the health service, education and the religious setting. A greater degree of professionalisation, highlighted in Chapter 10, means that not only are police better able and prepared to take on difficult child abuse investigations but also that they are discovering hitherto un-envisaged benefits to be derived from change. Counted amongst the benefits are a greater level of status in such work and a higher level of dynamism amongst staff working in child protection.

Bibliography

Abel, E.L. (1984) 'Smoking and pregnancy', *Journal of Psychoactive Drugs*, 16: 327–38.

Advisory Council on the Misuse of Drugs (2003) *Hidden Harm: Responding to the needs of children of problem drug users*. London: Advisory Council on the Misuse of Drugs.

Advisory Council on the Misuse of Drugs (2007) *Hidden Harm Three Years On: Realities, challenges and opportunities*. London: Advisory Council on the Misuse of Drugs.

Alder, C. and Wundersitz, J. (1994) *Family Conferencing and Juvenile Justice: The way forward or misplaced optimism?* Canberra, ACT: Australian Institute of Criminology.

Alderson, J. (1979) *Policing Freedom*. Plymouth: Latimer Trend.

Alison, L. (2000) 'What are the risks to children of parental substance misuse?', in F. Harbin and M. Murphy (eds) *Substance Misuse and Child Care: How to understand, assist and intervene when drugs affect parenting*. Lyme Regis: Russell House.

Anderson, S., Kinsey, R., Loader, I. and Smith, C. (1994) *Cautionary Tales: Young people, crime and policing in Edinburgh*. Aldershot: Avebury.

Angus, S. (2001) 'An enquiry into Youth Offending Team practitioners' understanding of restorative justice processes and the role of the victims', unpublished dissertation.

Anon. (2005) 'Internet porn users to face jail', *Guardian*, 30 August.

Arendt, R., Angelopoulos, J., Salvator, A. and Singer, L. (1999) 'Motor development of cocaine-exposed children at age two years', *Pediatrics*, 103: 86–92.

Aubrey, C. and Dahl, S. (2006) *Children's Voices: The views of vulnerable children on their service providers and the relevance of services they receive*. Dartington: Research in Practice.

Aye Maung, N. (1995) *Young People, Victimisation and the Police*, Home Office Research Study No. 140. London: HMSO.

Bailey, R. and Williams, B (2000) *Inter-agency Partnerships in Youth Justice: Implementing the Crime and Disorder Act 1998*. Sheffield: University of Sheffield Joint Unit for Social Service Research.

Balloch, S. and Taylor, M. (eds) (2001) *Partnership Working*. Bristol: Policy Press.

Bancroft, A., Wilson, S., Cunningham-Burley, S., Backett-Milburn, K. and Masters, H. (2004) *Parental Drug and Alcohol Misuse: Resilience and transition among young people*. York: Joseph Rowntree Foundation.

Banton, M. (1964) *The Policeman in the Community*. London: Collins.

Barnard, M. and Barlow, J. (2002) 'Discovering parental drug dependence: silence and disclosure', *Children and Society*, 17: 45–56.

Barnard, M. (2003) 'Between a rock and a hard place: the role of relatives in protecting children from the effects of parental drug problems' *Child and Family Social Work*, 8, 291–9.

Barnard, M. (2007) *Drug Addiction and Families*. London: Jessica Kingsley.

Barrett, D. (ed.) (1997) *Child Prostitution in Britain. Dilemmas and practical responses*. London: Children's Society.

Barrett, G., Sellman, D. and Thomas, J. (eds) (2005) *Inter-professional Working in Health and Social Care*. Basingstoke: Palgrave Macmillan.

Barton, C. (2003) *Restorative Justice: The empowerment model*. Sydney: Hawkins Press.

Bateman, D. and Chiriboga, C.A. (2000) 'Dose-response effect of cocaine on newborn head circumference', *Pediatrics*, 106: E33.

Bates, J. (2005) 'Embracing diversity and working in partnership', in R. Carnwell and J. Buchanan (eds) *Effective Practice in Health and Social Care: A partnership approach*. Maidenhead: Open University.

Bates, T., Buchanan, J., Corby, B. and Young, L. (1999) *Drug Use, Parenting and Child Protection: Towards an effective interagency response*. Lancashire: University of Central Lancashire.

Bateson, G. (1973) *Steps to an Ecology of Mind*. St Alban's: Paladin.

Bauman, P.S. and Levine, S.A. (1986) 'The development of children of drug addicts', *International Journal of Addictions*, 21: 849–63.

Bayley, D.H. (1994) *Police for the Future*. New York: Oxford University Press.

Bayley, D.H. (1996) 'What do police do?', in W. Saulsbury, J. Mott and T. Newburn (eds) *Themes in Contemporary Policing*. London: Independent.

Bays, J. (1990) 'Substance abuse and child abuse: Impact of addiction on the child', *Pediatric Clinics of North America*, 37: 881–904.

Bazemore, G. and O'Brien, S. (2002) 'The quest for a restorative model of rehabilitation: theory-for-practice and practice-for-theory', in L. Walgrave (ed.) *Restorative Justice and the Law*. Cullompton: Willan.

Becker, H.S. (1963) *Outsiders: Studies in the sociology of deviance*. London: Free Press.

Behling, D.W. (1979) 'Alcohol abuse as encountered in 51 instances of reported child abuse', *Clinical Pediatrics*, 18: 87–91.

Berger, P. and Luckmann, T. (1966) *The Social Construction of Reality*. London: Penguin.

Bernstein, V., Jeremy, R., Bans, S. and Marcus, J. (1984) 'Interaction and infant behavior at 4 months', *American Journal of Drug and Alcohol Abuse*, 10: 161–93.

Berry, J. (1992) *Lead Us Not Into Temptation: Catholic priests and the sexual abuse of children*. New York: Doubleday.

Bichard, M. (2004) *Bichard Inquiry Recommendations. Progress Report*. London: Home Office.

Bignell, V. and Fortune, J. (1984) *Understanding Systems Failures*. Manchester: Manchester University Press.

Bittner, E. (1991) 'The function of the police in modern society', in C.B. Klockars and S.D. Mastrofski (eds) *Thinking About Police*. New York: McGraw-Hill.

Black, R. and Meyer, J. (1980) 'Parents with special problems: alcoholism and heroin addiction', *Child Abuse and Neglect*, 4: 45.

Blow, K. and Daniel, G. (2006) 'Whose story is it anyway?', in A. Vetere and E. Dowling (eds) *Narrative Therapies with Children and Families*. London: Routledge.

Bibliography

Blumer, H. (1971) 'Social problems as collective behaviour', *Social Problems*, 18(3): 296–306.

Blunkett, D. (2002) quoted in *Guardian*, 2 October.

Bott, E. (1968) *Family and Social Networks*, 2nd edn. London: Tavistock Publications.

Bowcott, O. (2003) 'Row over Vatican order to conceal priests' sex abuse', *Guardian*, 18 August.

Bowling, B. and Philips, C. (2002) *Racism, Crime and Justice*. Harlow: Longman.

Brady, G. (2005) 'ADHD, diagnosis and identity', in C. Newnes and N. Radcliffe (eds) *Making and Breaking Children's Lives*. Ross on Wye: PCCS Books.

Braithwaite, J. (2002) *Restorative Justice and Responsive Regulation*. Oxford: Oxford University Press.

Brannen, J. and O'Brien, M. (eds) (1996) *Children in Families: Research and Policy*. London: Falmer Press.

Brisby, T., Baker, S. and Hedderwick, T. (1997) *Under the Influence: Coping with parents who drink too much: a report on the needs of the children of problem drinking parents*. London: Alcohol Concern.

Brongersma, E. (1984) 'Aggression against paedophiles', *International Journal of Law and Psychiatry*, 7: 79–87.

Brown, S. (2005) *Understanding Youth and Crime*. Buckingham: Open University Press.

Bryant, C. (1999) 'Psychological treatment of priest sex offenders', in Thomas G. Plante (ed.) *Bless Me Father for I Have Sinned: Perspectives on sexual abuse by Roman Catholic priests*. Westport, Connecticut: Praeger.

Burck, C. (2003) 'From parentification to expertise: therapeutic work with children in the context of domestic violence', in *Resisting Abuse: From shame to self-empowerment*. Book of contributions to the International Conference in Family Therapy, Bled, Slovenia.

Burkett, E. and Bruni, F. (1993) *A Gospel of Shame: Children, sexual abuse and the Catholic church*. New York: Viking.

Burman, E. (1994) *Deconstructing Developmental Psychology*. London and New York: Routledge.

Burnett, B.B. (1993) 'The psychological abuse of latency age children: a survey', *Child Abuse and Neglect*, 17: 441–54.

Burns, E., O'Driscoll, M. and Watson, G. (1996). 'The health and development of children whose mothers are on methadone maintenance', *Child Abuse Review*, 5: 113–22.

Butler, I., Robinson, M. and Scanlon, L. (2006) *Children and Decision Making*. London: National Children's Bureau.

Byng Hall, J. (2002) 'Relieving parentified children's burdens in families with insecure attachment patterns', *Family Process*, 41: 375–88.

Byrne, L. (1996) *Local Government Transformed*. Manchester: Baseline Books.

Calder, M. (ed.) (2004) *Child Sexual Abuse and the Internet: Tackling the new frontier*. Lyme Regis: Russell House.

Campbell, D., Bianco, V., Dowling, E., Goldberg, H., McNab, S. and Pentecost, D. (2003) 'Family therapy for childhood depression: researching significant moments', *Journal of Family Therapy*, 25(4): 417–35.

Casado-Flores, J., Bano-Rodrigo, A. and Romero, E. (1990) 'Social and medical problems in children of heroin-addicted parents: a study of 75 patients', *American Journal of Diseases in Children*, 144: 977–9.

Catalano, R.F., Haggerty, K.P., Fleming, C.B., Brewer, D.D. and Gainey, R.R. (2002) 'Children of substance abusing parents: current findings from the Focus on Families project', in R.J. McMahon and R.D. Peters (eds) *The Effects of Parental Dysfunction on Children*. New York: Kluwer Academic/Plenum Publishers.

Chapman, S. (2004) *Sociology*. Letts Education, London.

Christie, N. (1977) 'Conflicts as property', in *British Journal of Criminology*, 17: 1–19.

Christie, N. (1986) 'The ideal victim', in E.A. Fattah (ed.) *From Crime Policy to Victim Policy: Reorienting the criminal justice system*. Basingstoke: Macmillan.

Christie, N. (1998) 'Between civility and state', in V. Ruggiero, N. South and I. Taylor (eds) *The New European Criminology: Crime and social order in Europe*. London: Routledge.

Cockburn, T. (1998) 'Children and citizenship in Britain', *Childhood*, 5(1): 99–117.

Cohen, S. (1972) *Folk Devils and Moral Panics*. Oxford: Martin Robinson.

Cohen, S. and Young, J. (eds) (1973) *The Manufacture of News: Deviance, social problems and mass media*. London: Constable.

Coleman, R. and Cassell, D. (1995) 'Parents who misuse drugs and alcohol', in P. Reder and C. Lucey (eds) *Assessment of Parenting: Psychiatric and psychological contributions*. London: Routledge.

CED (1984) *Collins English Dictionary*, ed. Smart. London: Harper-Collins.

Commission for Social Care Inspection (2006) *Supporting Parents, Safeguarding Children: Meeting the needs of parents with children on the child protection register*, www.csci.org.uk/publications

Cooklin, A. (2001) 'Eliciting children's thinking in families and family therapy', *Family Process*, 40(3): 2922–312.

Cooper, J. and Vetere. A. (2005) 'The effects of domestic violence: trauma, resilience and breaking the cycle of violence', in C. Newnes and N. Radcliffe (eds) *Making and Breaking Children's' Lives*. Ross on Wye: PCCS Books.

Corby, B. (2000) *Child Abuse: Towards a knowledge base*. Maidenhead: Open University Press.

Crawford, A. (1998) *Crime Prevention and Community Safety*. London: Longman.

Crawford, A. and Newburn, T. (2003) *Youth Offending and Restorative Justice: Implementing reforms in youth justice*. Cullompton: Willan.

Cross, N., Evans, J. and Minkes, J. (2003) 'Still children first? Developments in youth justice in Wales', in *Youth Justice*, 2(3).

CSO (1994) *Social Focus on Children*. London: HMSO.

Cullen, R. (2004) *personal correspondence via email*. London: Youth Justice Board.

Cullen, R. (2005) *personal correspondence via email*. London: Youth Justice Board.

Cusick, L., Martin, A. and May, T. (2003) *Vulnerability and Involvement in Drug Use and Sex Work*. HORS 268. London: Home Office.

Daniel, G. (2003) 'From parentification to expertise: therapeutic work with children in the context of parental mental illness', In *Resisting Abuse: From shame to self-empowerment*. Book of contributions to the International Conference in Family Therapy, Bled Slovenia

Daniel, G. and Wren, B. (2005) 'Narrative therapy with families where a parent has a mental health problem', In A. Vetere and E. Dowling (eds) *Narrative Therapies with Children and Families*. London: Routledge.

Day, E., Porter, L., Clarke, A., Allen, D., Moselhy, H. and Copello, A. (2003) 'Drug misuse in pregnancy: the impact of a specialist treatment service', *Psychiatric Bulletin*, 27: 99–101.

Demarest, S. (1999) 'Foreword', in Thomas G. Plante (ed.) *Bless Me Father for I Have Sinned: Perspectives on sexual abuse by Roman Catholic priests*. Westport, Connecticut: Praeger.

Dempsey, D. and Benowitz, N. (2001) 'Risks and benefits of nicotine to aid smoking cessation in pregnancy', *Drug Safety*, 24: 277–322.

Department for Education and Skills (2004a) *Every Child Matters: Change for Children*. London: Stationery Office.

Department for Education and Skills (2004b) *Safeguarding Children in Education*. London: Stationery Office.

Department for Education and Skills (2006a) *The Common Assessment Framework for Children and Young People: Practitioners' guide*. London: Stationery Office.

Department for Education and Skills (2006b) *Working Together to Safeguard Children under the Children Act 1989*. London: Stationery Office.

Department for Education and Skills, the Home Office and the Department of Health (2005) *Every Child Matters: Change for Children – young people and drugs*. London: Stationery Office.

Department of Health (1989) *The Care of Children: Principles and practice in regulations and guidance*. London: HMSO.

Department of Health (1991) *The Children Act Guidance and Regulation*. London: HMSO.

Department of Health (1995) *Child Protection: Clarification of arrangements between the NHS and other agencies: Addendum to Working under The Children Act 1989*. London: HMSO.

Department of Health (2000) *Framework for the Assessment of Children in Need and their Families*. London: Stationery Office.

Department of Health (2002) *Safeguarding Children*. London: Stationery Office.

Department of Health (2003) *What to Do if you are Worried a Child is Being Abused*. London: Stationery Office.

Department of Health (2004) *2004 National Report to the EMCDDA by the Reitox National Focal Point: United Kingdom. New developments, trends and in-depth information on selected issues*, www.emcdda.europa.eu

Derren, S. (1986) 'Children of substance abusers: a review of the literature', *Journal of Substance Abuse Treatment*, 3: 77–94.

Dickson, N. (2003) 'To see ourselves as other see us', Keynote speech to ADSW Annual Conference.

Dignan, J. (2005) *Understanding Victims and Restorative Justice*. Maidenhead: Open University Press.

Dorling, D. (2005) 'Prime suspect: murder in Britain', in P. Hillyard et al. (eds) *Criminal Obsessions: Why harm matters more than crime*. London: Crime and Society Foundation.

Drucker, E. (1990) 'Children of war: the criminalization of motherhood', *The International Journal on Drug Policy*, 1: 10–12.

Earley, L. and Cushway, D. (2002) 'The parentified child', *Clinical Child Psychology and Psychiatry*, 7(2): 163–78.

Economist (2006a) 'Muslim schools', 9 September, p. 32.

Economist (2006b) 'Public money private beliefs', 15 April, p. 37.

Eiden, R., Foote, A. and Schuetze, P. (2006) 'Maternal cocaine use and caregiving status: group differences in caregiver and infant risk variables', *Addictive Behaviors*, 32: 465–76.

Elliott, E. and Watson, A. (2000) 'Responsible carers, problem drug takers or both?' in F. Harbin and M. Murphy (eds) *Substance Misuse and Child Care: How to understand, assist and intervene when drugs affect parenting*. Lyme Regis: Russell House.

Emsley, C. (1996) 'The history of crime and crime control institutions c 1770–c1945', in M. Maguire, R. Morgan and R. Reiner (eds) *The Oxford Handbook of Criminology*. Oxford: Clarendon Press.

Ennew, J. (1986) *The Sexual Exploitation of Children*. Cambridge: Polity Press.

Fals-Stewart, W., Kelley, M.L., Cooke, C.G. and Golden, J.C. (2003) 'Predictors of the psychosocial adjustment of children living in households of parents in which fathers abuse drugs: the effects of postnatal parental exposure', *Addictive Behaviors*, 28: 1013–103.

Family Justice Council (2007) *Report to the President of the Family Division*.

Famularo, R., Kinscherff, R. and Fenton, T. (1992) Parental substance abuse and the nature of child maltreatment', *Child Abuse and Neglect*, 16: 475–83.

Famularo, R., Stone, K., Barnam, R. and Wharton, R. (1986). 'Alcoholism and severe child maltreatment', *American Journal of Orthopsychiatry*, 56: 481–5.

Fanshel, D. (1975). 'Parental failure and consequences for children', *American Journal of Public Health*, 65: 604–12.

Farrington, D. (2007) 'Childhood risk factors and risk-focussed prevention', in M. Maguire, R. Morgan and R. Reiner (eds) (2007) *The Oxford Handbook of Criminology*. Oxford: Oxford University Press.

Fawzy, F.I., Coombs, R.H. and Gerber, B. (1983) 'Generational continuity in the use of substances: the impact of parental substance use on adolescent substance use', *Addictive Behaviors*, 8: 109–14.

Feeley, M. and Simon, J. (1992) 'The new penology: notes on the emerging strategy of corrections and its implications', *Criminology*, 30(4): 449–74.

Feeley, M. and Simon, J. (1994) 'Actuarial justice: the emerging new criminal law', in D. Nelken (ed.), *The Futures of Criminology*. London: Sage.

Fido, M. and Skinner, K. (1999) *The Official Encyclopaedia of Scotland Yard*. London: Virgin Press.

Finkelhor, D. and Asdigian, N.L. (1996) 'Risk factors for youth victimization: beyond a lifestyles/routine activities theory approach', *Violent Victimisation*, 11(1) (Spring).

Finkelhor, D., Wolak, J. and Berliner, L. (2001) 'Police reporting and professional help seeking for child crime victims: a review', *Child Maltreatment*, 6(17).

Fitzgerald, M. Stockdale, J. and Hale, C. (2003) *Young People and Street Crime: Research into young people's involvement in street crime*. London: Youth Justice Board.

Focht-Birketts, L. and Beardslee, W. (2000) 'A child's experience of parental depression: encouraging relational resilience in families with affective illness', *Family Process*, 139: 417–34.

Foley, P., Roche, J. and Tucker, S. (2001) *Children in Society*. Basingstoke: Palgrave.

Forrester, D. (2000) 'Parental substance misuse and child protection in a British sample: a survey of children on the child protection register in an inner London district office', *Child Abuse Review*, 9: 235–46.

Fout, J.C. and Shaw Tantillo, M. (eds) (1993) *American Sexual Politics: Sex, gender, and race since the Civil War*. London: University of Chicago Press.

Fuller, Richard C. and Myers, Richard R. (1941) 'The natural history of a social problem', *American Sociological Review* 6: 320–9.

Gallagher, B. (1998) *Grappling with Smoke. Investigating and managing organized child sexual abuse: A good practice guide*. London: NSPCC.

Gallagher, B. (1999) 'Institutional abuse', in N. Parton and C. Wattam (eds) *Child Sexual Abuse; Responding to the experiences of children*. Chichester: Wiley.

Garbarino, J. and Gilliam, G. (1980) *Understanding Abusive Families*. Lexington: Lexington Books.

Garland, D. (2001) *The Culture of Control: Crime and social order in contemporary society*. Oxford: Oxford University Press.

Garrett, P. (2004) 'Talking child protection. The police and social workers "Working Together" ', *Journal of Social Work*, 4(1): 77–97.

Giannetta, J. (1995) 'Cocaine-exposed children follow-up through 30 months', *Journal of Developmental and Behavioral Pediatrics*, 16: 29–35.

Gibbons, J., Conroy, S. and Bell, C. (1995) *Operating the Child Protection System: A study of child protection practice in English Local Authorities*. London: HMSO.

Gilligan, R. (2000) *Promoting Resilience: A resource guide on working with children in the care system*. London: British Agencies for Adoption and Fostering.

Glaser, D. and Frosh, S. (1988) *Child Sexual Abuse*. London: Macmillan.

Gledhill, R. (2005) 'Catholic Church admits abuse claims up by 50%', *The Times*, 28 June, p. 20.

Gonsiorek, J.C. (1999) 'Forensic psychology. Evaluations in clergy abuse', in Thomas G. Plante (ed.) *Bless Me Father for I Have Sinned: Perspectives on sexual abuse by Roman Catholic priests*. Westport, Connecticut: Praeger.

Goodey, J. (2005) *Victims and Victimology: Research, policy and practice*. Harlow: Longman.

Gopfert, M., Webster, J. and Seeman, M. (eds) (2004) *Parental Psychiatric Disorder*. Cambridge: Cambridge University Press.

Gorell Barnes, G., Thompson, P., Daniel, G. and Burchardt, N. (1995) *Growing up in Stepfamilies*. Oxford: Clarendon Press.

Gorin, S. (2004) *Understanding what children say: Children's experiences of domestic violence, parental substance misuse and parental health problems*. London: National Children's Bureau, for the Joseph Rowntree Foundation.

Graham, J. and Bowling, B. (1995) *Young People and Crime*. London: Home Office.

Green, C. (2001) *The New Understanding ADHD*. Ealing: Random House.

Green, J.R. and Klockars, C.B. (1991) 'What police do', in C.B. Klockars and S.D. Mastrofski (eds) *Thinking About Police*. New York: McGraw-Hill.

Greer, C. (2003) 'Sex crime and the media: press representations in Northern Ireland', in P. Mason (ed.) *Criminal Visions: Media representations of crime and justice*. Cullompton: Willan.

Grubin, D. (1998) *Sex Offending against Children: Understanding the risk*. Police Research Series Paper 99. London: Home Office.

Hain, P. and Hebditch, S. (1978) *Radicals and Socialism*. London: Institute for Workers' Control.

Haines, K. (1998) 'Some principled objections to a restorative justice approach to working with juvenile offenders', in L. Walgrave (ed.) *Restorative Justice for Juveniles: Potentialities, risks and problems*. Leuven, Belgium: Leuven University Press.

Haines, K. and Drakeford, M. (1998) *Young People and Youth Crime*. London: Macmillan.

Hall, S., Crichter, C., Jefferson, T., Clarke, J. and Roberts, B. (1978) *Policing the Crisis: Mugging, the state and law and order*. London: Macmillan.

Hallam, S. (1999) 'Effective and efficient policing: some problems with the culture of performance', in A. Marlow and B. Loveday (eds) *After Macpherson*. Lyme Regis: Russell House.

Hallsworth, S. (2005) *Street Crime*. Cullompton: Willan.

Harrington, V. and Mayhew, P. (2001) *Mobile Phone Theft*, Home Office Research Study No. 235. London: Home Office.

Harthill, R. (2000) 'Inner circle', in *Guardian Society*, 13 December.

Hartless, J., Ditton, J., Nairn, G. and Phillips, S. (1995) 'More sinned against than sinning: a study of young teenagers' experience of crime', *British Journal of Criminology*, (35)1.

Hawtin, A., Banton, R. and Wyse, D. (2000) 'Children at risk' in D. Wyse, and A. Hawtin (eds) *Children: A multi-professional perspective*. London: Arnold.

Hebenton, B. and Thomas, T. (1997) *Keeping Track? Observations on sex offender registers in the US*. Police Research Group, Crime Detection and Prevention Series Paper 83. London: Home Office.

Hendrick, H. (1994) *Child Welfare: England 1872–1989*. London: Routledge.

Her Majesty's Inspectorate of Constabulary (1998) *Winning the Race*. London: HMSO.

Herjanic, B.M., Barredo, B.H., Herjanic, M. and Tomelleri, C. (1979) 'Children of heroin addicts', *International Journal of the Addictions*, 14: 919–31.

Hill, M., Laybourn, A. and Brown, J. (1996) 'Children whose parents misuse alcohol: a study of services and needs', *Child and Family Social Work*, 1: 159–67.

Hillman, M. et al. (1990) *One False Move: A study of children's independent mobility*. London: Policy Studies Institute.

Hirschi, T. (1969) *Causes of Delinquency*. Berkeley: University of California Press.

Hogan, D. (1998) 'Annotation: The psychological development and welfare of children of opiate and cocaine users: review and research needs', *Journal of Child Psychology and Psychiatry*, 5: 609–20.

Hogan, D. and Higgens, L. (2001) *When Parents Use Drugs: Key findings from a study of children in the care of drug-using parents*. Dublin: Children's Research Centre, Trinity College.

Holdaway, S., Davidson, N., Dignan, J., Hammersley, R., Hine, J. and Marsh, P. (2001) *New Strategies to Address Youth Offending: The national evaluation of the pilot Youth Offending Teams*. London: HMSO.

Home Office (1965) *Report of the Committee on the Prevention and Detection of Crime* (Cornish Report). London: HMSO.

Home Office (1967) *Police Manpower, Equipment and Efficiency*. London: HMSO.

Home Office (1990) *The Victim's Charter*. London: Home Office.

Home Office (1991) *Safer Communities: The local delivery of crime prevention through the partnership approach* (Morgan Report). London: Home Office.

Home Office (1993) *Police Reform: A police service for the twenty first century*, Cm. 2281. London: HMSO.

Home Office (1995) *Review of the Police Core and Ancillary Tasks: Final report* (Posen Report). London: HMSO.

Home Office (1997) *No More Excuses: A new approach to tackling youth crime in England and Wales*. London: HMSO.

Home Office (1998a) *Crime and Disorder Act Guidelines*. London: HMSO.

Home Office (1998b) *Speaking up for Justice: Report of the Interdisciplinary Working Group on the Treatment of Vulnerable or Intimidated Witnesses in the Criminal Justice System*. London: Home Office.

Home Office (1999) *The Government's Crime Reduction Strategy*. London: HMSO.

Home Office (2002a) *Justice for All*. London: Home Office.

Home Office (2002b) *Narrowing the Justice Gap. Consultative Document*. London: Home Office.

Home Office (2004) *Bichard Inquiry Recommendations*. London: Home Office.

Home Office (2005a) *The Victimisation of Young People: Findings from the Crime and Justice Survey 2003*. London: Home Office.

Home Office (2005b) *Young People and Crime: Findings from the 2004 Offending, Crime and Justice Survey*. London: Home Office.

Home Office (2006) *A Co-ordinated Prostitution Strategy and a Summary of Responses to Paying the Price*. London: Home Office.

Home Office and Youth Justice Board (2000) *The Referral Order: Guidance to Youth Offending Teams*. London: HMSO and Youth Justice Board.

Home Office, Department of Education and Science, Department of Employment, Department of he Environment, Department of Social Security, Department of Trade and Industry, Department of Transport, and Welsh Office (1990) *Crime Prevention: The Success of the Partnership Approach* (Home Office Circular 44/1990). London: Home Office.

Home Office, Department of Education and Science, Department of the Environment, Department of Health and Social Security and Welsh Office (1984) *Crime Prevention*, (Home Office Circular 8/1984). London: Home Office.

Home Office, Lord Chancellors Department, YJB (2002) *Referral Orders and Youth Offender Panel: Guidance for Courts, Youth Offending Teams and Youth Offender Panels*. London: Home Office, Lord Chancellors Department, YJB.

Home Office, Northern Ireland Office and Scottish Office (1993) *Inquiry into Police Responsibilities and Rewards*, Cm. 2280 (Sheehy Report). London: HMSO.

Hough, M. (1985) 'Organizations and resource management in the uniformed police', in K. Heal, R. Tarling and J. Burrows (eds) *Policing Today*. London: HMSO.

Householder, J., Hatcher, R., Burns, W. and Chasnoff, I. (1982) 'Infants born to narcotic-addicted mothers', *Psychological Bulletin*, 92: 453–68.

Howitt, D. (1995a) *Paedophiles and Sex Offences Against Children*. Chichester: John Wiley and Sons.

Howitt, D. (1995b) 'Pornography and the paedophile: is it criminogenic?', *British Journal of Medical Psychology*, 68: 15–27.

Hoyle, C. (2002) ' Securing restorative justice for the "non-participating" victim', in C. Hoyle and R. Young (eds) *New Visions of Crime Victims*. Oxford: Hart.

Hoyle, C. and Young, R. (eds) *New Visions of Crime Victims*. Oxford: Hart.

Hughes, O.E. (1994) *Public Management and Administration*. New York: St Martins.

Hurt, H., Brodsky, N.L., Betancourt, L., Braitman, L.E., Malmud, E. and Itzin, C. (2000) *Home Truths about Child Sexual Abuse*. London: Routledge.

Jackson, S. and Scott, S. (1999) 'Risk anxiety and the social construction of childhood', in D. Lupton (ed.) *Risk and Sociocultural Theory: New directions and perspectives*. Cambridge: Cambridge University Press.

James, A. and Prout, A. (1997) *Constructing and Reconstructing Childhood: Contemporary issues in the sociological study of childhood*. London: Falmer.

James, A., Jenks, C. and Prout, A. (1998) *Theorising Childhood*. Cambridge: Polity.

Jaudes, P.K., Ekwo, E. and Van Voorhis, J. (1995) 'Association of drug abuse and child abuse', *Child Abuse and Neglect*, 19: 1065–75.

Jefferson, T. and Shapland, J. (1994) 'Criminal justice and the production of order and control', *Journal of Criminology*, 34(3).

Jenkins, P. (1998) *Moral Panic: Changing concepts of the child molester in modern America*. New Haven, Connecticut: Yale University Press.

Johnson, B. and Petre, J. (2002) 'Pope accepts Boston Cardinal's resignation', *Daily Telegraph*, 14 December.

Johnson, J.L., Boney, T. and Brown, B.B. (1991) 'Evidence of depressive symptoms in children of drug abusers', *International Journal of the Addictions*, 25: 465–79.

Johnstone, G. (2002) *Restorative Justice: Ideas, values, debates*. Cullompton: Willan.

Jones, T., Newburn, T. and Jones, T. (1994) *Democracy and Policing*: London: PSI.

Jubb, R. (2003) *Youth Victimisation: A literature review*. London: NACRO.

Kandel, B. (1990) 'Parenting styles, drug use and children's adjustment in families of young adults', *Journal of Marriage and the Family*, 52: 183–96.

Kauffman, C.J. (1988) *Tradition and Transformation in Catholic Culture*. New York: Macmillan.

Kearney, P. and Ibbetson, M. (1991) 'Opiate-dependent women and their babies: a study of the multi-disciplinary work of a hospital and a local authority', *British Journal of Social Work*, 21: 105–26.

Kelling, G., Pate, T., Dieckman, D. and Brown, C. (1974) *The Kansas City Preventive Patrol Experiment: A summary report*. Washington DC: Police Foundation.

Kennison, P. and Fletcher, R. (2005) 'Police', in G. Barrett, D. Sellman and J. Thomas (eds) (2005) *Inter-professional Working in Health and Social Care*. Basingstoke: Palgrave Macmillan

Kennison, P. and Read, M. (2003) 'Policing the Internet, part one: the Internet and child protection', *Community Safety Journal*, 2(2).

Kettle, M. and Hodges, L. (1982) *Uprising*. London: Pan.

Kinsey, A.C., Pomeroy, W.B. and Martin, C.E. (1948) *Sexual Behaviour in the Human Male*. Philadelphia: W.B. Saunders.

Kinsey, R., Lea, J., and Young, J. (1986) *Losing the Fight Against Crime*. Oxford: Blackwell.

Kitzinger, J. (1988) 'Defending innocence: ideologies of childhood', *Feminist Review*, 28: 77–87.

Kitzinger, J. (1996) 'Media constructions of sexual abuse risks', *Child Abuse Review*. 5(5): 319–33.

Kitzinger, J. (1997) 'Who are you kidding. Children, power and the struggle against sexual abuse', in A. James and A. Prout (eds) *Constructing and Reconstructing Childhood*. London: Falmer Press.

Kitzinger, J. (1999) 'The ultimate neighbour from hell? Stranger danger and the media framing of paedophiles', in B. Franklin (ed.) *Social Policy, the Media and Misrepresentation*. London: Routledge.

Klee, H. and Jackson, M. (1998) *Illicit Drug Use, Pregnancy and Early Motherhood: Report to the Department of Health Task Force to Review Services for Drug Users*. Manchester: Centre for Social Research on Health and Substance Abuse.

Klee, H., Wright, S. and Rothwell, J. (1997) *Drug Using Parents and their Children: Risk and protective factors*. Manchester: Centre for Social Research on Health and Substance Abuse.

Kolar, A.F., Brown, B.S., Haertzen, C.A. and Michaelson, B.S. (1994) 'Children of substance abusers: the life experiences of children of opiate addicts in methadone maintenance', *American Journal of Drug and Alcohol Abuse*, 20: 159–71.

Kroll, B. and Taylor, A. (2003) *Parental Substance Misuse and Child Welfare*. London: Jessica Kingsley.

Kumpfer, K.L. (1999) 'Outcome measures of interventions in the study of children of substance-abusing parents', *Pediatrics*, 103: 1128–44.

Kumpfer, K.L. and DeMarsh, J.K. (1985) 'Family environmental and genetic Influences on children's future chemical dependency', in S. Ezekoye, K. Kumpfer and W. Bukoski (eds) *Childhood and Chemical Abuse: Prevention and intervention*. New York: Hayworth Press.

Laming, Lord (2003) *The Victoria Climbié Inquiry*. London: Stationery Office.

Laming, Lord (2007) 'The Victoria Climbié Memorial Lecture', *Memorial Lecture Newsletter*, 26 February. Middlesex: Victoria Climbié Foundation.

Lansley, S., Goss, S. and Wolmar, C. (1989) *Councils in Conflict*. London: Macmillan.

Lea, J. and Young, J. (1993) *What is to be Done about Law and Order?* London: Pluto.

Leach, P. (1999) *The Physical Punishment of Children: Some input from recent research*. London: NSPCC.

Leishman, F., Cope, S. and Starie, P. (1996) 'Reinventing and restructuring: towards a "new policing order" ', in F. Leishman, B. Loveday and P. Savage, *Core Issues in Policing*. Harlow: Longman.

Lemert, E. (1951) *Social Pathology*. New York: McGraw-Hill.

Leopold, B. and Steffan, E. (1997) *Special Needs of Children of Drug Users*. Germany: Council of Europe Publishing.

Lester, B.M., LaGasse, L. and Brunner, S. (1997) 'Database of studies on prenatal cocaine exposure and child outcome', *Journal of Drug Issues*, 27: 487–99.

Little, M. (1997) 'The re-focusing of children's services: the contribution of research', in N. Parton (ed.) *Child Protection and Family Support: Tensions, contradictions and possibilities*. London: Routledge.

Liverpool Health Authority (2001) *In a Different World: Parental drug and alcohol use. A consultation into its effects on children and families in Liverpool*. Liverpool: Liverpool Health Authority.

Loftus, J.A. (1989) *Sexual Abuse in the Church: A quest for understanding*. Aurora, Ontario: Emmanuel Convalescent Foundation.

Loftus, J.A. (1994) *Sexual Misconduct amongst Clergy: A handbook for ministers*. Washington DC: Pastoral Press.

Loftus, J.A. (1999) 'Sexuality in priesthood', in Thomas G. Plante (ed.) *Bless Me Father for I Have Sinned: Perspectives on sexual Abuse by Roman Catholic priests*. Westport, Connecticut: Praeger.

London Child Protection Committee (2003) *London Child Protection Procedures*, 2nd edn. London: LCPC.

Lothstein, L. (1999) 'Neuropsychological findings in clergy who sexually abuse', in Thomas G. Plante (ed.) *Bless Me Father for I Have Sinned: Perspectives on sexual abuse by Roman Catholic priests*. Westport, Connecticut: Praeger.

Loveday, B. (1995) Reforming the police: from local service to state police? *Political Quarterly*, 66(2).

Loveday, B. (1996) Crime at the core', in F. Leishman, B. Loveday and S. Savage, *Core Issues in Policing*. Harlow: Longman.

Lupton, D. (ed.) (1999) *Risk and Sociocultural Theory: New directions and perspectives*. Cambridge: Cambridge University Press.

Luthar, S.S. and Cushing, G. (1999) 'Neighborhood influences and child development: a prospective study of substance abusers' offspring', *Development and Psychopathology*, 11: 763–84.

Lyon, C. (2003) *Child Abuse*. Bristol: Family Law.

McCold, P. (1999) 'Towards a holistic vision of restorative justice: a reply to Walgrave', paper presented at the 4th International Conference on Restorative Justice for Juveniles. Leuven, Belgium, October 24–27.

McConville, M. and Shepherd, D. (1992) *Watching Police Watching Communities*. London: Routledge.

McIlroy, D. (2004) 'Style or substance: Does the reputation of the church matter?' *Cambridge Papers*, 13(1). www.jubilee-centre.or/online-documents accessed on 5 August 2005.

McKegany, N., Barnard, M. and McIntosh, J. (2002) 'Paying the price for their parents' addiction: meeting the needs of the children of drug-using parents', *Drugs: Education, Prevention and Policy*, 9: 233–46.

Mackintosh, M. (1993) 'Partnership: issues of policy and negotiation', *Local Economy*, 7(3): 210–24.

McLaughlin, E. and Muncie, J. (1996) *Controlling Crime*. London: Sage.

MacLeod, M. (1996) *Talking with Children about Child Abuse*. London: Childline.

MacLeod, M. (1999) 'Don't just do it. Children's access to help and protection', in N. Parton and C. Wattam (eds) *Child Sexual Abuse*. Chichester: Wiley.

McNeill, P. and Townley, C. (1993) *Fundamentals of Sociology*. Cheltenham: Stanley Thornes.

Macpherson, W. (1999) *The Inquiry into the Matters Arising from the Death of Stephen Lawrence*, Cm. 4262. London: Stationery Office.

Macrory, F. and Harbin, F. (2000) 'Substance misuse and pregnancy', in F. Harbin and M. Murphy (eds) *Substance Misuse and Child Care: How to understand, assist and intervene when drugs affect parenting*. Lyme Regis: Russell House.

MacVean, A. (2000) 'Just another job for the police: the criminalisation of child sexual abuse and a new role for the police', unpublished PhD, Brunel University.

MacVean, A. and Spindler, P. (eds) (2003) *Policing Paedophiles on the Internet*. Goole: New Police Book Shop, Benson Publications.

Maguire, M. et al. (2001) *Risk Management of Sexual and Violent Offenders: The work of Public Protection Panels*. Police Research Series Paper 139. London: Home Office.

Manuel, G. (1999) 'Beginning an intervention in clergy abuse', in Thomas G. Plante (ed.) *Bless Me Father for I Have Sinned: Perspectives on sexual abuse by Roman Catholic priests*. Westport, Connecticut: Praeger.

Marshall, T. (1999) *Restorative Justice: An overview*. London: Home Office.

Martin, D., Chatwin, C. and Porteous, D. (2007) 'Risky or at risk? Young people, surveillance and security', *Criminal Justice Matters*, 68 (Summer).

Matza, D. and Sykes, G. (1957) 'Techniques of neutralization', *American Sociological Review*, 22: 664–70.

Maung, N. (1995) *Young People, Victimisation and the Police*. Home Office Research Study 140. London: HMSO.

Mead, G.H. (1934) *Mind, Self and Society*. Chicago: University of Chicago Press.

Melrose, M. (2007) 'The Government's new prostitution strategy: a cheap fix for drug-using sex workers?', *Community Safety Journal*, 6(1): 18–26.

Metcalf, C.M. (2006) 'Making sense of sex offenders and the Internet', unpublished PhD thesis: Brunel University.

Metropolitan Police Service (2004) 'Victoria Climbié Inquiry Recommendations Progress Grid', unpublished internal document.

Metropolitan Police Service (2005) 'Community Partnership Project Final Report', unpublished.

Miers, D. (1977) *State Compensation for Criminal Injuries*. London: Blackstone Press.

Miers, D. (2001) *An International Review of Restorative Justice*. London: Home Office.

Miers, D. (2004) 'Taking the Law into their own hands', in A. Crawford and J. Goodey (eds) *Integrating a Victim Perspective within Criminal Justice: International debates*. Dartmouth: Ashgate.

Minuchin, S. (1974) *Families and Family Therapy*. London: Tavistock Publications.

Moore, J. (1985) *The ABC of Child Abuse Work*. Aldershot: Gower.

Morgan, J. and Zedner, L. (1992) *Child Victims: Crime, impact and criminal justice*. Oxford: Oxford University Press.

Morgan, R. and Newburn, T. (1997) *The Future of Policing*. Oxford: Clarendon Press.

Morgan Report (1991) *Safer Communities: The local delivery of crime prevention through the partnership approach*. London: Home Office.

Morris, A. and Maxwell, G. (2001) *Restorative Justice for Juveniles: Conferencing, mediation and circles*. Oregon: Hart.

Moss, H.B., Vanyukov, M., Majumder, P.P., Kiriski, L. and Tarter, R.E. (1995) 'Prepubertal sons of substance abusers: influences of parental and familial substance abuse on behavioral disposition, IQ and school achievement', *Addictive Behaviors*, 20: 345–58.

Mullender, A., Hagues, G., Imam, U., Kelly, L., Malos, E. and Regan, L (2002) *Children's Perspectives on Domestic Violence*. London: Sage.

Muncie, J. (2004) *Youth and Crime*. London: Sage.

National Youth Agency (2006) 'Knives, guns and gangs', *Spotlight*, 37 (September).

Newburn, T. (1995) *Crime and Criminal Justice Policy*. Harlow: Longman.

Newburn, T. (2007) 'Youth crime and youth culture', in M. Maguire, R. Morgan and R. Reiner (eds) (2007) *The Oxford Handbook of Criminology*. Oxford: Oxford University Press.

Newburn, T., Crawford, A., Earle, R., Goldie, S., Hale, C., Masters, G., Netten, A., Saunders, R., Sharpe, K. and Uglow, S. (2001) *The Introduction of Referral Orders into the Youth Justice System*. RDS Occasional Paper 70. London: Home Office.

Newman, T. (2004) *What Works in Building Resilience?* Essex: Barnardo's.

Newnes, C. and Radcliffe, N. (2005) *Making and Breaking Children's Lives*. Ross on Wye: PCCS Books.

Nichtern, S. (1973) 'The children of drug users', *Journal of the American Academy of Child Psychiatry*, 12: 24–31.

Nolan, Lord (2001) *The Nolan Review on Child Protection in the Catholic Church in England and Wales*. London: Roman Catholic Church.

Norman, C.A. (1994) 'Not in families like us: the social construction of child abuse in America', paper presented at Emerging Theories/Merging Practices in Gender Studies, The Ninth National Graduate Women's Studies Conference. University of California at San Diego, April 14–17. Available Online at www.consultclarity.com/conference.html. Visited 8 November 2003.

O'Byrne, M. (1981) 'The role of the police', in D.W. Pope and N.L. Weiner (eds) *Modern Policing*. London: Croom Helm.

Oliver, I. (1997) *Police, Government and Accountability*. London: Macmillan.

Ornoy, A., Michailevskaya, V., Lukashov, I., Bar-Hamburger, R. and Harel, S. (1996) 'The developmental outcome of children born to heroin-dependent mothers, raised at home or adopted', *Child Abuse and Neglect*, 20: 385–96.

Osofsky, J.D. (ed.) (1997) *Children in a Violent Society*. New York: Guilford Press.

Ottaviani, Cardinal A. (1964) *On the Manner of Proceeding in Cases of Solicitation*. Rome: Vatican Press.

Pain, R. (2003) 'Youth, age and the representation of fear', *Capital and Class*, 80 (Summer): 151–71.

Parrott, L. (2005) 'The political drivers of partnership', in R. Carnwell and J. Buchanan (eds) *Effective Practice in Health and Social Care: A partnership approach*. Maidenhead: Open University Press.

Parrott, L. (2006) *Values and Ethics in Social Work Practice*. Exeter: Learning Matters.

Parton, N. (1991) *Governing the Family: Child care, Child protection and the state*. London: Macmillan.

Parton, N. (ed.) (1997) *Child Protection and Family Support: Tensions, contradictions and possibilities*. London: Routledge.

Parton, N. and Wattam, C. (1999) *Child Sexual Abuse: Responding to the experiences of children*. Chichester: Wiley.

Parton, N., Thorpe, D. and Wattam, C. (1997) *Child Protection: Risk and the Moral Order*. London: Macmillan.

Pearce, J., Williams, M. and Galvin, C. (2003) *'It's someone taking a part of you': a study of young women and sexual exploitation*. London: National Children's Bureau.

Pearson, G. (1983) *Hooligan: A history of respectable fears*. Basingstoke: Macmillan.

Petre, J. (2005a) 'Paedophile priests cost the Catholic Church £1M for a decade of abuse', *Daily Telegraph*, 1 July.

Petre, J. (2005b) 'Paedophiles "turning Christian to target children in church" ', *Daily Telegraph*, 7 May.

Phillip, P. and Hooper, J. (2005) 'Scandal of sexual abuse by priests shocks Brazil's 125 million Catholics', *Guardian*, 26 November, p. 22.

Phillips, A. and Chamberlain, V. (2006) *MORI Five Year Report: An analysis of youth survey data*. London: Youth Justice Board

Phoenix, J. (2002) 'In the name of protection: youth prostitution policy reforms in England and Wales', *Critical Social Policy*, 22(2): 353–75.

Phoenix, J. (2004) 'Rethinking youth prostitution: national provision at the margins of child protection and youth justice', *Youth Justice*, 3(3): 152–68.

Pinkerton, J. (2001) 'Developing partnership practice', in P. Foley, J. Roche, and S. Tucker (eds) *Children in Society*. Basingstoke: Palgrave.

Pitts, J. (2005) 'Youth justice election briefing', *Community Care*, March.

Pitts, J. and Bateman, T. (2005) 'Youth crime in England and Wales', in T. Bateman and J. Pitts (eds) *The RHP Companion to Youth Justice*. Lyme Regis: Russell House.

Plante, T.G. (ed.) (1999) *Bless Me Father for I Have Sinned: Perspectives on sexual abuse by Roman Catholic priests*. Westport, Connecticut: Praeger.

Plante, T.G., Manuel, G. and Bryant, C. (1996) 'Personality and cognitive functioning among hospitalised sexual offending Roman Catholic priests', *Pastoral Psychology*, 45: 129–39.

Police Review (1992) 1 May, p. 799.

Pollack, L. (1983) *Forgotten Children: Parent–child relations 1500–1900*. Cambridge: Cambridge University Press.

Porteous, D. (1998) 'Young people's experience of violence: findings from a survey of school students', in A. Marlow and J. Pitts (eds) *Planning Safer Communities*. Lyme Regis: Russell House.

Potter, J. (1996) *Representing Reality: Discourse, rhetoric and social construction*. London: Sage.

Prime Minister's Strategy Unit (2004) *Alcohol Harm Reduction Strategy for England*. London: Cabinet Office.

Reid, S. (2005) 'The Devil's work?', *Daily Mail*, 17 June.

Reiner, R. (1991) *Chief Constables*. Oxford: Oxford University Press.

Reiner, R. (1992) *The Politics of Police*. London: Harvester Wheatsheaf.

Rennie, D. (2002) 'Cardinal defiant over child abuse crisis', *Daily Telegraph*, 13 April.

Renvoize, J. (1993) *Innocence Destroyed. A study of child sexual abuse*. London: Routledge.

Richter, K.P. and Bammer, G. (2000) 'A hierarchy of strategies heroin-using mothers employ to reduce harm to their children', *Journal of Substance Abuse Treatment*, 19: 403–13.

Ricks, L. (2005) *Circles of Support and Accountability in the Thames Valley: The first three years April 2002 to March 2005*. London: Quaker Communications.

Rodgers, B. and Pryor, J. (1998) *Divorce and Separation: The outcomes for children*. York: Joseph Rowntree Foundation.

Roe, S. and Man, L. (2006) *Drug Misuse Declared: Findings from the 2005/06 British Crime Survey – England and Wales*. Home Office Statistical Bulletin. London: Home Office.

Rose, N. (1989) *Governing the Soul*. London: Routledge.

Rossetti, S. (1995) 'The mark of Cain: Reintegrating pedophiles', *America*, 173(6): 9.

Royal College of Physicians (1995) *Alcohol and the Young*. London: Royal College of Physicians.

Rubington, E. and Weinberg, M.S. (1971) *The Study of Social Problems: Five perspectives*. New York: Oxford University Press.

Russell, D. (1984) *Sexual Exploitation: Child abuse and sexual harassment*. Beverley Hills, California: Sage.

Ryan, M. (1999) *The Children Act 1989*. Aldershot: Ashgate.

Scarman, L. (1981) *The Brixton Disorders 10–12 April 1981: Report of an inquiry by the Rt. Hon. The Lord Scarman OBE*. London: HMSO.

Scarman, L. (1982) *The Scarman Report: The Brixton disorders 10–12 April 1981*. Harmondsworth: Penguin.

Schon, D. (1987) *Educating the Reflective Practitioner*. San Francisco: Jossey-Bass.

Schuetze, P. and Eiden, R. (2006) 'The association between maternal cocaine use during pregnancy and physiological regulation in 4- to 8- week old infants: an examination of possible mediators and moderators', *Journal of Pediatric Psychology*, 31: 15–26.

Sherman, L. and Strang, H. (2007) *Restorative Justice: The evidence*. London: Smith Institute.

Siddiqui, G. (2006) 'Breaking the taboo of child abuse', in *Child Protection in Faith-based Environments. A guideline report*. London: Muslim Parliament of Great Britain.

Silverman, J. and Wilson, D. (2002) *Innocence Betrayed: Paedophilia, the Media and Society*. Oxford: Blackwell.

Singer, L.T. (1999) 'Advances and redirections in understanding effects of fetal drug exposure', *Journal of Drug Issues*, 29: 253–62.

Singer, L.T., Arendt, R., Minnes, S., Farkas, K., Salvator, A., Kirchner, L. and Kleigman, R. (2002) 'Cognitive and motor outcomes for cocaine-exposed infants', *Journal of the American Medical Association*, 287: 1952–60.

Sipe, A.W.R. (1990) *A Secret World: Sexuality and the search for celibacy*. New York: Bruner/Mazel.

Sipe, A.W.R. (1995) *Sex, Priests and Power: Anatomy of a crisis*. New York: Bruner/Mazel.

Sipe, A.W.R. (1999) 'The problem of prevention in clergy sexual abuse', in Thomas G. Plante (ed.) *Bless Me Father for I Have Sinned: Perspectives on sexual abuse by Roman Catholic priests*. Westport, Connecticut: Praeger.

Skidmore, P. (1995) 'Telling tales: media, power, ideology and the reporting of child sexual abuse in Britain', in D. Kidd-Hewitt and R. Osbourne (eds) *Crime and the Media*. London: Pluto.

Small, J.A. (1999) 'Who are the people in your neighbourhood? Due process, public protection, and sex offender notification laws', *New York University Law Review*, 74: 1451–94.

Smart, C., Neale, B. and Wade, A. (2001) *The Changing Experience of Childhood*. Cambridge: Polity.

Smith, D. (2004) *The Edinburgh Study of Youth Transitions and Crime: The links between victimization and offending*. Edinburgh: School of Law, Edinburgh University.

Smith, D., McVie, S., Woodward, R., Shute, J., Flint, J. and McAra, L. (2001) *The Edinburgh Study of Youth Transitions and Crime: Key findings at ages 12 and 13*. Edinburgh: University of Edinburgh.

Smith, J. (2003) *The Nature of Personal Robbery*, Home Office Research Study 254. London: Home Office.

Soloski, J. (1989) 'News reporting and professionalism: some constraints on the reporting of news', *Media, Culture and Society*, 11: 207–28.

Soothill, K. and Walby, S. (1991) *Sex Crime in the News*. London: Routledge.

Soothill, K. et al. (1998) 'Paedophilia and paedophiles', *New Law Journal*, 12 (June): 882–3.

Sowder, B.J. and Burt, M.R. (1980) *Children of Heroin Addicts: An assessment of health, learning, behavioral and adjustment problems*. New York: Praeger.

Spector, M. and Kitsuse, J. (2001, 1st edn 1987) *Constructing Social Problems*. New Jersey: Transaction.

Stenson, K. (1999) 'Crime control, governmentality and sovereignty', in R. Smandych (ed.) *Governable Places: Readings in governmentality and crime control*. Aldershot: Dartmouth.

Stone, B. (1998) *Child Neglect: Practitioners' perspectives*. London: NSPCC.

Swann, S. and Balding, V. (2001) *Safeguarding Children Involved in Prostitution. Guidance Review*. London: Department of Health.

Sykes, G. and Matza, D. (1957) 'Techniques of neutralisation: a theory of delinquency', *American Sociological Review*, December: 664–70.

Tarter, R.E., Schultz, K., Kirisci, L. and Dunn, M. (2001) 'Does living with a substance abusing father increase substance abuse risk in male offspring? Impact on individual, family, school and peer vulnerability factors', *Journal of Child and Adolescent Substance Abuse*, 10: 59–70.

Taylor, A. (1993) *Women Drug Users: An ethnography of a female injecting community*. Oxford: Clarendon Press.

Taylor, I., Walton, P. and Young, J. (1973) *The New Criminology*. London: Routledge.

Taylor, S. (1989) 'How prevalent is it?', in W. Stainton Rogers, D. Hevers and E. Ash (eds) *Child Abuse and Neglect: Facing the challenge*. London: Batsford.

Templeton, L., Zohhadi, S., Galvani, S. and Velleman, R. (2006). *Looking Beyond Risk: Parental substance misuse scoping study*. Edinburgh: Scottish Executive.

Thomas, J. (2005) 'Issues for the future', ch. 15 in G. Barrett, D. Sellman and J. Thomas (eds) *Inter- professional Working in Health and Social Care*. Basingstoke: Palgrave Macmillan.

Thomas, T. (2000) *Sex Crime: Sex offenders and society*. Cullompton: Willan.

Thomas, T. (2003) 'Sex offender community notification: experiences from America', in *Howard Journal of Criminal Justice*, 42(3): 217–28.

Trinder, L., Beek, M. and Connolly, J. (2002) *Making Contact Work: How parents and children negotiate and experience contact after divorce*. York: Joseph Rowntree Foundation.

Turning Point (2006) *Bottling It Up: The effects of alcohol misuse on children, parents and families*. London: Turning Point.

Umbreit, M. (2001) *The Handbook of Victim–Offender Mediation: An essential guide to practice and research*. San Francisco: Jossey-Bass.

Valios, N. (2007) 'Street smart' *Community Care*, 19 April: 30–1.

Velleman, R. and Orford, J. (1999) *Risk and Resilience: Adults who were the children of problem drinkers*. Amsterdam: Harwood Academic Publishers.

Victim Support (2003) *Survey of Crimes against 12–16-year olds*. London: Victim Support

Walgrave, L. (1998) 'What is at stake in restorative justice for juveniles?', in L. Walgrave (ed.) *Restorative Justice for Juveniles: Potentialities, risks and problems for research*. Leuven: Leuven University Press.

Walker, A., Kershaw, C. and Nicholas, S. (2006) *Crime in England and Wales 2005/6*. London: Home Office.

Ward, L. (2005) 'Churches to attend ritual abuse summit', *Guardian*, 12 July.

Wardhaugh, J. and Wilding, P. (1993) 'Towards an explanation of the corruption of care', *Critical Social Policy*, 37: 4–31.

Warren, M. (2004) 'Top US school accused of sex abuse cover up', *Daily Telegraph*, 12 June.

Wasserman, D.R. and Leventhal, J.M. (1993) 'Maltreatment of children born to cocaine-dependent mothers', *American Journal of Diseases in Children*, 147: 1324–8.

Weatheritt, M. (1986) *Innovations in Policing*. London: Croom Helm.

Websdale, N. (1999) 'The social construction of "stranger-danger" in Washington state as a form of patriarchal ideology', in J. Ferrell, and N. Websdale (eds) M*aking Trouble: Cultural constructions of crime, deviance, and control*. Hawthorne, New York: Aldine de Gruyter.

Weingarten, K. (2003) *Common Shock*. New York and London: Dutton.

Wetherell, M., Taylor, S. and Yates, S. (2001) *Discourse Theory and Practice*. London: Sage.

Whincup, P. (2001) 'Age of menarche in contemporary British teenagers: surveys of girls born between 1982 and 1986'. Available online at www.pubmedcentral.nih.gov/articlerender.fcgi?artid=31261. Visited 8 September 2003.

White, H.R., Johnson, V. and Buyske, S. (2000) 'Parental modelling and parenting behaviour effects on offspring alcohol and cigarette use: a growth curve analysis', *Journal of Substance Abuse*, 12: 287–310.

Wikstrom, P.H. and Butterworth, D.A. (2006) *Adolescent Crime: Individual differences and lifestyles*. Cullompton: Willan.

Wilcox, A. and Hoyle, C. (2004) *Youth Justice Board Restorative Justice Projects: The national evaluation of the Youth Justice Board's Restorative Justice Projects*. London: Youth Justice Board.

Wilkins, L. (1964) *Social Deviance*. London: Tavistock.

Wilkinson, E. (2002) *Restoring Young Victims: The role of support in encouraging participation in reparation schemes*. Trafford: Trafford YOT and Victim Support.

Williams, B. (1999) *Working with Victims of Crime: Policies, politics and practice*. London: Jessica Kingsley.

Williams, M. (1983) 'The problems of children born of drug addicts', *Journal of Maternal and Child Health*, 8: 258–63.

Wilson, C. (2005) *Circles of Support and Accountability in the Thames Valley: The first three years April 2002 to March 2005*. London: Quaker Communications.

Wilson, D., Sharp, C. and Patterson, A. (2006) *Young People and Crime: Findings from the 2005 Offending, Crime and Justice Survey*. London: Home Office.

Wilson, J.Q. (1968) *Varieties of Police Behaviour*. Cambridge, Massachusetts: Harvard University Press.

Wilson, K. (2002) *Child Protection Handbook*. London: Harcourt.

Winlow, S. and Hall, S. (2006) *Violent Night: Urban leisure and contemporary culture*. Oxford: Berg.

Wood, M. (2005) *The Victimisation of Young People: Findings from the Crime and Justice Survey 2003*. Home Office Findings 246. London: Home Office.

Wright, P., Turner, C., Clay, D. and Mills, H. (2006) *Involving Children and Young People in Developing Social Care. Practice Guide 6*. London: SCIE.

Young, J. (1998) *The Criminology of Intolerance: Zero-tolerance policing and the American prison experiment*. London: Middlesex University.

Young, M. (1991) *An Inside Job*. Oxford: Clarendon Press.

Young, R. (2002) 'Testing the limits of restorative justice: the case of corporate victims', in C. Hoyle and R. Young (eds) *New Visions of Crime Victims*. Oxford: Hart.

Youth Justice Board (2001a) *Good Practice Guidelines for Restorative Work with Victims and Offenders*. London: YJB.

Youth Justice Board (2001b) *Risk and Protective Factors Associated with Youth Crime and Effective Interventions to Prevent It*. London: YJB.

Youth Justice Board (2003a) *Professional Certificate in Effective Practice (Youth Justice)*. London: YJB.

Youth Justice Board (2003b) *Research Study Conducted for the Youth Justice Board by MORI January–March 2003*. London, YJB.

Youth Justice Board (2006) *Developing Restorative Justice: An action plan*. London: YJB.

Youth Justice Board (2007) www.youth-justice-board.co.uk

Zehr, H. (2002) *The Little Book of Restorative Justice*. New York: Good Books.

Index